Millennial Sex: I've Never Done This Before

A. Lea Roth & Nastassja Schmiedt

For the Tufts community with love

♡ Lea & Nastassja

Spring Up Press

www.timetospringup.org

Third Edition, November 2015

ISBN: 1518873421
ISBN-13: 978-1518873423

To Sam, who always appreciated
a good story, and to Nastassja,
who made it all possible.
- A. Lea Roth

To the moments unseen,
and to Lea, who showed me
that love is real.
- Nastassja Schmiedt

SPECIAL THANKS TO:

Nicola Schmiedt

Angel Schmiedt

Aaluk Edwardson

Renee' Vallejo

Victoria Rozier

Giavanna Munafo

CONTENTS

PREFACE

At your age, you're going to have a lot of urges. You're going to want to take off your clothes, and touch each other. But if you do touch each other, you *will* get chlamydia... and die.

Coach Carr teaches Sex Ed, Mean Girls (2004)

Millennial sexuality is a two-sided coin, subject to much speculation and titillation from the arbiters of media and culture. On one hand, we millennials were raised in a hyper-sexualized culture saturated with explicit media from the time we were young children. Yet we were also raised in a culture grappling with the internalized shadow of Puritanical sexual shame. In the height of the culture wars of the 1980s & '90s, we were the children whose innocence & sexual purity were defended. When it came to sex education, Coach Carr's iconic message was echoed in the hushed voices of our shame-based caregivers and peers:

>*"Nobody needs to see that."*
>*"Don't have sex until you're married."*
>*"Don't have sex with the wrong person."*
>*"Don't have sex with too many people."*
>*"Don't be a slut."*
>*"Don't be a prude."*
>*"Your virginity is like a new car; if you dent up your sexuality, no one will want to marry you."*

This advice has not served us well. The effects of our sex-negative acculturation include a legacy of sexual illiteracy, unsafe sex, and what the authors would argue is an intensification of the rape culture older generations also passed down to us. In a perverse twist on previous generations' aims to "protect our children," nowhere is this rape culture more evident than in our schools, a new shocking story of egregious violation, of sexual betrayal and the complicity of relevant authority figures emerging each week, each day as the movement to end sexual violence, bullying, and harassment grows.

Where did our young people learn to do these things to each other? In a sex-negative culture saturated with extremely graphic and accessible sexual material. No, porn didn't make them do it. But their attitudes of sexual entitlement, their willingness to dehumanize and objectify the bodies of those they deem vulnerable came from the unexamined legacies of a history of patriarchal colonization put into a crucible of sexual shame.

We have a serious vacuum when it comes to sexual education in the United States[1], and yet we know so much—too much—of the sexual status quo, of the racialized fetishization and conquest mentality celebrated in our mainstream media. We know too little of consent, of sexual intimacy, of shared pleasure, of making love; of healthy, mature sexuality, because many of us have rarely—if ever—experienced it firsthand.

But Millennials are having sex. We now live in not just a digital culture, or a "hookup culture," but a digital hookup culture, which, like internet porn, takes everything to the next level. Cruising

---

[1] The case for starting sex education in kindergarten (PBS)
http://www.pbs.org/newshour/updates/spring-fever/

culture has intensified and become mainstream, with millennials engaging in online sexual marketplaces like Tinder, Grindr, Okcupid, and even the sketchy 'Casual Encounter' bowels of Craigslist. Here, we fall back on the scripts and scenes we have learned to eroticize, and the legacy of a de-historicized rape culture that has served as the linchpin of centuries of racial and sexual subjugation emerges.

We are fresh out of a century of industrialization and digitization that has stripped many of us of connection to our own cultures, histories, and identities within our materialist postmodern society. Yet this is no excuse to plead ignorance of our context: the defining feature and potential of our post-historical moment is to be self-reflexive, literate of our past; to dialogue with it, to choose our fate moving forward, lest we recreate the sins of our forefathers and squander our own evolutionary potential. We are the inheritors of this culture; we are shaped by its scripts and mythologies. These dynamics live on within us, to the degree that we choose to carry them, or, through our silences, to allow them to permeate our culture unchecked.

As two queer and gender diverse female survivors of sexual assault in a long-term relationship, these are the issues we, the authors, have engaged with for years: issues of intimacy and sexuality, trauma and healing, and we are pleased

---

[2] Tinder and the Dawn of the Dating Apocalypse (Vanity Fair) http://www.vanityfair.com/culture/2015/08/tinder-hook-up-culture-end-of-dating

to be able to serve as a conduit in bringing what we have learned to a broader culture struggling with the same issues. We come from the trenches of the Movement to End Campus Violence, as well as the daily struggle for the freedom of women, people of color, and LGBT people in 21st century America, and as we set upon a journey towards our own freedom, we asked ourselves what we could do to imagine and create a better future for ourselves and our communities. We came up with a sex-positive solution that wouldn't merely demonize the scripts of our culture, but instead would inspire people to new possibilities of sexual engagement: we decided to write some erotica.

Informed by the most common fantasies of Millennials[3], as well as our own subjective experiences and those of friends we've been fortunate enough to discuss these sorts of things with over many cups of coffee, glasses of wine, and occasionally something a little stronger, we wrote a book. Let's be discreet and call it an erotic novel. Erotica engages the imagination rather than any of the material senses we may associate with sexual activity. There is no shame in reading erotica; no shame in fantasy: whatever shame you find within these pages is your own.

We strive to make the characters we write as human, as multidimensional as possible, while manifesting scenes that are archetypal, that are larger than any one of us in that they exist as the

---

[3] 11 Completely Unexpected Facts About How Millennials Really Watch Porn (Mic.com) http://mic.com/articles/121846/11-unexpected-things-you-didn-t-know-about-millennials-and-porn

sexual mythologies of our culture. Real people, three-dimensional people are not like the mythical specimens that populate the stereotypes and scripts we each hold about "people like us," or "people like them," nor are they able to be reduced to their most vulnerable and painfully human moments. We feel that too often the moments that shape who we are exist in the unspoken shadows, in the quiet space of our inner being, unnoticed and unresolved. These are the moments we explore through the perspectives of our characters, through their hopes and fantasies, traumas and desires; through things they've never done before.

It is from this context that we present to you the first volume of the Millennial Sex Trilogy: "I've Never Done This Before." We hope you enjoy it, but more than anything, we hope it inspires the reader to reconnect their heart, soul, body, and desire to the most powerful sexual organ of all: the mind, and to have more honest and trusting communication about sexuality with their friends, families, and of course, sexual partners.

With Love,

Nastassja Schmiedt & A. Lea Roth

August 2015
Miami Beach, Florida

1: ERIN

Consent

Trigger Warning: Power Play

Part One

Erin looked up from the Welcome Prospective Students letter she was skimming and snuck another glance at Quinn, the lanky blond sitting in the seat next to her at the monotonous *Your Path to Medical School* pre-pre-med lecture. It was the second day of her prospective student weekend visit to Blakeley College and she was still undecided over whether she'd enroll here next fall, or end up at Ohio State with her high school friends.

She and Quinn had found themselves in the same tour group yesterday, and then had spent the Sustainability Mixer, the Philosophy open house, and now this pre-premed event together. They had an odd affinity for each other that was quickly turning to clear flirtation. They had connected so well yesterday; their mutual attraction was evident to both of them, it seemed, and Erin had begun to imagine a romance, a fling, a hook-up blossoming between them during the weekend they were at Blakeley.

She had fantasized last night about kissing him, about maybe going further with him. She had gotten turned on thinking about how he had grabbed her arm at lunch; how his hand felt on her skin… how he might touch her if they had sex—but her worries about whether her roommates would notice and what they might think had stopped her from touching herself.

She wondered how people masturbated at college, sharing space with roommates. What if you wanted to be alone?

Or to be alone with someone?

Just like at her house, you could never be sure of any privacy, she thought.

Quinn caught her eye and gave her a slight smile before looking up at the Dean speaking again. He moved his foot to brush against hers, the corners of his mouth curling slightly.

Quinn was from Portland. He was a vegan, had gone to a magnet arts school, and was different from any boy Erin knew or dated in Ohio. He was interested in philosophy and biochemistry, and like her, thought he'd be pre-med but wasn't sure. He made her ex, Chad, look like a dumb redneck. "Good riddance," she thought, "I'll be at college, meeting people more interesting than he can imagine, and he'll be flying a stupid plane," but a pang of guilt coursed through her stomach when she thought of Chad telling her he was joining the Air Force; how she'd broken up with him, telling him that maybe he was comfortable putting his life in danger but she couldn't support it.

Maybe she was a bad person.

No, she was ready to move on with her life, ready for college, ready to date new people. Chad and Friendly High were her past—even though she still had five weeks left until graduation, and he'd be around until he left for Basic Training in July. "Can't we stay together until I leave?" Chad had asked her, hoping that she would end up deciding to wait for him while he enlisted. After all, they'd been together for almost three years and were one of the most serious couples at Friendly High.

Blakeley College had great student to teacher ratios, fascinating academic departments, and an eclectic, welcoming student population, but one of the main reasons Erin was leaning towards choosing it was to put Friendly, Ohio and Chad and high school altogether behind her. She was comfortable enough there, but she had always known she belonged somewhere else. Somewhere like Blakeley, where people were interesting and different—where there were people like Quinn.

She looked over at him again. He was pale and angular, with white blonde hair. It rained a lot in Portland, he had told her. She thought he looked like Draco Malfoy, then chided herself for being such a childish nerd. Quinn was both serious and funny, and seemed so mature for a high school student. She hoped he ended up at Blakeley, although he had told her he was leaning towards matriculating at an experiential wilderness philosophy school back in the Pacific Northwest.

Feeling bold and not wanting to make Quinn feel uncomfortable about playing footsie with her, Erin rested her hand on his knee for a second, giving him a little smile. He smiled back, more broadly, and without hesitation put his entire arm over her shoulders, surrounding her with warmth. She was very attracted to him, she acknowledged, even though he was different from how she described her type to her friends. Maybe College Erin had a new type—or no type at all.

Quinn returned his arm to his side, and they both scooted closer to each other, shoulders pressed together. Suddenly, nonchalantly, he took her hand in his and her stomach fluttered. The lecture droned on about AP credits and focus areas, volunteering and student research opportunities, but it was all subsumed by the giddy buzz in Erin's head. Being romantic, physically affectionate with someone besides Chad felt so new, so shocking to her, and yet this was what she had imagined going away to visit college might be like, what she wanted to leave some possibility for when she had ended things with Chad. People around them began to stir, to stand up, and Erin realized the talk was over. She and Quinn remained seated for a moment.

"Well... I'm not sure I want to be a doctor. This sounds hella tedious," he said, breaking the ice.

She laughed, and responded, "Yeah, I'm not sure either."

"What's your schedule like now?" he asked, finally untangling his fingers from hers.

She replied, "I have a break for lunch until the Study Abroad Fair this afternoon. You?"

"I have a break too," he said, "but I'm not hungry—I've been eating all day at these open houses." Quinn looked down for an instant, then his eyes darted to meet hers, and he added, "I don't want to make you uncomfortable... but I'd like to spend more time alone with you and my host is out at classes all day so I have the room to myself. Would you want to come hang out?"

He looked nervous, and irresistibly cute.

"That sounds nice. I'd like to spend more time with you too," she responded.

As they filed out of the crowded room, she felt him brush against her from behind. Was it an accident? It happened again as they pushed into the bustling hallway, and he placed his hand on her hip for a fraction of a second. A little thrill shot through her.

Quinn was forward, but Erin was surprised to realize how much she was into it. She and Chad had been together for months—almost a year—before things got explicitly sexual, and they had gone slowly, only going all the way after homecoming this year. Their relationship was nice, predictable, and she had cared about him and felt like he cared about her, but she had never felt sharp, piercing desires with him the way she was starting to feel with Quinn.

Erin had thought sex could be more than a biological function, more than a physical exchange—and it *was* more, in her head—but that hadn't really translated to her experiences with Chad, and she had never been with anyone else. While she was away, visiting college, could be a perfect time to have an experience with someone else, someone she might only meet this weekend and never see again; someone who she had chemistry, not a friendship, with. She wanted to have an experience with someone who wasn't Chad, someone who didn't think he knew her so well; someone who met her as she was now, as an adult.

Was that someone Quinn? Perhaps.

Although Erin wasn't sure what she wanted to do with him, she was pleased that there now seemed a real possibility of *something* happening. She barely knew him, but there was no denying that she wanted him, and it seemed like he wanted her too. Was he a virgin? He probably wouldn't have been so comfortably and physically affectionate with her if he were, she thought. Would they have sex? Was he more experienced; into radical west coast things that alternative, sex-positive vegans did?

"Chill out, Erin," she told herself, taking a deep breath.

Quinn was telling her about his Sustainability Club back home, how they had taken a boat up to British Columbia to see the impact of drilling on the fragile shoreline and wildlife. He was somehow earnest and cool, intriguing and bland. She told him about the trip she had taken to Louisiana with her church group last summer to clean up after the big oil spill, and by the time she had gotten to the part about the orphaned manatees, they had reached the dorm where he was staying.

Quinn fumbled with the keys, and opened the door for her.

The dorm was a mess, and the occupant's belongings were piled in the corners to make room for a twin size inflatable mattress on the floor where Quinn had slept the previous night.

Quinn sat down on one corner of the airbed with a laugh. "Well, welcome to my lounge," he said.

She sat down in the middle of the bed; feeling as though this had become strangely intimate—and they hadn't even kissed yet!—but maybe that's what college was like.

As though he had read her mind, Quinn said, "Erin, could I kiss you?"

She responded impulsively by leaning forward herself and putting her hand against his shoulder, and he kissed her, softly at first, then more forcefully, clasping his hand in her hair as a passionate make out built between them.

Erin grew breathless as he pulled her closer, before she pushed away and said, "Quinn… I want you to know that this is a little new for me. I really like you, but I just ended a relationship with someone I was with for a long time."

"Do you not want to go so fast?"

"No, no, I like you. I think you're really attractive, and this is nice. I just wanted you to know that this is different for me—I want it to be different." She wasn't sure what she meant, and felt a bit foolish.

"Well, I'm a different kind of guy," he chuckled.

He traced his finger over her lips, caressing her cheek. Again, she felt a shock, a surge of desire, and she gasped slightly. This was what she had been looking for: passion.

She hadn't wanted Quinn to get the wrong impression, and she still wasn't sure how far she wanted to go with him, but she was glad things had become physical.

Quinn smiled, and leaned in to kiss her again.

She ran her hands through his soft hair, and they began to make out again, his hands exploring her body, hers clutching at his t-shirt. As she drew closer, he fell back until she was lying atop him. Even though she was on top, he was forceful, even aggressive, grabbing her arms, her neck, her hair, her hips, her breasts.

Erin felt a little taken aback. She hadn't expected this from this thin alternative peacenik, but it turned her on in a way Chad's fumbling petting never had and she felt herself growing wet with desire, and grasping at Quinn in return. She felt him shift his hips beneath her and could feel him growing hard, pressed against her thigh. This was much closer to the passionate sex she had fantasized about, and she wanted to see what would happen. She wanted to have sex with him. What felt like a wave of energy swept through her, and she pressed against him in return.

"I want you," she gasped.

"You sound surprised," Quinn teased.

"I am! But I do!"

She kept kissing him, and an aching need for him swept through her, starting from the pit of her stomach—mixed with butterflies of nervousness, of fear. Was she really going to have sex with him? He was practically a stranger! They had just met!

Quinn wrapped his arm around her, pinning her against his chest, holding her by the hair with his other hand. Her legs parted, straddling him, and he began to grind against her.

Second thoughts raced through Erin's head, and she felt her body tensing. Sure, he seemed nice, and this seemed like a safe environment for experimentation, but should she be afraid? Was this a bad idea? She thought she wanted to have sex with him, but he was already strangely physically dominating, and it was their first time together.

She liked it, but she wasn't sure if she should.

"Erin, do you know about safe words?" Quinn asked abruptly.

"What?" Now was an odd time to return to their earlier conversation about theory of language, she thought.

"You know, like if you're with someone— sexually—and you don't like what's happening and you want it to stop, you say a safe word, so that person knows what you want and don't want. Like, you could say 'lollipop' if you want it to stop, or 'orange' if you want to slow down or back off on something."

"Ok... that makes sense..." Erin was a little puzzled about what the confusion might be, but then again she didn't know what to expect and appreciated that he was letting her in on his way of communicating sexually before things went further. At least he was open to stopping if she wanted to, so she wouldn't have to go through with anything she didn't like.

"I... I have something to tell you too. I like rough sex," Quinn said, a little bashful.

Erin froze.

"I think something's wrong with me," he continued, "It's hard for me to do it any other way. I think I watched too much porn when I was 13 or something, and you seem like a nice person and I don't want to do anything bad to you..."

Quinn trailed off, looking nauseously self-conscious now, his eyes downcast. He took a deep breath, and his eyes met hers for an instant before drifting to some point above her left shoulder as he continued, determined to get it all out, "But... I like to be dominant. Maybe even to hurt you... My ex... was into it, and we learned how to communicate about it. That's why safe words are so important to me, and why I wanted to tell you about this before we went even farther. Because I'm really into you too, as you can tell, and I don't want to freak you out or upset you. Are... you into that... at all? I thought about bringing it up before, but I didn't want to be presumptuous."

Quinn had somewhat released the arm pinning Erin against him, but she was hyperaware of its pressure on her back, of his erection pressing against her. Although she had felt a chill of fear at his saying the words "hurt you," she couldn't deny that she felt turned on. Her fantasies sometimes got more violent; being pinned down, tied up, fucked impersonally... but she had never really let herself imagine acting them out—and certainly not with Chad!

She hadn't let herself acknowledge consciously that this was something she was into, perhaps—but she sometimes touched herself, thinking about a man—an attractive man, but one she didn't know too well; even a stranger—holding her down and fucking her hard. Whenever this happened, she'd orgasm quickly and powerfully— when push the thought from her mind, self-conscious about why it excited her. But if Quinn wanted to do it like that, and didn't want to force her to do anything she wasn't into… Maybe it could be the perfect opportunity to act on these desires, to explore them with someone she liked.

She swallowed. "I could be into that. Thank you for telling me... before…"

"Of course! I don't want to scare you. It's only good if we can trust each other and communicate. Do you remember the safe words?"

"Um... 'lollipop' to stop and 'orange' to slow down... "

"Do you still want me?" asked Quinn.

"Yes… I do," Erin whispered in his ear.

Part Two

At that, Quinn wrapped his arms around Erin and flipped her over in one sudden move, so she was on her back. He held her in a chokehold, her throat pressed against his shoulder, her arms pinned against her sides by his other arm.

She felt powerless, pinned under his body, unable to move, knowing that he wanted to take her... Her hands rested on his back, and she could feel his hardness pushing against her. Fear swirled through her. This was what she was supposed to be afraid of—but she liked him; she was trusting him, and although she could tell him to stop, she didn't want to.

He kissed her again, fiercely, pulling her head back by the hair and pressing his erection into her stomach. She moaned, and struggled against him, finding herself still unable to move. Waves of arousal swept through her, and she went limp, letting him overpower her.

Quinn released her, and sat up. He was straddling her, pinning her down with his hips. They looked at each other, faces flushed, breathing hard—Quinn's hair was a mess, and Erin could feel her body shaking with excitement; her eyes wide, her breath coming in gasps, her chest heaving.

Quinn began pulling off her shirt. She complied with his efforts, sitting up halfway, then tugging off his shirt herself. He was lean, fit, pale; not muscular, but strong. She was still wet, she could tell—her jeans were uncomfortable against her. Her hips were bucking, but her knees were shaking too. She tried to calm herself, but she could feel him on top of her, pinning her down, and her mind kept shouting, "He's going to fuck me! He's going to fuck me!" She was aroused by the thought, but couldn't tell if this arousal was more tinged with anticipation, or fear.

"You're beautiful," Quinn said. He was looking down at her, almost lovingly, it seemed; lying in her bra beneath him.

Erin was calmed by his words, by the look in his eyes. He liked her, after all. He wasn't just trying to have sex with her—he had invited her over, and asked to kiss her, but she was the one who had been fantasizing about him, and who had said she wanted to have sex! Still, she was nervous. She and Chad had been having sex somewhat regularly for the last few months, but this felt all new, as though she had no idea what might happen.

Quinn continued to gaze at her, a harder look in his eyes now as he slowly unbuckled his belt and slid it out of his pant loops. He folded it over in his hands, and for a second she flinched, thinking he was going to hit her with it—her dad had hit her with his belt once when she was much younger, when she had climbed on top of a plate of glass he was installing and had broken it, 'nearly killing herself,' as he had put it. In what seemed like a blind rage, he had struck her, shouting 'you could have died!' until her mom heard her cries coming from the backyard and had stopped him, furious with both of them. It was one of her most vivid childhood memories, from back at the old house. Was that what Quinn meant by 'hurt her'? Did he want to hit her? Like 50 Shades of Grey? She had read the book on her phone over Christmas Break, and it had kept her entertained, but she wasn't sure if she liked it; if she would really want to do that, let alone have a relationship like that. Quinn set his belt on the side of the bed, and she felt somewhat foolish. Why had she thought he would want to do that? Did that mean she wanted him to? Or that she was afraid of it?

He stood up, towering over her as he unbuttoned and unzipped his khakis, letting them fall down and then stepping out of them. He was wearing black boxer briefs and she could see the outline of his penis straining against them.

"Take off your pants," he commanded.

Erin nodded, unbuttoning them and sliding them down her legs as he watched.

"Suck my cock."

Again, a burst of arousal. She had never been *commanded* to do anything sexually, and it thrilled her to hear the words from Quinn's lips, to imagine obeying him, submitting to him, letting him take charge— but her throat felt constricted.

Did she want to suck his cock? She wanted to see him naked; she liked doing it sometimes, and it would probably make her more comfortable sexually with him, but she was nervous about what he might expect, nervous about not doing it right.

She rose to her knees, and he grabbed her chin, looking into her eyes, asking, "Hey, is this ok? Are you into this?"

She nodded.

"Are you scared?"

She nodded again.

"Do you trust me?"

She shrugged, and nodded once more.

"I'm trusting you too…" he said, "I'm trusting that you'll tell me if you don't like what's happening, ok? You can tell me if you want to stop, or if you would like something else better."

"Ok," Erin said quietly. She liked that he knew what he wanted, so she didn't have to think so much about what to do. It stressed her out and turned her off to try to figure out what to do next while she was having sex.

She reached to caress Quinn's hips and bulge before tugging down the waistband of his boxers. His cock sprang free, and it was as pale as the rest of him, maybe a little shorter than Chad's, but definitely thicker. She stroked it with her hand and looked up at him.

"I didn't say to touch it, I said to suck it. As much as you can fit in your mouth," said Quinn. His face was stern, his voice clipped.

Erin still felt a rush of excitement at the dirty talk, but she felt anxious about what else he might want her to do, about whether she'd be able to tell if it was what she wanted too.

She dropped her hands to her sides and leaned forward, opening her mouth and licking the tip of his penis before enveloping the head with her lips, easing her tongue along its underside, sliding forward until she felt resistance at the back of her throat. She began rocking, sliding her mouth up and down his shaft. She tried to fit more with each push, gagging slightly.

Quinn groaned, placing his hand on her head. "That's right, choke on it," he said. He left his hand on her head, but refrained from pushing her onto him, letting her control the pace and depth.

Erin felt a surge of desire; she wanted to feel him on top of her, inside her, commanding her to receive him, to take more of him.

She also felt a bit self-conscious. Did she really want him to talk to her like that?

Erin could tell Quinn was trying not to push her too far too fast, while expanding her comfort zone significantly. She closed her eyes and tried to fit more of him in her mouth, starting to choke and feeling tears well behind her closed eyelids. Her throat clenched and she panicked for a moment, but she ached for him, and part of her wanted to swallow all of him, to deep throat him, to let him use her in this way.

She could hear his breathing deepen as she bobbed up and down, still gagging but trying to relax, to release her resistance.

Suddenly she felt his hand clench in her hair and pull her head off of him. "I want to fuck you," he gasped.

Quinn pushed her down onto her back before she could react, pulling down her underwear in one swift movement as she tried to catch her breath.

Kneeling between her legs, he reached over and pulled a condom from his wallet, tearing open the wrapper with his teeth and sliding it over himself fluidly.

Erin could feel that she was wet for him and looked into his eyes as he lunged down on top of her, surprising her by wrapping his hand around her throat. Instinctively she grabbed his wrist with her hands and began to struggle as he pushed her knees apart and pressed his erection between her legs.

He was not strangling her, she realized, just holding her down. Her panic subsided a little and turned to arousal as she felt him pressing at the entrance to her vagina and realized how ready she was for him.

She could hear her breath coming in little frantic cries as she strained against him. She was naked now—and he was on top of her, hard between her legs. She wanted him to take her, to pound into her. She wanted to feel how much he desired her.

Erin couldn't help but try to keep her legs closed to protect herself, and Quinn struggled to position himself against her. She felt internal conflict swirling within. Part of her felt defenseless, vulnerable; her knees spread by his, his body on top of hers, his hand around her throat. She felt scared, and for a second, thought about telling him to stop—but a larger part of her was begging him to fuck her, to push her past her comfort zone.

"I want to try this. I can stop it at any time," she told herself.

Quinn paused for a moment and looked her in the eyes, asking again, without words this time.

Erin nodded, and without breaking eye contact, he thrust deeply into her and she cried out. She could feel his thick cock stretching her, and her whole body tensed and relaxed at the same time. As she was adjusting to it, he thrust again, and again, until the whole thing was inside her; buried deep, filling her.

She melted beneath him, gasping, breathing deeply, tears in her eyes. She began to grind into him, wanting him faster, harder, more. He paused for a moment, looking down at her before taking his hand from her throat, pinning her wrists on either side of her head, and continuing to pump in and out of her roughly, his hips slapping against her, her moans sounding like cries.

Erin lay there, taking him, struggling slightly to move her wrists and hips for a more comfortable angle as she bounced against the air mattress. There was some pain, but it also felt good, and more than that, it felt exciting to feel like Quinn wanted her, needed her like this, and that she could take him, could enjoy it too. She felt like a real adult woman.

Quinn sped up, pounding in and out of her violently, and Erin let out a sharp scream as she tightened around him, pulling him in. He let go of one of her wrists, putting his hand over her mouth to stifle the noise, and she instinctively brought her free hand to his hip, bracing herself against him as they furiously thrust themselves together. She felt like he was opening her up, swirling her into a tornado, consuming her. Her eyes closed, and she felt completely present in her body; letting go, surrendering to him.

Quinn let out a groan. With several long, firm strokes, he came inside of her, collapsing on top, removing his hand from her mouth. He let go of her wrist, but it was as though she could still feel his fingers digging into her.

Erin lay there, stunned by how explosive it had been. She was gasping, feeling him still inside of her. She was definitely still turned on, her hips rocking against him, but she was unsure what she wanted to do now.

Quinn lay on top of her, and she tentatively wrapped her arms around him, stroking his hair with her hand.

She was shocked by how things had developed between them, and was surprised by how much she had enjoyed it, once she let herself relax. Quinn seemed like such an adult, knowing what he wanted and telling her plainly, giving her a chance to say yes or no, and respecting her ability to consent to something that would have otherwise been outside her realm of comfort; not assuming it would be ok, going for it, and then apologizing, or expecting her to guide the whole experience, as Chad had often done.

Erin felt still, peaceful, lying there under Quinn, his penis softening inside her. Again she marveled at how quickly their relationship had developed, and how close she now felt to him. Despite this being a hook up—or perhaps because it was a hook up—she had felt freer to express herself to Quinn, and through being with him, she had become acquainted with an entirely new side of herself.

Quinn lay on top of her for a few moments, breathing deeply, before he pulled out, rolling to his side, and taking off the condom. "Are you ok? How are you? Did you come?" he asked.

"I... uh... wow... I'm good. That was intense. I've never done anything like that before, but I guess I liked it... Um, no, though, I didn't... come," Erin replied. She felt somewhat in a daze.

"Do you want to? I can touch you if you'd like," he offered.

"Ok..." she said tentatively, still aching between her legs.

Quinn slipped his arm under her shoulders, pulling her close to him and holding her by the hair, gently this time. He reached down with his other hand and began to stroke her, caressing her clit with his thumb, sliding his fingers in and out of her.

Erin had always felt self-conscious when Chad fingered her, but she let herself relax, opening to Quinn, replaying what had happened in her head, and after just a few moments she felt herself begin to shake uncontrollably.

Quinn held her firmly by the back of her neck, and she let go as she had never done before, even with herself; thinking of him, surrounding her, overpowering her. She could hear herself moaning, and it sounded like someone else as she felt wave after wave of orgasm spread through her body, hot and magnetic.

Quinn held her close as the shaking continued. He whispered in her ear, "That's right, come for me. Let go," until she relaxed completely against him, finally still.

They lay close for several more minutes, her chest heaving, her heart racing, until she started laughing.

"What is it?" Quinn asked.

"It's just... you make me feel like I've never really had sex before. It makes me look forward to college!"

"Maybe I'll come here after all," Quinn said with a little smile, tucking her hair behind her ear and kissing her on the cheek.

2: J

Trust

Trigger Warning: Discussion of Campus
Sexual Violence and Childhood Molestation

Part One

"Get some! Get some!"

J's friends began to pound their fists on the edge of the table, each of the five laughing and joining in on the chant started by Mac and Usa, who were on the basketball team and used every chance they could to start scenes like this. J's eyes darted around the cafeteria, seeing the mostly white students at neighboring tables begin to side-eye the group of loud black studs, sliding their chairs away a fraction of an inch.

"Shut up, fools!" J hissed. She looked to TZ, Kayla and Raimee to de-escalate. They were on the track and gymnastics teams, and for whatever reason, were often less inclined to make a scene.

"What's the matter, they ain't seen more than one of us at a time before?" Mac laughed, returning to her chicken strips and taking a bite while making a face at a nearby table that was still staring.

The group had begun eating meals together somewhat recently, although they had each known of each other separately for most of their time at Highland University. They each stood out in their own niches of campus but were often confused for each other by the rest of the student body.

"We might as well form our own crew," J had declared to Mac and Kayla when the three found themselves ostracized to the corner at the Dean's Honor List Banquet last semester. They took her suggestion to heart, inviting Usa, TZ and

24

Raimee over to Mac's apartment to smoke weed that evening after skipping out early on the Banquet.

Somehow they had wound up talking about what they would be called if they were a boy—or girl?—band, since they didn't seem to fit into any categories as individuals, but as a group, they made their own category; appearing nearly as coherent in their gender presentation as Boyz II Men or Destiny's Child, but in their own way. How was it that, if they didn't fit in to any other group, they fit in with each other, J wondered. She had never been around a group of people who seemed like her before. They weren't girls, and they weren't boys; they were bois, like some of the people she followed on Instagram.

> *"Hol up, We Dem Bois,*
> *Hol up, hol up, hol up,*
> *We makin' noise,"*

J had sung, high on THC and companionate intimacy. Then and there, they decided they would call themselves "dem bois," and from then on, they'd been a crew.

The other five already had an informal affection for each other as peer athletes, but J's addition to the cohort of queer black women had really cohered them as a friend group outside of any one team or niche. They had hung out almost every day since, becoming more and more comfortable taking up space around campus.

"We're the highest and flyest motherfuckers at Highland; that's what they're looking at," Usa would say whenever their presence drew unwarranted attention from their peers.

They each seemed to grow more confident in their presentation throughout the year, and the effects on J's sense of self had been seismic. During her first year at college, J kept a low profile, focusing on her schoolwork and keeping to herself, wearing more and more masculine clothing as the year went on. No matter what she did, she stuck out like a sore thumb in her classes and walking around campus. Even as she felt more like herself, more like the person she imagined herself to be, people couldn't seem to see *her* behind the front, behind the sweats, the jerseys, even the dapper khakis and button-downs she liked to wear sometimes. At least back in Atlanta, people knew her, even though she had to wear stupid girl shit to keep Pops happy and fit in at school, at church.

Ever since she found dem bois, that had all changed. Even though she wasn't on a team, and wasn't cut like them, the others respected her style, respected her vibe. Her clothes seemed to fit her better when she was with them, although she often had a sinking feeling that she was no more the J they knew than the Janelle she had been at Madison Polytechnic High School for Achievement. The real her was somewhere in between the person that Aliya, her best friend from Madison High, had known and loved, and the person dem bois saw as their man from the ATL... and, somehow, the 'Janelle' her Pops still saw as his little girl.

J looked up from her fries to see the group all staring at her.

"Don't leave us hanging, you haven't gone on a date all year!" Raimee said.

"Who's the girl and what makes her so special?" Kayla added.

J was the longest-standing single member of the group. Indeed, she had little to no exploits whatsoever to add to their regular play-by-plays of conquests with girls on their teams, girls in the city, girls from back home, girls they were dating. J would allude to things from high school, but she felt duplicitous, like they'd laugh at her if they knew her most intimate experiences were sleepovers with Aliya where they had held each other, did each other's hair, even kissing sometimes—well, twice—after high school graduation.

J returned her attention to the table. Finally she had something to dish, but she didn't want to give them the wrong idea. She didn't know what the idea was herself, as she was still giddy over even having asked beautiful Cata to get together with her outside of class, outside of the library.

"Um, you know, it's that girl from my bio class. My lab partner. The one I told y'all I thought was trying to get with me... I think she is, and, you know, I don't wanna stand in the way, so I asked her out," J said. She could feel herself blushing, and tried to play it cool.

"Ayyyy!" they collectively broke out in a roar again, but quieter this time.

Mac leaned in, "What happened, like specifically? We need a play by play, we gotta figure out whether she's into you or just wants that D..."

"What?" Usa interrupted, "You know, and I hope that girl knows, she ain't got no D! Is she gay?"

"You know what I mean." Mac muttered.

J cut her off, saying, "Yo, it ain't like that! It's a date, man. The goal is to figure that out. I don't know what she's thinking. I wish I did, but all I know is that she said yes to going to the step show with me tomorrow, and... and we're going to get some ice cream."

It sounded juvenile, girly as she said it out loud, and Raimee interjected, "Aww, so cute. Are you gonna lick her ice cream cone?"

Raimee liked to brag about going down on her "bi-curious" track teammate for hours, and when they were talking about sex, used every chance she could to bring it up.

"You know, the first time Tina and I.." she continued.

"Shut up about you and Tina!" TZ, the other member of the track team, snapped. "We wanna hear about J's girl. What's her name? How did you ask her out? Is she gay?"

"She's not my girl!" J responded defensively. "Her name is Cata."

"Oh, she's Spanish? You're definitely gonna get some!" Raimee burst out, doing a little samba in her seat.

TZ punched her shoulder, saying "Shut up, bro, don't talk about her that way. That's offensive."

Raimee held up her hands, but let it go. J was glad TZ had shut Raimee down so she didn't have to.

"She's Colombian. And she's not like that. It's not like that. I think she might like me, but I don't know if she's gay or whatever. She never mentioned any boyfriend, and I told you about her flirting with me, but I don't know, man."

"Let's see a picture!" Mac exclaimed, and they began to browse through Catalina de la Rosa's Instagram on TZ's phone.

"Gay or not, she's fucking hot!" Kayla chimed in.

J hoped they couldn't tell she was blushing, still. The banter continued as they got up, cleared their trays, and left the cafeteria, going their separate ways in the night.

* * * * *

As J walked past Feinholtz Library on the way to her dorm, she thought about how she and Cata had studied for their midterm together last weekend, staying until the library closed at 2 AM, sharing Pringles, Gushers, and an energy drink from the vending machine. Cata had looked gorgeous in those purple sweatpants and that white tank, her hair in a messy ponytail, leaning on J's shoulder, laughing, adorable and sleepy, as they stumbled out of the library together.

J had felt an overwhelming urge to kiss her then, to wrap her arms around her and never let go; to tell her how beautiful she was and how much fun the evening had been, but she didn't want to ruin what they had shared, and so she had pulled away and said, tactfully, "Alright, so I'll see you in class on Monday. Goodnight, Cata."

Her name lingered on J's tongue. Cata had looked at her, and for a moment J could have sworn that Cata wanted to kiss her too, before she backed away and said, "You know, you're getting close, but it's CAH-tuh, not Caah-tuh"

It sounded the same to J, and she had replied, "Alright, girl, I'll work on it, but you know it's my southern accent. I can't help it! Maybe that's how we say it in Atlanta."

"Si, pero you're in Florida now!" said Cata. She flashed J a cute smirk, poking fun at her; flirting, it seemed, but you could never really tell when it came to women...

They had parted ways, and J replayed each moment over and over again in her head, feeling like she had kept it together surprisingly well—and it seemed like Cata could actually be into her too! But was she queer, or just friendly?

They had sat next to each other at the midterm on Monday, exchanging anxious smiles. Cata finished her exam before J and left first, so they hadn't spoken again until Wednesday's field module trip to the Botanical Preserve. Cata was J's partner, and although she had seemed a bit upset when she arrived to class, they sat next to each other on the bus, and laughed and brushed against each other as they collected samples from the wetlands, talking about high school and their favorite movies on the ride back and as they stood around waiting for their classmates. J's stomach had knotted when Cata spontaneously gave her a hug on the bus, conspicuously aware of the scent of Cata's hair, the warmth of her body pressed against J for an instant.

J thought that besides Aliya, Cata was the closest thing she had ever had to a girlfriend, and that their weekly companionate forays into dissection, genetic splicing, and problem sets were the closest things to dates she had experienced since coming to college. After the study session and field trip went so well, J had resolved that the next time she saw Cata, she would to ask her to do something outside of class to see if there was anything more between them. If it was just in her head, she didn't want to fall for Cata any further than she already had.

It happened that day; on Thursday, after class, while clearing up their books together, that Cata had casually asked what J's plans for the weekend were. J, tongue-tied, said that she was going to the step show tomorrow, and without asking Cata about her plans, she blurted out, before she lost her nerve, "Would you want to go with me? I think you're really cool, and think it would be great if we could hang out outside of studying sometime. Maybe we could get some ice cream or something too... There's a great place just off-campus."

Cata's face seemed blank, unreadable for a moment, then she smiled and said, "Yeah, that sounds interesting. Let's go."

"Ok, I'll pick you up at your dorm at 8 and we can walk over together. Text me the address?" J added. Cata gave her a little smile and confirmed, then left the classroom hurriedly.

Reviewing what happened, J wondered why Cata had paused. What had she thought in that moment?

Was it because it was a gay date?

Or because she wasn't sure if she wanted to be friends like that outside of class, to spend their Friday evening together?

Or because J had invited her to something so black— Why hadn't she just asked if they could see a movie together? What would it be like at the step show, a crowd of people… a crowd of black people? Would Cata be uncomfortable?

Should J try to make it more of a date, or less of a date?

What if the whole thing was too black and too gay and Cata never wanted to talk to her again?

Would she ask to switch to a new lab partner?

J decided she was probably overthinking it. There was nothing she could do anyway, save to feel it out once it was happening.

The step show was outside this year, in Courtyard Commons and J realized that if they snuck out to the patio above the math department they would have a private view. She remembered the access code her Calc TA had given her to set up for their Departmental Picnic last spring—it was the first six digits of pi, and she didn't think they'd changed it.

Should she set up a picnic?

She didn't want it to seem too premeditated.

Maybe a bottle of wine?

She didn't want it to seem like she was trying to get Cata drunk.

Maybe flowers? Should she bring her flowers?

There were so many things that could go wrong.

J ran through scenarios in her head all night, and all Friday morning. Her other classes seemed dry, unimportant. She wondered if Cata was thinking about her, if she remembered that they'd made plans.

Part Two

After her last class, J returned to her dorm and sat on the bed. Would Cata come back to her room? She should clean just in case, she thought.

She straightened up the odds and ends, smoothed her bed, and picked up and folded the clothing on the floor, thinking nervously about how it was only four hours until she was going to go pick Cata up. Four hours. What was she going to do with herself?

J's stomach grumbled. She picked up a packet of Ramen noodles from the shelf and went to the dorm kitchen, where she found her floor-mate Darnell bent over a textbook in the adjacent lounge.

"Hey, man," she said.

Darnell responded, "What's popping, bro? Friday night!"

She began to prepare the Ramen, putting some water to boil, and offered, "I got a date tonight."

It was true, but she still felt anxious, as though she were misleading people. What if Cata didn't feel the same way and found out J had been calling it a date?

"Congrats, man!" said Darnell, "Is she pretty? It's—she's a girl, right? I ain't never seen you go on a date..."

"Yeah, it's a girl, dude! She's perfect," said J, "The problem is just figuring out whether she likes me."

"Well, imma be here all night with this Accounting textbook. She's my girl this weekend, until I pass this midterm on Monday," Darnell said.

He looked back to his textbook, and J opened the packet of Ramen, adding the block of noodles to the boiling water, poking it around with a fork. She checked the time.

Darnell looked up, and said abruptly, "Oh, I got that new shit from Colorado I was telling you about! You're gonna love it! I can't smoke this weekend or I'd invite you over to try it out. You want me to drop some off later? You gonna be around?"

"Yeah, I'll take my usual," said J. She spent too much money on weed, but Darnell was a good dealer, and always made her feel like it was worth it. She added, "I'll be around for the next few hours. Stop by whenever you get a chance. I can't wait to try it."

J finished preparing the Ramen, and said, "Good luck, bro," to Darnell as she moved to leave the room.

"Good luck to you, my man!" Darnell shot back, "I'll be sending you my mojo, since I won't be using it tonight."

"You can keep your mojo. Use it on that test! I got my shit on lock," J retorted. Darnell laughed.

She left the common room and returned to her room to eat the Ramen while watching an episode of Real Housewives of Atlanta. The world the show was set in was nothing like her Atlanta, but it reminded her of the parts of Atlanta she disliked and made her less homesick. Plus, the women's problems were nothing like her own, so it was a welcome distraction.

When the episode finished, J began to browse through the music on her laptop, absent-mindedly putting together a playlist of songs that reminded her of Cata. She thought that maybe she'd burn her a CD, then thought better of it as she found herself pulling together the most cheesily romantic subset of her iTunes Library.

She heard a soft knock at the door, and she opened it to let Darnell in. He tried to be inconspicuous, but J could smell a waft of dank herb coming off of him even before he pulled the baggie of weed from his pocket. He passed it to her, and she slipped him a thin roll of ten and twenty dollar bills.

"I promise you, this stuff is so dope," he said. "Morning Sunrise, it's called. My buddy in Colorado swears by it. It's his favorite new strand. They imported it after it swept the Cannabis Cup over in Amsterdam last year. It's a hybrid; heavy indica feel, clear head high—and twenty-five percent THC. Twenty-five fucking percent! You gotta let me know what you think of it."

Darnell returned to the lounge, saying it was too tempting to hang out with her without being able to roll a nice joint from the new supply.

J looked at the baggie, took a whiff of the buds, and thought about rolling herself a small j while she waited. She decided it would probably make her more anxious about the date. She wanted to try the new strand in a relaxed environment, and she didn't want to show up high at Cata's door. She tucked the new stash away in the hand-painted air sealed time capsule TZ had given her for her last birthday, and checked the time again. Finally, it was after 7!

J began to get dressed, pulling on her nice khakis and a black button-up shirt. She added her favorite green kicks and a jade floral bow tie, smoothing back her dreads. She looked at herself in the mirror and thought she looked pretty handsome. She hoped Cata would think so.

She checked her phone, noticing that Cata had texted her:

Bingsley Hall 204, see u later!

J hit reply, then sat there for a minute, unsure what to say, settling on:

On my way.

She decided not to add an emoji—she didn't want to seem overeager.

J had asked for Cata's number when they became lab partners, but all their previous texts had been more formal, deciding where and when to meet to study together. It felt like a big step to be sending personal messages, even if they were still curt and logistical.

J walked to Cata's dorm and entered the building. She could hear her heard pounding in her ears as she wandered through the halls, looking for room 204. She got turned in circles, but eventually found it. Her hands were shaking slightly, and she wiped her sweaty palms on her khakis before knocking on the door three short times.

She glanced at her phone. It was 7:58. She hoped she wasn't too early, that it wasn't weird to show up on time. The show wasn't until 8:30. She heard a noise inside, and Cata opened the door.

J's stomach turned. Cata was naked, hair wet, wrapped in a towel.

"Sorry! I got back from dinner late and just got out of the shower! I hope you don't mind waiting a little bit, come in!" exclaimed Cata with an apologetic grin.

J thought she looked both adorable and extremely sexy. She pulled herself together enough to say, awkwardly, "Well, I would give you a hug, but..."

Cata laughed, and repeated, "Come in so I can finish getting ready!" She beckoned J in.

J stepped into the room, and it was surprisingly messy, desk cluttered with stacks of papers, clothes in piles on the floor. Posters of Audrey Hepburn, elegant cigarette extender in hand, and Marilyn Monroe, flirtatious and wild, decorated her walls alongside pictures with friends, and dub step music was playing over the speakers. J noticed q-tips, make-up, and various little tools spilling from a worn gold leopard print beauty bag on top of Cata's dresser, next to a mound of little bottles of nail polish.

"Nice space," J said. She was pleased to be inside Cata's temple.

Cata responded, "Sorry it's such a mess!"

She was opening drawers, gathering clothes, pulling a black lace bra from the top of a pile of laundry. When she noticed J still standing by the door, she added, "You can sit on the bed if you want."

J complied with the suggestion, smoothing the rumpled quilted kaleidoscope blanket at the foot of the bed and perching uncertainly, hands clasped.

Cata went over to the bathroom she shared with her suite-mate, and J did a double take as she watched her legs and shoulders emerging from the towel as she walked away.

This was going ok, she thought, although Cata was already so much more than J had imagined. That was a good thing, she acknowledged, as it would have been difficult to be friends with, let alone date, the Cata of her imagination.

The bathroom door was slightly ajar, and J could see a sliver of Cata's back, of her upper thigh silhouetted in the fluorescent bathroom lighting as she hurriedly dressed. J looked away, then back, then away, fixating her attention on the blanket's intricate pattern to distract herself.

Why had Cata left the door open? It seemed more carelessness than seduction, and J didn't want to leer. The music was pulsing, robotic and sensual, and J listened to it, bemused to think that perhaps this was what Cata was listening to on her headphones before and after class.

Cata emerged from the bathroom, hair falling in loose curls around her shoulders, wearing a short pink tube skirt and draped black halter top, with black high-top converse.

"Wow, you look great!" J said.

Cata laughed slightly and said, "Oh my god, no! My hair's all wet and I couldn't find the skirt I wanted, but thanks..." She added, as an afterthought, "It's Friday, want to take a shot?"

It was J's turn to laugh, taken aback. "Yeah, sure, I'm down," she said.

Cata took a half full bottle of Bacardi Limón from her dresser, along with two fluorescent plastic shot glasses, which she filled, handing one to J.

"To new friends," Cata said as they clinked their glasses together.

J took the shot, coughing slightly at the burning aftertaste, and Cata, who had downed hers in one quick gulp, said, "Sorry I don't have a chaser! Want another?"

"Yeah, ok," J replied, head spinning slightly from more than just being in Cata's presence now. Maybe this would help her relax.

They took another shot. The music seemed more vivid, deeper to J. She felt her head bob to the grinding bass line. She wanted to dance with Cata, to feel her body pressed against hers, but she stayed seated on the foot of the bed.

"Ready to go?" Cata said, turning with a flourish as she set the bottle on the top of the dresser, shaking out the shot glasses. She bustled around the room, turning off the music and the lights in the bathroom, picking up her keys.

"Yeah, let's go," said J.

Cata held the door open for J and they shared a brief moment of intense eye contact. It felt like Cata was really, finally looking at J, seeing her.

Cata closed and locked the door behind them, her keys and student ID hanging from a thin lanyard under her top.

J's eyes flicked over Cata's ass, shapely and beautiful in the fitted skirt. It mesmerized her for a moment, then she cleared her throat and put her hands in her pockets.

"So... How are you?" J offered.

They began to walk down the hallway, making their way across campus to the quad.

"Oh, you know. Still adjusting to being at school. I was Skyping with my friends in Miami this afternoon, and I guess I'm feeling pretty homesick. I'm excited to see the show. One of my friends is a stepper. Not here, though. They're all dancers; they're at dance school together in Miami. I used to be a dancer. Well, I am a dancer. I just haven't decided whether I'm going to be a dancer here."

Cata was a very expressive speaker, gesturing exuberantly with her hands as she spoke, nearly hitting J several times as they walked down the hallway side by side.

"Oh, so you're a dancer?" J asked rhetorically. Cata's sensuality, her posture; the lithe and vibrant way she moved all made sense now. "What kind of dance?"

"Yeah, I always will be a dancer," replied Cata, "It's in my bones. I've been doing it since I was a little girl. I did ballet, then jazz, then some salsa, then in high school I got more into hip hop and contemporary mixed with, you know, jazz. And some other stuff."

"Wow, you're a real dancer!" said J.

"Now I just dance when my friends and I go clubbing in town. I have a fake, so I can get in,"

41

Cata looked slightly distracted, and changed the topic slightly, asking J, "What's your creative passion?"

J hadn't considered herself a creative person for some time, but when Cata asked, she remembered how much she had enjoyed singing in the gospel choir at church, in the chorus at school back home, how she still sung in the shower, and she responded, "Well, I guess I'm a singer, but not like how you're a dancer. I just like to sing sometimes."

"You have to sing for me!" burst out Cata.

"Uh… What?" replied J.

"Yeah, sing something for me! Don't be shy," insisted Cata.

J had Chris Brown's "Excuse me, Miss" playing in her head from the playlist she had compiled earlier. They were now outside, on an isolated part of the path across campus, and she decided to go for it.

"Should I talk about her smile?
Or what about her style?
I'm out of time, she's out the door, I gotta go for mine,
I think I'll say,
Yo, I don't know your name but excuse me, miss,
I saw you from across the room,
and I gotta admit that you got my attention,
you makin me want to say ooh,"

J sang, then laughed. She was pleased that it had actually come out sounding pretty good, then again, it had been her favorite song when she was 12 and she knew it forward and back.

Cata clapped her hands, then patted J on the back heartily.

"Touché," Cata said.

Feeling confident, flirtatious, J offered, "I'm glad you liked it. Maybe sometime you can dance for me."

A slight hush fell, and it seemed they were both acknowledging that they weren't just new friends, that this was a date, that there was an undeniable attraction between them, although what that attraction meant to each of them remained unclear.

Cata smiled at J, sneaking a look over at her, pushing back her hair, and saying, "Maybe."

* * * * *

They arrived at the Commons, and it was already packed with students, swarming, seated in packs, crowding for a place to see the patio at the center.

"Come with me," J said, taking Cata's hand and guiding her through the crowd to the front of the Carlsby Hall of Mathematics, which bordered the courtyard. The building was still open, students working on problem sets in conference rooms, custodians cleaning the floor.

J cracked the door open, slipping inside, Cata following behind.

Cata's hand felt soft in hers, and J noted their fingertips parting, hands sliding apart as they entered inside the building.

"What are we...?" Cata began.

J held her finger to her lips, and said, "Follow me," heading up a flight of stairs.

They reached a landing, and before them was a locked door to the grad student lounge. Cata was eying J quizzically, but without a pause J entered the door code, and said, "Ta-da!" opening the door and revealing the attached patio with a view of the courtyard and crowd below.

"How did you...?" Cata started to ask.

J replied, "I've been here a while. I know people." She paused, then added, "in the math department."

They proceeded out to the patio, J relieved to have made it this far without any mishaps, and pleasantly surprised that being with Cata felt like being with a friend. A startlingly attractive friend who gave her butterflies each time she looked at her, but a friend nonetheless.

They stood along the railing, shoulder to shoulder, watching the show assemble below.

"So how are you liking Highland? I mean, besides that bio midterm that slayed us both." J asked.

"I don't know," Cata said, "I told you I've been feeling homesick— for Miami, for dance. I even miss my family, and I thought I wanted to go to school outside Miami to get some space from them. It's been like two months now, and I still only hang out with a group of guys and girls from my high school. Actually, we went to middle school together, but they're not really my closest friends to be honest; they're just like, the people I know here. We used to go clubbing every weekend in town, which was fun, but now they're all pledging Greek houses except me, so if we're on campus on the weekend, we end up hanging out at the two frats the guys are in; Sigma Chi and Delta Ep. That's where they all are tonight."

"Yeah, that's kind of the main scene, until you get to know people who live off-campus." J replied.

The show started below, but they could still hear each other over the noise. They leaned close, and continued their conversation.

"I went last weekend to a party at Sigma Chi and it was so crowded," said Cata, "Every time I started dancing, a brother would think I was trying to get with him and would grab me, you know. So I don't know if I really want to hang out there anymore; it's better at the clubs where there's space to dance... alone." She looked disgusted.

J's stomach twisted, to think of these drunk guys groping, fondling Cata against her will, assuming she was there for them. A lot of girls were interested in picking up frat guys, though, and J noted that Cata was not one of them; the note of disdain in her voice, the insinuation that she'd rather dance alone. Was it because she was queer? Or because she was used to being assaulted, to having people assume she was there for their sexual validation?

"I'm sorry you experienced that. I think they're gross too; the frat parties. I went a couple times my freshman fall too, and it's pretty grimy. Crowded and impossible to get a drink. Not that I drink much, but I did more then."

Cata looked troubled, and J asked, "You ok?"

"I shouldn't tell you this," she started, eyes downcast, "but I don't know who else to talk to. I told you why I don't like to hang out at Sigma Chi, but Delta Ep... something bad happened to my friend there last weekend."

Cata started nervously playing with the tips of her hair. The corner of her mouth twisted a little, and J listened quietly as she continued, "My friend Alejandra. She was in the hospital, then left campus. She went back to Miami this week. She's gone. And they're all hanging out there, at the Beach Party tonight anyway, like it doesn't even matter."

"What happened?" J couldn't help but ask, although she had heard too many stories not to have some idea. "You don't have to tell me."

Cata, on the verge of tears, eyes fixed on the movement below, let it spill out.

"Ok, so we were at the party there last Saturday, Ale and I and the rest of the group. The guys too. Jorge and Eddy are pledges there, with the other guys from the baseball team. This guy, this brother, was flirting with her, and brought her a drink. He was cute; we thought it was ok, but I think there was something in it, because she started acting weird. I thought she was just drunk. I thought she left to go home. She told me, 'I gotta go,' and ran off."

Cata turned to face J, continuing her confession, "I should have gone with her. She went to the bathroom, and the guy followed her, and he said she could lie down in his room until she felt better, and he took her there. She doesn't really remember any more, but she thinks there were two of them, and they... did things to her, made her do things... They put a blanket over her and left her naked on the porch with the words "drunk slut" written on her forehead. She woke up there, and she can't remember who they were. None of the guys will say who they were; they don't want to turn on one of their own, especially a teammate. I saw him; I saw him give her the drink, but I don't remember what he looks like. I was drunk too, and all these white guys look the same. Jorge and Eddy say they don't know anything about it, but they're in the house! How can they not know? How can they still be there tonight? How can they choose that over Ale? I had to talk to the police on Tuesday, and they just asked if she drank a lot; if this was normal for her, and if I drank a lot too, and that was why I couldn't even remember what he looked like. They said we should all be more careful. And that I should be more careful so it doesn't happen to me too."

She began to cry, covering her face, her words ending with, "Sorry!"

J had listened quietly to the story, watching flickers of pain dance across Cata's face, coiled rage building in her stomach, her chest. She thought about how they had hung out in the library the night before this happened to Cata's friend; it had been so sweet and innocent, and this could have just as easily happened to Cata. J wanted to be able to protect Cata, to watch out for her; for someone to always be there to watch out for her, just as Cata wished she'd been able to watch out for Ale.

"Can I... Do you want a hug?" J asked.

Her instinct was to put her arm around Cata, to hold her, but especially considering the subject matter and the sexual ambiguity between them, she didn't want to do anything violating. Cata nodded, and turned, burying her face in J's shoulder. J wrapped her arms around her, holding her close to her chest, as Cata cried, "It just seems like everyone is being raped. It's all anyone is talking about, in the news, in orientation; they're just like 'Don't get raped' over and over. Don't forget your whistle; don't forget to tell your buddy where you're going. Upperclassmen saying 'I was raped; don't let it happen to you,' but Ale knew all that! We went to all that together, and it still happened! If everyone knows that, why does it keep happening? She couldn't have done anything different besides stay home, and it makes me feel like if I go out, I'm asking for it to happen to me too."

"No, no, no," J finally said into Cata's ear as she trailed off in a sob. "It's not your fault, and it's not her fault either. That was a stupid thing of them to say, but fuck the police, and fuck Delta Ep. I'm sorry that happened to your friend, and I'm glad you're ok. You're safe."

Cata burrowed against J's shoulder; her sobs intensified, and J held her tight, somewhat in disbelief—but grateful— that Cata was opening up to her like this. Cata continued, tearfully, "I'm not. Look at me. Guys have always stared at me, touched me without asking, tried to grind with me, asked me to do things with them, assumed I want to have sex with them, and I don't want to be with any of them, and it keeps happening and I just know that someday one of them is going to rape me."

She buried her head in J's shoulder again, sniffling.

J held her tight, unsure what to say besides, "I wish I could keep you safe."

Cata seemed calmer, having told J her fear, and she pulled back, wiped her eyes, and said bitterly, "Did you know at Delta Ep they call freshmen rape bait? Like just for coming here, just for being a girl, you're asking for it to happen to you."

"That's fucked up."

Cata shook her head, watching the show for a moment, and J didn't know what to say. She wondered if Cata would think her friends were too aggressive, too sexual, too objectifying, too bro-y. Dem bois could be a lot, but she knew that under their front, each one of them loved women deeply and wanted to fall in love, to sweep a woman off her feet and treat her right (especially sexually!). Hell, they were women—and quite a bit more, she acknowledged.

They were athletes, but there were reasons they didn't hang out with, didn't fit in with, the rest of their teams socially. Something bad had happened to TZ too, last year, before J had known the group, and the swimming, track, and crew teams involved had all pretended nothing had happened. TZ's own assistant coach had written out an incident report, but then torn it up, saying, "Let's just try to put this behind us and have a good season. Do you think you can do that? Can you try to forget this happened and move on? Maybe steer clear of the crew team, don't make any more problems for yourself."

J hadn't known what had happened for months, but the others all alluded to it darkly, and eventually Raimee dished, telling J that TZ had been hooking up with a swimmer... until her boyfriend found out, and he and several members of the crew team cornered TZ down by the track and field house after hours and beat her bloody, saying that if it happened again, they'd "do something that would make her never want to fuck again."

Gossip had spread through the three mostly white teams, that the guys had "put TZ in her place" over the affair, and when TZ had shown up to practice the next day, black eye and open gashes, there had only been hushed whispers and averted eyes. The unspoken consensus was that by sleeping with the swimmer, TZ had been asking for it. J and TZ had gotten a lot closer over the summer, messaging over gchat almost every day, and TZ had finally told her more about it, although she didn't like to talk about it much.

Male sexual entitlement infuriated dem bois, as did the freedom to violence that many all-male spaces on campus seemed to enjoy, whether it was in the frats or on the teams, and even women's complicity in it was so upsetting to the group after "the incident," as they referred to it, that they had all nearly completely stopped hanging out with their teams afterwards, and had found solidarity together, feeling safer in numbers.

"They can't take all of us, it's better if we roll as a crew," Mac said, and stood by it, even though she and Usa fit in well and were mostly accepted by their own team, the women's basketball team.

Each lost in their own thoughts, J and Cata watched the show until Cata started again, "I just keep thinking of Ale, in Miami, with her parents. It's Friday, it happened almost a week ago. How is she dealing? It's bad enough for me. The others just pretend nothing happened, but how am I supposed to talk to her? How can I be there for her when she's not even here, when I am, and when what happened is so bad that neither of us wants to talk about it?"

J's mind wandered to a more distant memory, of Aliya, crying on J's bed in eighth grade, saying she was afraid to be home over the summer, afraid to be around her uncle. That he had done bad things to her, and now that everyone at school was talking about boyfriends and girlfriends, kissing and hook-ups, Aliya didn't know what to say. She felt invisible, like there was something wrong with her, like she didn't know how to tell anyone what happened and still be Aliya, still share any of those normal experiences with them.

She and J, both quiet and uncomfortable with sex, had become much closer after that. They talked about what happened to Aliya more openly as the years went by, as their intimacy and maturity deepened (but avoided the topic of J's sexuality and what it might imply about the closeness between them). Aliya had told her, "I'm just so glad I can talk to you about this, that you don't make me feel like a freak because this happened, or like I'm broken now and can never be whole," especially after she told her sister, her mother, even her brother, and they all averted their eyes and never mentioned it again.

"I... uh... well, that happened to my high school girlfriend," J said. She decided that 'girlfriend' was more accurate than any other word to describe Aliya, and that it clarified her interest in women to Cata. Cata was watching her closely, and it was J's turn to look downward, to clench her hands on the railing, to lower her voice. She continued, "but it happened when she was a little girl... and everyone either pretended nothing had happened, or they couldn't look at her the same... and what helped her was just being able to talk about it, for me to listen, to not see that as too shameful to talk about, because we all have things we're ashamed to talk about, you know, and just because you're not talking about it doesn't change what happened, doesn't change that she's thinking about it and has to deal with it every day."

Cata nodded, and moved her hand to rest over J's.

J's heart leapt. This could still be a friendly consolation, but Cata's hand was pressed against hers, thumb tracing softly along the edge of her palm, holding her hand.

"Did you ever have a boyfriend? Or... girlfriend?" J asked, changing the subject slightly, interested in Cata's context for their budding closeness.

"No!" Cata said, with a laugh. "I didn't date in high school."

J was surprised, since she had assumed that someone like Cata would have a full romantic life, with no shortage of admirers.

"Well, that must have been by choice, because I think you're the most beautiful woman I've ever seen," J said with a nervous smile.

Cata laughed again, seeming flattered, and said, "Maybe things would have been different if there was someone like you around," leaning over and giving J a kiss on the cheek.

J was surprised, startled even, and when she abruptly turned to look at Cata, the two found themselves nose to nose, and there was a moment of nauseous unclarity, of heady expectation and the promise of intimacy, before J closed her eyes and leaned forward, giving Cata a soft kiss on the lips.

Everything seemed to collapse into itself, and J could have sworn she saw fireworks go off behind her closed eyelids, feeling Cata's lips pressed against hers before they separated. They leaned close together for another moment, both smiling shyly, acknowledging that this had been incontrovertibly intimate, incontrovertibly queer.

Without another word, J put her arm around Cata. Cata rested her head against J's shoulder, and together they watched the Alphas and Thetas dance off below.

* * * * *

The show finished, and they stood still for another minute or so, cuddling, watching the crowd disseminate, until it grew a little awkward and they separated, smiling sheepishly. J wasn't sure what to say, how to continue now that this was so clearly romantic between them. They had kissed! Should she kiss her again?

Cata broke the silence, "So you mentioned getting ice cream? I'd like that."

J replied, quickly, "Yeah! Have you been to The Scoop yet?"

Cata shook her head, and they started to make their way down from the patio, across campus to the landmark ice cream shop that was a staple of campus life (and a common casual date locale for the student body). It also happened to be just across the street from J's upperclassmen dorm on the edge of campus. J told Cata about the viral video "High at Highland" that had come out last spring, and specified that The Scoop was the ice cream shop where the video's protagonist had taken a nap in between giant multi-flavored ice cream cones.

"Of course I saw that!" Cata laughed, recognizing the bench in front of the store where he had fallen asleep as they walked up.

J held the door for Cata, and they entered the shop, taking their place in line.

"You order first, I don't know what to get," Cata said.

J proceeded to order her usual, a scoop of raspberry cocoa implosion.

"Cup or cone?" the freckled server asked.

J was about to say cone, then realized that licking an ice cream cone while talking to Cata would probably come across as uncomfortably sexual, and said, "Cup, please."

Cata didn't seem to share her concerns, ordering a scoop of mint chocolate chip and adding, "Cone!"

J looked at Cata again, standing next to her, and marveled at the fact that she was a person like anyone else, that she existed outside of class, outside of J's fantasies, outside J's wildest imagination of what her perfect girl would be like. Just for existing, she was all that, and it was a wonder to stand next to her, to behold her in her daily magnificence.

Cata smiled at her, breaking J's reverie. J pulled out her wallet and said, "I got it," handing her card to the server, and collecting her cup.

"Wanna sit on the bench?" J suggested.

Cata agreed, and they went outside and sat side by side.

Cata pretended to fall asleep, licking her ice cream cone as she slouched over on the bench as the "High at Highland" guy had done, and J laughed.

"You know," said J, "right after that video came out, my friends and I got super high and got an ice cream bucket from the scoop to share, and we actually passed out too. We were watching a movie, and we all just fell asleep, and woke up like an hour later. Maybe there's something in the ice cream."

"Maybe it's the weed!" Cata said, licking her ice cream cone.

J tried not to stare.

"Do you smoke?" J asked her. She hoped Cata would be interested in trying out some of that Morning Sunrise she had picked up from Darnell earlier.

"Sometimes, just with friends and at parties though. Not much," said Cata.

"Do you like it?" asked J.

"I guess," replied Cata ambivalently, "It's usually when I'm drinking too and I get tired though. You?"

"I'm a bit of a stoner," J said, outing herself. She hoped Cata wouldn't disapprove. "I told you I didn't drink much, but my friends and I really like to smoke. I actually just got this new stuff, from Colorado, that's really supposed to be a clear head high that doesn't make you tired at all, and I was hoping to try it out tonight... If you'd like to join, I would really like that."

"Yeah, ok. I told you about the situation with my friends, so I don't really have other plans," said Cata.

"My dorm is actually right there, it's the second window from the right, three floors up."

"Great location!"

"I got lucky in the housing draw." J continued to take little spoonfuls of her ice cream, sneaking glances over at Cata.

She couldn't believe Cata wanted to come back and hang out in her room. Her ice cream bowl sat in her lap, held between her knees, her one hand free, resting on her knee next to it, and she felt Cata slide her hand to rest on hers, locking their fingers together. J moved her hand to rest between them at a more comfortable angle, and continued to scoop tiny bites of ice cream from her cup with her other hand, wishing she had just gotten a cone.

A girl walked up, and Cata said, "Hey, Mariana!" holding J's hand a little tighter but not letting go.

They exchanged pleasantries before the girl gave J a little wave and went inside.

"Sorry I didn't introduce you. She's from my freshman writing seminar," Cata said.

J noted that although Cata seemed a little uncomfortable under the girl's scrutiny, she had made a point of not hiding their intimacy, not hiding that they were together. She felt a swelling of—was it pride?—within her. Cata wasn't ashamed to be seen with her, to be seen with her romantically in public. Whatever happened between them didn't need to be kept a secret, as so many of dem bois' trysts and affairs were. It was real.

They finished their ice cream, more flirtatiously, holding hands, making eyes at each other, laughing, and J said, "So you want to come hang out?"

"Yeah."

Part Three

They disposed of their garbage, releasing each other's hand but walking closely as they made their way across the street and up into the dorm, shoulders bumping together, making small talk. Reaching J's floor, Cata remarked how much nicer the upperclassmen dorms were, and J showed her the lounge and the kitchen as they walked to her room. As they peeked into the lounge, Darnell looked up, then did a double take, pointing at Cata, while looking at J.

J motioned for him to cut it out, and Cata glanced between the two of them before J stammered, "Uh, Cata, this is my friend Darnell. Darnell, this is Cata. See you later."

She steered Cata out of the room before Darnell could say anything embarrassing, and caught Darnell's eye as he gave her two thumbs up. J pulled out her key, opening her door, holding it for Cata to enter. She felt as though now she was letting Cata into her own sanctuary, with its sparse decorations and homey comfort. She was glad she had cleaned.

J entered, and leaned over to plug in the string of lights she had hung across the ceiling. They provided a softer light than the fluorescent bulbs supplied by the school.

When she straightened up and turned back to Cata, it was as though they were pulled together magnetically, communicating wordlessly. Their bodies drew together. J's hand found its way into Cata's hair, her other around her waist, and they began to kiss passionately, with a hot intensity, hips and breasts pressing together.

Cata's hands were on her chest, her neck, around her waist. As the sexual tension that had built between them discharged, J noted Cata clutching at her, letting out a soft moan as their lips and tongues danced together, pushing her hips against J's.

J's hands were on Cata's hips, and they began to wander up her sides before finding their way to her breasts, caressing them softly, then firmly grabbing them as Cata pressed against her. For an instant, she returned to herself, scarcely believing that this was happening; Cata was clutching at her, wanting her like this; she was touching Cata's breasts, kissing Cata's lips.

J felt drunk, although she knew the alcohol they had consumer earlier was out of her system. She was intoxicated by Cata's smell, the feel of her body. She dizzied J, and they held on to each other desperately until they fell apart, gasping, looking at each other, laughing self-consciously at what had happened. So Cata really *was* into her like that, J thought triumphantly. What would happen now?

"Should I roll that blunt?" J asked.

"Yeah. That sounds good." Cata's face was flushed, her hair tousled from their kissing.

It was quiet, and Cata offered, "My friends, the dance ones, are the ones I used to smoke with in Miami. They like to watch dance videos while they're getting high."

"Want to show me some?" J asked, "I'd love to see the kind of dance you're into."

"Well, these are more what I'm inspired by. I'll find some good ones from *So You Think You Can Dance*."

J pulled out her smoking tray and sat in her desk chair with it in her lap, taking a blueberry-flavored cigarillo paper and grinding up some of the new weed. Cata took off her shoes, and sat cross-legged on the edge of the bed. She pulled out her phone, browsing through dance clips on YouTube.

"This is a good one! Come close and watch," Cata said, tilting her screen towards J.

J moved over to the bed to sit next to her. They watched an animation krumping performance, and J was genuinely impressed.

"What is this from?" she asked.

"It's a dance competition," Cata replied, "A dancer from my studio was on it last season! All the dancers love it."

J finished rolling the blunt, tapping it, twisting the tip, and handed it to Cata. Completing her pre-smoking ritual, J got up and opened the window, turning on the outward-facing box fan, then dropped the towel from its hook on the door, pushing it to cover the crack under the door with her foot to prevent smoke from escaping the room. She finished off her preparations with a spray of Ozium over the entire doorframe, then returned to sit next to Cata on the bed.

Cata held up the blunt, admiring the even way it was rolled, saying, "This almost looks like a Cubano! I don't think I can smoke this much, but cheers!"

She brought it to her lips, and J lit the tip, watching as Cata closed her eyes and inhaled, taking a long slow draw and holding it for a few seconds before exhaling smoothly, letting out a little cough at the end. She took another small pull, and passed it to J, saying, "That tastes pretty good."

J couldn't wait to try the Morning Sunrise Darnell had told her so much about. She lifted the blunt to her lips, taking a deep pull, feeling it swell within her, warming her and heightening her senses from the inside. He was right; it felt like a ball of golden energy was rising through her chest. She exhaled and took another deep pull.

They continued to pass the blunt back and forth, watching at least two more videos, laughing, awestruck by the performances, drifting into giddy bliss until their attention turned back towards each other and they began to shotgun the smoke, breathing into each other's mouths, adding a little kiss at the end.

"I'm pretty high," Cata finally said, refusing the blunt as J passed it back to her.

J took one more drag, feeling pretty high herself, then snuffed out the smoldering end in the ashtray on the smoking tray. She got up, placing the tray on her desk, and looked back at Cata, sitting on the edge of her bed, watching her.

"Do you wanna watch another video, or... or should I play some music?"

"Play some music."

J turned to her laptop, feeling a pulse of anxiety at what her music choice would say about the mood. She had been mortified when she finished the playlist for Cata earlier, swearing she wouldn't show it to her, but now that the situation had developed in this way it seemed like the best option. Her "chill zone" playlist wouldn't set the right tone, and the "dem bois get it" playlist was much too sexual. With a sigh, she pressed play on the "Songs for Cata" playlist, hearing "Can't Take My Eyes Off Of You," start to play as she returned to sit next to Cata on the edge of the bed.

"I... really like you," J said, reaching up to stroke Cata's cheek, scarcely believing that they were now at a place where she could say and do such things.

Cata blushed, looking down, before putting her hand on J's thigh and saying, "I like you too."

J leaned forward to kiss her, and their lips met softly as the music played in the background.

"If you feel like I feel,
please let me know that it's real.
You're just too good to be true,
Can't take my eyes off of you."

Slowly, sensuously their hands caressed each other, sitting side by side. They were somewhat uncomfortably turned to face each other. Cata solved the problem when, to J's amazement, she stood up and climbed onto J's lap, straddling her, knees on either side of J's thighs. They began to kiss again, a rawness and desperation now filling them as they clutched at each other, filled with need for each other but unsure how to act on it, unsure what they were each desperate for. J's hands caressed Cata's body, wrapped around her, stroking her back, her thighs.

* * * * *

"I can be your fantasy"

The music played in the background, upbeat and melodic.

Cata was pressed against her, grinding, her skirt pushed up by J's hands caressing, grasping. Sliding up the insides of her thighs, J's thumbs brushed against the laced edges of her underwear and Cata let out a little moan.

J didn't want to push her luck, but she also wanted this to be all it could be, and to not let her lack of experience and confidence stand in the way of what was possible between them, if Cata wanted to go there too. They were kissing, passionately, and Cata's hands were clutching at J's sides, pulling her into her. The next step would make it sex, J thought.

"May I...?" J looked up at Cata, who smiled and ran her hand through her disheveled hair, then leaned forward and whispered in J's ear, "Yes, touch me, please."

J felt a burst of desire shoot through her. That was the sexiest thing she had ever dreamed of experiencing, and they hadn't even done anything sexual yet.

"Dontcha, dontcha, dontcha want me"

J gasped as she lightly ran her thumbs over Cata's panties, stroking her from front to back.

Cata wanted her to touch her. Cata was sitting in her lap, legs spread, kissing her neck, stroking her chest, her shoulders, her back. Cata felt warm, soft, and as J's fingers ran over what felt like her vagina, there was a small spot of dampness.

J felt a sharp rush.

Cata was wet for her. She turned Cata on. Cata wanted to take things further. And now? She was going to give Cata the best experience of her life, even if she had never done anything like this before. If she had, by some miraculous turn of fate, by what must have been divine intervention, found herself between the legs of the most beautiful girl she had ever seen, let alone spoken to, she could figure out how to take it from here.

"Help me, Jesus," she said internally. She felt a pang of shame over invoking Jesus's blessing of her foray into homosexual depravity, but she decided that her own personal Jesus would be happy for her to be having such an important milestone.

Cata moaned again, lips parting as she kissed J, and J slipped her thumbs into her panties, feeling softness, tufts of hair, then, as she stroked gently, unmistakably, Cata's vagina. It was wet, she hadn't imagined it, and Cata let out a little cry in her ear, arms wrapped tightly around J, as her thumb slid over the opening.

Cata had to be the sexiest woman in the world. And it seemed like she wanted to have sex with J!

"Swimming through your galaxy,
Starstruck on all of you"

J stroked gently upwards until she found a little bump—was that her clitoris? Her vagina felt different from J's. Softer, more compact. She felt like a girl. Well, woman.

J felt like she had pretty manly genitals, for a female. Sometimes she thought of herself with a penis, but didn't think she'd actually prefer it to what she had. Hers worked ok. But they didn't feel erotic like this. J had never imagined that she could feel such arousal just from stroking something so utilitarian as genitals. She had thought that they were ugly, but could feel good if used in the right way. That was before she had interacted with Cata's genitals. They felt like a masterpiece. J flinched as Maxwell's "Hey Lover" came on—she was a little bit embarrassed, but not enough to stop what she was doing or change the music.

J brushed her thumb over the bump again, spreading the wetness around, and Cata let out another little cry, "Ay!"

It seemed like J had found her clitoris. They stopped kissing, breathing heavily against each other. J's head rested on Cata's shoulder, looking down at her perfect breasts, still covered by her lacy bra. With one thumb, J continued to stroke Cata lightly, but she removed her other hand and placed it on Cata's hip, feeling her grinding against her, then tracing with her fingertips up Cata's stomach and over her breast.

She couldn't believe Cata was letting her touch her like this, wanted her to touch her like this.

Cata sat up and leaned back a little, arching her back, and reached behind herself to unfasten her bra. With her free hand, J slipped the bra's straps from one shoulder, then the other, kissing the newly exposed skin. Cata's naked shoulders were beautiful. J's jaw dropped slightly as the bra fell from Cata's breasts, revealing their lovely curve, their dark nipples. J gently grazed them with her hand, the nipples hardening under her touch, then leaned forward and kissed them with an open mouth, her lips closing over each nipple and flicking it with her tongue. It was almost like she was in a trance, enchanted by Cata, guided by her own body and desire. Cata was making soft noises of pleasure, relaxing against J's shoulder, hips moving rhythmically, her hands at J's sides again.

"This is more than a crush"

It felt like Cata was opening for her, her vagina softening, swelling as J continued to trace it with her thumb.

J pressed her thumb directly against the opening to Cata's vagina, and Cata let out a deeper moan, then whispered in J's ear, "Be gentle. I've never done this before. I'm... a virgin."

J felt surprised that this gorgeous woman didn't have as much experience as she had expected, but she was a freshman, a Catholic, and she obviously didn't do this with everyone.

J was pleased, and a little confused. What did that mean?

Did she not want J to go inside, or was she giving her the go ahead to go inside?

Did she mean she had never been touched?

Or that she had never done something like this with a girl?

She probably meant that she hadn't been penetrated... Did this make J her first, or did fingering not count?

Was she saving herself for some guy?

Did she have any sexual experience with guys? With... girls?

What counted as virginity?

One question led to another, and they all made J nervous. J definitely had never done this before, but she was unclear about what that meant to Cata. These questions all opened the door to questions about J's past and sexual experiences that she preferred to remain untouched for now.

"That's ok, baby," J tried out a new term of endearment, deciding that was the best way to address Cata's intimate disclosure. "We don't have to do anything you don't want to. Do you want me to go inside?" she continued, removing her hand from Cata's breast and brushing back her hair with it.

"Yes," Cata gasped, pushing her hips against J, causing the tip of her thumb to slip inside. J let out a moan this time. Her hand was pinned between her own pelvis and Cata's, her thumb beginning to penetrate Cata's softness, and it was as though she had a penis, the tip pressing into this beautiful woman, this virgin. Her vagina felt tight, hot, welcoming as J pushed her hips and hand forward, sinking her thumb all the way inside.

"I kissed you softly and you yearned for more"

Cata's head fell onto her shoulder and they began to hump against each other slowly, passionately, J's one arm wrapped around Cata now, holding her close as her thumb slid in and out.

> *"Into an ocean of love we both fell*
> *swimming in the timeless currents of pure bliss"*

Cata was grinding against her knuckles, wanting more it seemed, and J decided it was time for a change of pace. She wanted better access, to be able to see Cata and move freely, for Cata to be more comfortable, and so she first slowly withdrew her thumb, gliding it over Cata's clitoris a few times before pulling her hand from her underwear. J wrapped her newly freed arm around Cata too, supporting her lower and upper back, holding her against her hips, and in a fluid movement, stood up, lifting Cata and turning around to lie her down onto the bed. Cata clutched at her and wrapped her legs around her, holding herself up, then laughing as she fell onto her back, legs still wrapped around J's waist.

"That was smooth," she said.

J congratulated herself on not ruining the moment, on making it seem like she was suave and confident. "I thought you might be more comfortable lying down," J replied.

J was half standing, half lying on top of Cata, and Cata pulled her up onto the bed so their bodies were pressed together. Again J moaned, overcome by feeling Cata's nearly naked body, warm and soft, lying under her, legs and arms wrapped around her, holding her close. They kissed, passionately and J held herself on one elbow, one hand entwined in Cata's hair, her other hand exploring her breasts. Cata's hands caressed J's back, then reached down to her hips and ass, clutching her against her.

"When you want,
I'll be here baby
Longing to know ya"

J imagined she was dancing with Cata, grinding her hips against hers as they slowly kissed. Soon dancing turned to humping again and in that moment, J wished she had a penis to pull out and push into Cata's waiting vagina, to satisfy her and to feel what it would be like to be inside her, to really be her first.

Who knew if that's what Cata even wanted, though? Sure she was treating J more like a guy, but this was a pretty gay situation and she seemed pretty into it. She must have had the option to sleep with more than one guy if she had wanted to, and she had chosen not to. Instead, she had chosen J. If J had a penis, that would be the expectation, that she'd be trying to get Cata to let her penetrate her so she could come, but J wasn't doing this to get off, she was just grateful for the opportunity to make love to this beautiful woman, to please her, to share this magical experience with her.

J reached down, sliding her hand into the top of Cata's underwear and running her fingers over her. Cata moaned and her legs fell open. Her vagina was swollen, wet, a perfect flower dripping nectar. J's fingertips found her opening again, and as Cata gasped, "Yes," she began to sink two fingers into her. Cata felt snug, and there was some resistance that J gently pushed into.

"Ay, Ay!" Cata cried out softly, grasping at J's neck and back, pulling at her.

J began to slide her fingers in and out, her palm pressed over Cata's clit, and Cata's hips began to move against her again. A slow song was playing, and their bodies fell against each other in rhythm. J groaned, feeling Cata's breasts against her, her legs spread, their hips grinding together, her fingers penetrating her. It felt surreal, to have this beautiful woman opening to her, welcoming her intimately, desiring her, seeing her as a sexual partner, as an equal.

J saw a flicker of discomfort cross Cata's face, and thought maybe she'd taken the fingering too far, for someone who hadn't been penetrated before. She slowed down, resting her fingers halfway in and turning them slightly back and forth. Cata's moans resumed. J had thought women liked that, to feel you inside of them, but she had also heard girls complain about lovers who only focused on getting inside. She didn't want to be like that, and she wondered how she could show Cata that she wanted to please her, not just to get in, to get off.

"Can I take off your underwear?" she murmured to Cata.

Cata looked a little self-conscious but said, "Yeah, ok, if you want to."

"Ooh just the thought of you gets me so high. So high,"

J removed her hand and straightened up, looking down at Cata, whose eyes were closed, head turned to the side. J first unfastened and pulled off Cata's skirt, which was still bunched around her hips, then hooked her fingers in the waistband of Cata's panties, slowly tugging them down as Cata lifted her hips for her, gasping as she saw Cata's dark curls, her soft curves exposed. J had seen pictures of naked women; she had been in the locker room with teammates in high school and had changed with friends, but she had never seen a woman in this way: erotic, exposed, sexual, aroused, legs open for her. Instinctively she leaned forward and kissed Cata's lower abdomen, ran her hands over her thighs. Cata arched her back and moaned, then looked self-conscious.

"Sorry if it's..." Cata began.

J cut her off, "Don't be sorry about anything. You're perfect."

Cata smiled, and looked at her apprehensively.

J continued, feeling inspired to try another new thing she had fantasized about, "Could I kiss you... Down here? Would that be ok?"

Cata squirmed, a blush spreading across her cheeks, "Oh my god, you don't have to. You totally don't have to. Isn't that... gross... for you?"

J was surprised that Cata was so self-conscious about her body. Didn't she realize how gorgeous she was, what an honor it was to look at her, let alone touch her, let alone kiss her, lick her?

"No!" J burst out, "No, it's not gross! Definitely not gross. I'd love to do it. To try it with you."

Cata looked taken aback but reassured. She probably assumed J was more sexually experienced, that maybe this wasn't normal in her own circles, but there was a reason she wasn't dating anyone from those circles, a reason she was doing this with J, and that this must be normal to do with someone like J; a lesbian, a black stud.

"Ok... We can try it... If you want..." Cata continued, hesitantly.

"Are you sure, baby?" J continued, beginning to stroke up the insides of Cata's thighs, to trace her hip bones.

Cata nodded, closing her eyes again, looking slightly more comfortable.

"There's nothing I wouldn't do
just to get up next to you"

J leaned forward, kissing Cata's breasts, her abdomen, her hips, her upper thighs; tracing over all the soft curves of her naked body with her fingers, lips and tongue. Cata was moaning again, clearly aroused, and her legs spread slightly, allowing J to continue kissing onto her inner thighs, to stroke her curls and spread them with her fingertips, looking directly at Cata's inner lips, at her clitoris.

"Moment of truth," J thought, and remembered Raimee and Mac telling her, "Just lick it like an ice cream cone!"

She didn't want to pause and make Cata uncomfortable, so without further ado, she stuck out her tongue and licked from the base of Cata's vagina up to her clit, leaving her tongue resting on the small bump.

"Ah! Ah! Oh my god... Oh my god..." Cata burst out and J smiled.

It felt soft, slippery, with little tufts of hair tickling her nose, and it tasted and smelled rich and a little musty, private and acidic. She could see why people compared it to fish, but it wasn't unpleasant. She couldn't believe she was doing this, tongue lapping against Cata's clit, feeling Cata twist and grind against her, hearing her cries.

"Oh, J," Cata moaned, running her hand over J's dreads.

J felt a rush of energy between her own legs. Cata was moaning her name, she wasn't thinking of someone else. It was really J who turned her on like this. J licked at different angles, broad then small strokes, using the flat of her tongue then the tip, running over Cata's folds and opening, over her clit, watching and listening to see how she responded.

It seemed to be going well, J thought, as Cata's moans rose and fell, as she opened her legs wider, but J's neck and tongue were beginning to get a little bit sore.

"Gotta build up your endurance," she could hear Raimee saying.

J slowly licked over the entrance to Cata's vagina, using her hands to separate her labia, remembering what Raimee had said about how girls liked it when you penetrated them with your tongue. Should she try it? She prodded with the tip, Cata pushed forward against her, and she stuck out her tongue and pushed it in.

"Oh, oh!" Cata groaned, rocking against J's chin. She was tight at first, her opening tensed around J's tongue, but as they rocked together J felt her relaxing, letting her in, growing more wet, her lips swelling, until J's tongue grew tired from the motion and she licked upwards towards Cata's clit again.

Cata's moans deepened and her movements grew more frantic, clutching at J's head, shoulders, her thighs tensing, her head tossing back and forth, and J sped up, flicking her tongue over Cata's clit over and over, pressing her thumb into the base of her vagina.

"Ay! Ay! Ay!" Cata cried, louder, and J slipped her finger inside, taking Cata's clit between her lips and swirling her tongue over it from side to side.

Cata's body began to tense, to shake, to clutch at J's hair. Her outbursts turned into one long ecstatic cry as J continued to rhythmically lick and finger her. J felt completely overwhelmed by the sounds, the feelings, the sensations, and as Cata spasmed around her thumb, thrashing her hips up and down, legs clamped around J's neck, J realized she was coming too, moaning into Cata now, hips rocking against the bed, pressure building in her abdomen then releasing. Cata began to still, her moans subsiding into little cries, J's tongue still lapping against her gently until she gasped, "Enough!"

J ceased her movements, and rested there, still, head whirling for a moment, before slowly withdrawing her thumb from Cata's vagina, which was still contracting, spasming around it, and lifting her lips from Cata's clit. They were both gasping for air, chests rising and falling, and J was stunned. Cata had come, right? It definitely seemed like it... and J had even come too. J was still wearing her clothes; she hadn't even remembered to take off her shoes! She sat up and wiped her mouth on her sleeve, still tasting Cata on her lips.

Her head was spinning, and she looked down at Cata, lying peacefully now, eyes still closed, body shaking slightly. J had an overwhelming urge to hold her. She scooted up to lie next to Cata, swept her into her arms, and pulled the blanket over them both.

Part Four

Cata settled next to J, barely moving, eyes still closed. J's heart melted. Cata looked so beautiful resting on the pillow—almost angelic. J was stunned that Cata had let her get so close to her, and hoped she didn't feel they'd gone too far. It was technically their first date, after all, even though they'd known each other for about a month. It was unclear how Cata felt now, and J kissed her shoulder, then her hair, and said, "Was that ok? Are you ok?"

Cata finally stirred, opening her eyes and giving J a shy little smile, "I told you I was a virgin... I've just never felt like that with someone before."

J panicked internally. She seemed into it, but had J pushed her too much? Did she regret it?

"Was... that ok, though?" J continued.

Cata laughed, "Oh my god, yes! That felt amazing! You rocked my world. Was it... ok for you? You didn't mind?"

J felt a rush of relief, and said, "No, no, I didn't mind at all! It was really my pleasure. I think you're so special and beautiful, and it's an honor to make you feel good, to be close to you like this. Do you want some water or anything? A snack? I have some watermelon in the fridge..."

"You know, that actually sounds great," said Cata.

J leapt up from the bed, a little too quickly, tripping over herself trying to make Cata comfortable. She missed the feeling of her in her arms almost immediately.

She looked at Cata, lying there naked on her bed, half covered by the Falcons blanket Pops had given her for Christmas, and felt another knot in her stomach, this time one of giddy disbelief. Disbelief that she had had such an amazing date with Cata, that she had made love to her, that Cata had enjoyed it, and wanted to keep spending time with her. It felt too good to be true, too good to happen to someone like J, and yet, there she was—right in front of her. Naked.

"I'll get that then. It's in the kitchen. I'll be right back," J said. She felt a momentary impulse to add, "I love you," until her better sense told her to leave the room while she was ahead.

Outside, she shut the door behind her, and rubbed her hands over her face, reassuring herself that this was indeed happening, had indeed happened, and that Cata was now lying naked in her bed.

J walked to the kitchen lounge, where Darnell was still sitting, head in hands, one earbud in.

"Dude, that's the girl? She's super fucking hot!" Darnell said, noticing her in the door.

"Shhh!" J returned, motioning for him to zip it.

"No, but really!" he insisted, "She's still in there, isn't she? How's it going? That tree take you where you need to go?"

J grinned, allowing herself to receive his validation.

"Yeah, man, it went really well... It's going really well! And that shit is great, dude. I'm just getting some water."

"Water break! Gotta hydrate! That's great, man. I'm happy for you. I really am. Yo, I got a case of San Pellegrino to drink after practice; it's in the fridge. I know it says 'drink & die' but that's just to keep people from fucking with it. You should take some, roll in there like a baller, like, 'Yo, bitch I got you some sparkling water,' you feel me? Hot girls like that, like you know they're special."

She rolled her eyes, thinking that 'bitch' was hardly what she'd call Cata, and said, "Thanks, man, I'll take you up on that. Can I take two?"

"Don't get crazy now. Come by sometime this week after my test and we can hit the Volcano with some of that Morning Sunrise. It's good when you smoke it, but when you get that pure high with the vape? It's golden, man."

J took a bottle of sparkling water from the common fridge, along with the plastic bowl of watermelon she had brought back from the cafeteria earlier.

"I'll do that, catch you later bro."

As she walked to the door, Darnell made a lewd gesture with his hands and she shook her head, laughing, returning to her room just down the hallway, taking a deep breath before knocking softly and opening the door.

Cata was sitting on the bed, legs folded under her. She had put her clothes on, J noted with a twinge of disappointment, but then again, she supposed she hadn't expected her to lie around naked forever... although it certainly wouldn't be a problem if she wanted to.

Cata looked up at J and smiled, saying, "Hey," hair tangled, face still flushed.

J had never seen such a beautiful sight, and she walked over to sit next to Cata on the bed, holding out the bottle of San Pellegrino, setting the bowl of watermelon on the bedspread.

"Hey," J responded, with a flirtatious smile. She leaned in, giving Cata a kiss on the cheek, making her blush slightly. "Do you want to smoke some more of that blunt?"

"Yeah, sure."

As J bent over to pick up the blunt and lighter from the tray next to the bed, Cata continued, a bit self-consciously, "I hope you don't do this with all the girls..."

J couldn't help but laugh, then realized that could come across the wrong way.

"No," she started, "Definitely not. This is... special for me too."

Should she tell Cata that it had been her first time too? The playlist was still on in the background, and it seemed to answer to question for her, as in a moment of astounding serendipity, J. Cole's song "Wet Dreamz" came on:

"I ain't never did this before, no
And I ain't never did this before"

J groaned internally. It wasn't the first time that evening the music had caused her to cringe, but she decided it was a sign, and, handing the smoking materials to Cata, she continued, "You know, that was my first time too."

"What do you mean?" Cata said.

She lit the blunt, and took a hit.

J cringed again, before continuing, "I've never done that before."

Cata handed her the blunt, looking a bit skeptical, asking, "Which part?"

J took a hit before continuing, "All of it. I... haven't really dated, or been with anyone here at school."

"But you had a girlfriend in high school?"

J took another hit, passing the blunt back to Cata.

"Well, maybe it's a bit of an exaggeration to call her my girlfriend. We were very close, and it was... romantic, but we never had sex, no."

Cata started laughing hysterically. It seemed she had already started to feel the high, and J felt her stomach turn, worried that Cata was laughing at her, that she thought J was inexperienced, that she had misled her.

"What's so funny?" J asked.

"So you've never done anything like that before?" said Cata, gasping for air, " But it was so good!"

J felt a wave of relief. Rather than being amused, it seemed Cata was impressed. Well, perhaps impressed and amused.

"But how did you know what to do?" Cata continued, eating some watermelon. "Oh my god, this is delicious. This weed is really strong."

J was starting to feel the high too now, and she too started laughing, saying, "I don't know. I guess I just went for it and… uh, figured it out."

Her expectations had been confounded many times that evening, but nothing could have prepared J for what Cata was about to say.

"I want to try!"

It was J's turn to be dumbfounded, replying, "What?"

Cata looked more serious now, and she said, "You know, no one's ever taken me seriously as a... lesbian... before. My friends, my family always ask what guys I'm interested in, if I've finally found a guy, and I always say, 'I think I'm a lesbian,' and they just laugh and say, 'Come on, when are you going to stop being so picky?' And it's like, because I look like this, look like a girl... no offense... It's like they can't even consider the possibility that I could be... you know, a lesbian. Could be interested in women myself. Even my queer friends, they just see me as a straight girl, because, you know, look at me."

It was J's turn to laugh hysterically, and Cata's to look slightly offended.

"I mean it, I want to try! Have you ever had someone do that to you? Would you want to try it?"

J stopped laughing, and snuffed out the blunt, deciding they were high enough.

"Are you serious?"

"Yeah," Cata put her hand on J's thigh, "I really like you. You make me feel comfortable in my body, and I want to make you feel good, too."

Now Cata was seducing her... J's head spun slightly. She had never really considered that Cata might want to do that to her. Sure, J had wanted to do it for Cata, and didn't want to deny her the same sexual agency, but Cata's vagina was... pretty, and soft, and.... didn't smell bad.

J barely felt comfortable with her own body. What if she couldn't relax, couldn't open up to Cata as Cata had to her?

What if she ruined it all?

Or worse, what if Cata was disgusted, horrified?

What if it was too much and she decided she wasn't interested in women, in J, after all?

But here was the woman of her dreams, offering to give her head, saying she wanted to make her feel good... wait, had Cata said that she really liked her?

If ever there was a time to try it, it was now. She could feel comfortable with Cata; Cata had been so open with her. J wanted to respect Cata's ability to express her own boundaries and desires... and Cata wanted to reciprocate.

In another mortifying turn of events, the song J had added as an afterthought to the end of the playlist came on at this moment. It was Christina Aguilera's "Come on Over," and J leapt up to hit pause, but not before Cata started giggling.

J decided that things had heated up enough for the "dem bois get it" playlist to be appropriate. She hit play, then turned to face Cata, who was sitting on the bed, looking at her expectantly.

J swallowed. "I'd love to try it. Just… uh... Let me go to the restroom first."

"Ok, no problem." Cata bit her lip, and J felt a rush of desire.

She really did want to, and Cata wanted to... maybe it would be ok after all.

J rose and left the room again, going into the private bathroom right outside her door. She didn't have time to shave...

Cata hadn't shaved, so maybe that was ok, but Cata's hair was soft, not coarse and curled like J's.

No, it was ok for her to have hair; vaginas have hair, she told herself, but she didn't feel clean enough.

J turned on the sink and unbuttoned her pants, pulling them down slightly along with her boxers, putting some water in her hand and splashing it on her vagina, sort of wiping it off, trying not to get any water on her pants so it wouldn't look like she had wet herself.

She put some more water on a paper towel, and dabbed over herself with it, worried she had perhaps ruined the mood by leaving, but acknowledging that this would at least make her more comfortable with what was about to happen. She took another handful of paper towels and patted herself dry, running her hand over herself, and deciding it was ok. She pulled up her pants and washed her hands, then took a deep breath, pushing back her dreads.

Finally, she looked in the mirror, and told herself, "You got this," acknowledging that all she had to do was lie there and relax, but somehow it seemed even more daunting than what she had done before.

* * * * *

J returned to the room, and saw Cata perched on the edge of her bed. The music seemed louder, and as J closed the door behind her, Cata strode over to J, and kissed her, putting her arms around J's neck. J's hands rose to caress Cata's body, pressed against her, remembering how she had felt against her naked. She let out an involuntary moan as her hands ran over Cata's back, her sides, her ass.

Cata's hands slid down J's shoulders and pulled at the ends of her bow tie, tugging it open. She unbuttoned J's shirt, slipping her hands underneath it to caress J's sides, her waist, then slid two fingers into the front of J's waistband and led her towards the bed.

J was surprised by Cata's boldness, but then again, Cata was usually so confident in her body. In fact, it was one of the things that made her so attractive to J, who was more reserved, cautious. J figured Cata's newfound sexual panache made sense now that she felt more in control of the situation. J was happy to let her take charge. She turned J around, and pushed her to sit on the edge of the bed, then went to the laptop and pressed play on a song she had found on the playlist.

Beyoncé's "Rocket" began to play, and Cata said, "You asked if I'd dance for you."

She pulled back, flashing J a flirtatious smile with a hint of self-consciousness; striking a pose, then tossing her hair, turning away from J and beginning to move her body to the music. Beyoncé sang,

> *"Let me take this off,*
> *Will you watch me,*
> *don't take your eyes off it,*
> *Watch it, babe."*

Cata began to trail her fingers up her body, lifting her top off, hips moving enchantingly. She really was a good dancer, thought J, her movements powerful and sensual.

> *"Grab ahold, don't let go, Let me know that you ready..."*

J's heart was racing as she sat there, watching Cata put on a show for her. Cata lifted her hands above her head, then bent over, slipping out of her skirt.

> *"I just wanna show you now, slow it down..."*

Cata drew closer, dancing slowly, sexily. She pushed her hand through her hair and met J's eyes for a moment. J felt like she shouldn't be staring, her eyes fixated on Cata's hips, her stomach, her breasts, her collarbones... but Cata wanted her to watch!

She reminded J of Beyoncé in that music video... that scene that she had masturbated to several times of Beyoncé dancing as Jay-Z watched... The video had been about Beyoncé's fantasy, but J's fantasy was to be what someone like Beyoncé fantasized about... To be devoted to a beautiful woman, ready to please her, to study her every move, to satisfy her, to earn her trust and devotion in return.

J reflected on a conversation dem bois had rehashed many times over the nature of the perfect girlfriend. They had settled on "the Beyoncé"—the girl who was a lady in the street, but knew how to get freaky, and as Cata seemed to transform into a sexual goddess before J's eyes, she realized that somehow she seemed on the path to securing a Beyoncé as her own girlfriend.

"You rock hard, I rock steady."

Cata stepped forward, and used her hands to separate J's knees, lifting one leg up onto the bed to straddle her, hips swerving just above J's. J ran her hand up Cata's thigh, and Cata lowered herself to grind against J, caressing her, giving her a lap dance as Beyoncé sang,

"Hard rock steady rock hard,"

J's hands moved to Cata's hips, which rocked sensually. Her head fell forward to rest between Cata's breasts. Cata's skin was warm, and as her nipples grazed J's cheek, J let out a moan. She wanted to touch Cata again, to make Cata come, to hear her crying out in ecstasy, to feel her writhing at J's fingertips, to feel her come in her mouth again... but as her fingers trailed down Cata's abdomen, brushing over her panties, Cata grabbed J's wrists and returned her hands to rest against her gyrating hips. Cata smiled teasingly and leaned forward to push back J's dreads and whisper in her ear, "Just relax and watch. It's my turn."

J couldn't believe her luck. Whatever anxiety she felt was being transformed by Cata's confidence, by how sexy she was, how she looked in her underwear, how she moved... The fact that she was trying to seduce J only compounded her attractiveness.

"Rock it til water falls."

Cata began to tug J's unbuttoned shirt off her shoulders and down her arms, pulling off J's undershirt too, until J was in her sports bra, which, after looking up at J to confirm it was ok, she pulled off too with slight difficulty.

"Don't you know I give you the loving if you need it"

Cata moved her body sensuously, leaning over to kiss J's cheek, her neck, behind her ear. It was as though she was enveloping J; as though J were getting high off her touch, her smell, her taste. It was almost painful how much J wanted her; knots of desire twisting in her abdomen.

J moaned softly as Cata's fingertips caressed her chest, and Cata pushed her backwards, up onto the bed. J scooted back, and gasped when Cata climbed on top of her, straddling her. She was on all fours, hair trailing down onto J's neck and chest, body gliding up and down.

"Higher, harder"

Cata was moving to the music, lowering her hips onto J's and grinding against her as J reached up to trace her fingertips along her stomach and breasts, closing her eyes for a moment and feeling completely present in her body, in her desire for Cata. Her hips bucked, and Cata let out a little cry.

*"Dip me under where you can feel my river flow
and flow,
hold me until I scream for air to breathe…"*

They pushed against each other, hips
rolling, as passionate intensity built between them.
J closed her eyes, feeling the movement, the heat
between them. She wanted to make Cata feel good
in so many ways, to hold her against her as she
came again and again…

"Rock it, baby, til the water falls"

Cata was kissing her neck again with soft,
warm lips and hot breath. She began to trail soft
kisses down J's chest, her stomach, her hands
stroking J's abdomen, her hips as her mouth drew
closer to J's private place. Cata's ass rose in the air,
and J's fantasies took off… J had imagined herself
fucking a woman—although the specifics of what
that meant somewhat eluded her; had pictured the
woman of her imagination; sometimes Beyoncé,
now Cata—on all fours, moaning for her, and she
let out a groan, thinking about what it would be
like to fuck Cata, to push inside her, to make her
come that way too.

"I can't help but love the way we make love"

J felt her hips begin to rock, and she
groaned again. It felt like there was heat coming
from just below her navel, like Cata was pulling her
into her… Cata's fingers were unbuttoning her
pants, tugging at them, and J lifted her hips, letting
them slide down until she lay there in her boxers.
She wondered if Cata would pull them off too, but
instead she climbed atop J again. She was on her
knees, straddling J, and she continued to dance,

tossing her hair and sinking down against J as the song continued,

"Got me screaming to the Lord, boy
Kiss me, pray we don't overflow"

God, could it be true that Cata could see her, wanted her, J, as a masculine partner; someone to dance for, someone to take her out, to show her off and care about her—and fuck her, and make her come—and that she didn't mind that J was a woman, that she had a female body?

That she even… liked it?

Cata seemed turned on, her mouth open slightly, her eyes closed as she settled her hips on top of J's and began to ride her.

"I've been a bad, bad, bad girl."

J was enraptured, lying there, watching Cata, feeling drawn into her. She slowly slid her hands up Cata's thighs to hold her ass and her hips thrust upwards into Cata. She could feel their bodies cresting and falling against each other, energy pulsing between them. The song finished, and Cata smiled at her, a little self-conscious, settling back onto J's thighs. J didn't know what to say besides, "That was really sexy."

"I've never had anyone to dance for before," Cata said, "like this, anyway..."

J Holiday's "Bed," began to play, and J had a moment of appreciation for the value of the "dem bois get it" playlist. Cata continued rocking against her, riding her.

"Tonight you're having me your way," played in the background, and J felt waves of pleasure beginning to build between her legs, in her

abdomen as Cata bounced up and down, riding her. What if she came before Cata even went down on her? She had never heard of premature ejaculation being a problem for women, but leave it to her to get too excited just from pressing against Cata...

"Touching you like it's our first time"

As if she could tell that J was finally ready, Cata lifted herself up and began to tug J's boxers down. J wanted to feel Cata against her more than anything, but she couldn't help but panic at the thought of Cata seeing her naked, with her female body, her vagina, and she put her hand over Cata's, stopping her.

"Are you ok?" Cata asked, looking up, concerned.

"I... uh... you're sure? Sure you want to?" J asked nervously.

Cata seemed to intuit the cause of her anxieties, because she laughed a little, saying, "Don't worry, I know you're a girl! I'm into it, I promise."

Her hand was slowly tracing the front of J's boxers, making J moan softly, her hips twitching.

"Do you want me to keep going?" Cata said, teasingly. She lowered her head to the place her fingers were tracing and softly kissed across J's boxers. J moaned again, louder this time, a surge of aching desire shooting through her, and she gasped out, "Yeah, yeah."

Cata lifted herself up, slipping her fingers into J's boxers and pulling them down and off her legs.

"I love it, you love it, everytime that we touchin."

J felt naked, vulnerable, but she felt close to Cata, ready to feel her skin on skin, ready to let her touch J like she ached for. She closed her eyes, and felt Cata separate her knees gently, stroking her fingertips up her thighs until she grazed them over J's curls and J let out a sharp gasp, almost a cry. There was a pulsing, an aching between her legs, and for a moment, J's clit felt like an erection, a hard dick for Cata to stroke and suck. She felt a pulse of excitement burst through her, thinking about Cata's lips closing around her. Briefly, she mused at how it was possible for her to feel like a man, and also be a woman...

Cata knelt between her legs, stroking her softly, running her fingers from J's outside to her center until she rested them against her wetness.

"You really want me," she said, stating a fact, sounding pleased.

J responded, "More than anything."

Cata stroked her finger up to J's clit, circling it a few times, making J cry out again, before leaning forward and kissing J there, sticking out the tip of her tongue to press against it, her long hair cascading over J's thighs. J was startled by the new sensation, and let out a cry, surprised to hear the sounds Cata had made coming from her own mouth. She hoped Cata found it as arousing as she had.

"I want it, I want it, you want it, you want it"

Cata separated J's curls with her hands, and licked up and down with the tip of her tongue. She

92

was treating J's clit as though it were a tiny penis, taking the shaft between her lips and flicking her tongue, bobbing her head up and down. Again, J imagined her clit as an erection, and it was as though she could feel Cata's lips and tongue sliding up and down its length. J had felt on the verge of orgasm earlier, and she could feel it swelling in her again.

"*Ay ay ay gonna put my fingers in your hair, love you til your eyes roll back*"

She opened her eyes for a moment, and looked down. Cata was in her lap, giving her head, and although she hadn't imagined this, it was more of a fantasy than she could have ever dreamed up. She thought of Cata dancing, stripping for her, straddling her. She remembered how it had felt to make love to her, to be inside her, to taste her, to feel her legs wrapped around J's neck... and now? Cata was lying between her legs, licking her, kissing her gently, insistently.

J was breathing heavily, her body starting to tense. Cata's tongue lapped at her, taking her into her mouth. J cried out, her voice sounding higher than usual, and she reached down to put her hand in Cata's hair. She was going to come in Cata's mouth, she thought, with a rush of ecstasy. She could feel Cata moving against her as she released, her whole body convulsing, crying out, "Oh, oh!"

It felt apocalyptic, transcendent, obliterating. Her world collapsed into the awareness of her body, of Cata, and she shook for what felt like a minute as Cata continued to gently lick. With a deeper groan, J tensed all over, and another wave of bliss swept through her, before Cata's movements began to feel too intense against her sensitivity, and she slid her hand down to cover herself, pulling her hips back. Cata lifted her head, wiped her mouth on the back of her hand, and asked "Was that ok?"

J nodded wordlessly, gasping still, beckoning Cata to come close. Cata crawled up to lie against J's side, head on her chest. J wrapped her arms around Cata, holding her tight, giving her a kiss on the top of her head.

"Thank you, baby," she finally said, catching her breath. "Was that ok for you?"

Cata's hand rested on J's stomach, and she began to trail her fingers over J's chest.

"Yeah. It was new. I'm glad it was with you."

The two nested together quietly, J feeling Cata breathing softly against her. She was so grateful that they had found each other. Minutes passed, and they seemed to be drifting towards sleep.

Cata stirred. She looked up at J, and asked, "Would it be ok if I stayed here tonight?"

3: BRETT

Fetish

Trigger Warning: Racialized Language,
Racial Fetishization, Power Play

Part One

"FIT mature tech exec whiteboi seeks Dom BBC to put him in his place"

Brett sighed. He felt aroused and depressed, flipping through profile after profile, questioning his motives with each click. This really seemed to be about Jerry, he thought with each guy he looked at, about recreating what had happened with Jerry and giving it a different ending, one that didn't make Brett feel like such a weak, useless piece of shit. Hadn't he moved out to Palo Alto to get away from that? He felt dangerously close to recreating the scenario that had driven him out of DC, driven him out of politics altogether. He just didn't have the stomach for it anymore; the endless games, the manipulation, the one-upmanship, but most of all, for seeing how Jerry used and disposed of everyone around him.

"My wife won't put up with it any longer, Brett. She says it's too big a risk, and I agree, with midterms coming up and the Republicans looking for anything they can use to take me down. We're going to have to stop seeing one another like this."

What got Brett wasn't how casually Jerry had said this, lying in bed after a discreet lunch fuck at the Dupont Circle Hotel, but how little he saw Brett himself as a threat. After all, Brett knew people in the RNC, people who wouldn't hesitate to sling some mud Jerry's way come October... but Jerry couldn't imagine Brett having even that power over him. Didn't think he'd have the nerve to pull one over on Jerry, to out himself and take down Jerry's entire career. Brett's bosses, the DNC strategic development team, wouldn't care, and suspected it anyway. Coming out would probably even get him invited to a few more banquets, depicted on a few more campaign materials, but he already felt like enough of a token as the only black man on the team.

Jerry's conservative Indiana constituents would certainly care though, and being outed would lose him the election. Brett had thought about it for weeks, but in the end, had realized that he would be doing it vindictively, just to hurt Jerry, just to show him who was really boss. At the end of the day, he hadn't wanted to hurt Jerry, and even his stupid wife and kids, like that.

This convinced him that he no longer had the stomach for politics, for DC, and shredded up the last bit of validation he felt from being Jerry's down-low boyfriend, from being so close to power, from sucking its dick, taking it in his ass. Jerry had rarely sucked his dick, he now acknowledged, and had never taken him in the ass.

"I'm not that kind of guy, Brett!"

He had laughed dismissively the first time Brett had suggested he reciprocate, and Brett had accepted that he was just a top at the time, but really, what kind of guy did he think Brett was? Someone who took what he could get, and had enough sense to be grateful for it. Four years they had been together, the second half of Jerry's first term, and now the first half of his second, until Jerry... no, Jerry's wife, fucking Eleanor... had used the midterms as the reason to end things.

"I can't keep hiring boys in this town, it's going to catch up with me," he remembered Jerry saying soon after they had gotten together.

With a knot of self-loathing, Brett realized that maybe he had just been Jerry's 'boy' this whole time. And he hadn't even gotten paid for a job well done, for letting himself care, for letting himself support Jerry, being there for him, talking through the night about his job, colleagues, marriage, stress, stress, stress. Maybe Jerry felt he'd paid him what he was worth, with all the fancy hotel rooms, the meals, the bottles of champagne; trips to Martha's Vineyard, to the Bahamas, to Rehoboth Beach, even to Jerry's own fucking district. It had been a transaction. Validation for submission. Power for love. Fucking for being fucked.

At the end of the day, Jerry was a closet racist as well as a closet queer, Brett acknowledged. He had ignored the little comments, the small things that had suggested at Jerry's outdated conception of race in America for years. Given him credit for his willingness to make an exception for Brett, to let himself get close to Brett. It had begun to get under his skin after that time in Rehoboth Beach, when Jerry had pushed him over the table, pulled his pants down, and fucked him with barely any warning or lubrication, and then, as he was about to come, grunted, "Yeah, take that, boy!"

That moment, and how it made Brett feel, had highlighted Jerry's other daily insensitivities, but what had especially driven him crazy were Jerry's small comments distancing Brett from his blackness, as though to excuse why someone like Jerry would be with him. "You're such a hard worker, Brett. We need more young men like you," Jerry would say whenever policy issues regarding race came up between them, the insinuation being that other young (black) men were not hard workers and there ought to be less of them.

It had come to a head after the police shooting of that kid in Ferguson last year, and the media frenzy that had ensued. Brett and Jerry had been together in a hotel room, each doing some paperwork after Brett had blown Jerry, with the news on in the background. They were both drawn to the "Breaking News" alerts, the disturbing footage of riot cops and people packed in the streets. Brett had felt claustrophobic, his chest tightening, seeing all those people, nearly all black people, so filled with righteous anger, with contempt for a system that saw them as nothing better than cattle to be herded and kept off the streets, when they were trying to enact a cathartic group mourning that would give some semblance of closure to yet another irreconcilable racial tragedy in America.

"Don't get so worked up," Jerry had said, totally misreading the situation as Brett had begun to pace anxiously. "You're nothing like those people. You're a good one, Brett! You've worked hard to get where you are, unlike these looters and thugs."

"Those people are someone's constituents," Brett had hissed.

Jerry had replied, "Yeah, I have too many

like that myself."

His eyes had returned to his phone, checking his messages, but his comments had burned themselves into Brett's mind, his gut. They had only gotten together once after that, sexually, and Brett had hated it, unsure why he was going through with it except out of habit, because Jerry expected him to.

Jerry had taken over his body, his mind, and ending it was probably the best thing that could have happened for Brett, but feeling rejected by Jerry after all that seemed to also invalidate all the intimacy, the companionship they had shared, and had spiraled Brett into what seemed like a depression, drinking alone, listening to the angsty neo-soul stylings of Amy Winehouse whenever he could on his earbuds; finally realizing how much he hated his job, hated DC.

So when the DNC had also used the midterms as the reason for letting Brett go, saying they didn't need to keep around the whole staff for the "final lap," Brett had seen it as his excuse to make a change. A big change. A change of occupation and a change of coast. He had seen enough of how things worked out East; he was ready to go see how things could change out West. When he heard of the position directing Development for a major immigration policy think tank & advocacy nonprofit in Silicon Valley through the grapevine, he leapt at it, asked for the contact, flew out for the final round of interviews.

It had been his first time in California, and as his plane landed at the San Francisco airport, he decided that there would be no more lies here, didn't need to be any lies here. He would come out, from the beginning; at his job, to his friends, and on the scene. He wouldn't be ruled by shame and silence, guilt and complicity anymore. He was a new, free Brett.

He had sailed through the interview process, told by both principal interviewers separately that they loved him, and needed more "people like him," around the office. He didn't think they meant a solutions-driven problem solver with a proven track record, but instead suspected they were referring to people who were gay or black; or better, both. Brett was used to being patted on the back for being "a good one," with his suits and ties and UPenn class ring, but it was insidiously depressing to think that maybe what his colleagues saw in him was a black man—a gay black man—with a good attitude who would, in return for their benevolence, pat them on the back as "good ones." At any rate, he had gotten the job, terminated the lease on his brownstone in DC, and moved out to Palo Alto that month.

He hadn't called Jerry to tell him he was leaving town. Jerry had asked him not to contact him, and even though Brett knew he would want to make an exception for this news, he withheld it. Jerry would notice his absence eventually and would ask around and find out he was gone. Maybe then he would regret tossing Brett out like the morning garbage.

So now here he was, two months later, settled into a nice enough little house in San Mateo.

He was another Bay Area commuter, another San Francisco gay, another Silicon Valley up-and-comer. He felt like he was wearing a disguise; biking to work on nice days, wearing brighter colors, growing a beard. It seemed too pleasant to be true, too sharp a contrast to conservative dark suits and daily shaves, early mornings and brusque meetings, daily deadlines and clenched jaws. Politics.

At his new company, he was also working for a mission, on a campaign, but now his work involved bringing his "personal story" to the office to "shape the collective narrative."

A campaign staffer had once told him, "Unless you're the candidate, no one gives a fuck about your personal story. Just do your job."

Brett's new boss was fond of saying, "You're more than your job. You are your passion."

The move had been a success in giving him latitude to think of himself and his life in a whole new way, but paradoxically, it had only seemed to compound his internal "Jerry issues," as his new friend Brenda referred to them.

Brett had found a lot of success meeting women in the Bay Area, and although he had only known his college classmate Megan when he arrived in town, he had rapidly formed a small clique of close female friends between his colleagues and Megan's friends who reminded him of the snappy, independent women he had been close with in DC. What he hadn't been able to find was a date, or any guy he was remotely interested in dating who didn't remind him of Jerry.

There were a plethora of powerful, suit wearing older gay men swarming through Silicon Valley, and Brett was disgusted that this was now what aroused and intrigued him. It was clearly transference... Or was this just his new type? Had being with Jerry so long changed something inside of him, permanently oriented him to the validation of old white dick?

One thing was different though... Brett's fantasies of getting together with these men didn't end with him pleasing the master figure. They ended with the white man on his knees, either taking Brett in his mouth or ass.

Wasn't that what he wanted to do to Jerry, though? To... make him take Brett like that, to take Brett seriously, to respect his power? Even to punish him? It wasn't right to take that out on some other guy... unless the other guy wanted it, wanted to submit as Brett had, to work out his own issues with him so they could both move on.

But how could he tell what a guy was into just by picking him up in a bar, asking him on a date?

In DC, before Jerry, he had met nice guys, attractive guys; mostly black guys at the subset of DC bars that catered to that crowd, but he had been just looking to have a good time then, not to act out some weird fantasy.

Still hoping he could meet a nice guy, a normal guy, a guy he could relate to, he had asked Marco, a little Latino twink from his office, if there were any bars around where he could meet "guys more like himself."

Marco hadn't seemed to get the insinuation that he was looking for black guys, but instead said, "Sweetie, it's San Francisco! Every bar is a gay bar, except the gay bars. That's where the straight girls go to get away from the straight guys. What you're looking for is online now."

And so Brett had turned to Grindr.

"Welcome to the meatgrinder, honey!" Marco had responded when Brett told him he'd made a profile and was looking for advice on how to use the app from someone with more experience. "I call it grocery shopping. It's a different cut every night of the week!"

"I... I think I just want to meet one guy. Maybe like an ongoing thing, you know?" Brett had said, jarred by the insinuation.

"You say that now..." Marco trailed off, a wistful look on his face.

Brett had left his profile mostly blank. He uploaded pictures of himself shirtless, working out, in a suit, and had added the relevant measurements, and the carefully constructed phrase, "Professional looking to release a little steam." It sounded cheesy, but after seeing some of the other profiles, he thought keeping it simple and vague would serve his purposes and allow him to check out other guys in the meantime without deterring the guys he was looking for. Then he started to get the messages.

"I <3 ==== black guys"
"Need black cock now"
"White boi needs black daddy"
"You got that BBC I'm looking for?"

"Want a thug in my ass"

After a couple weeks on Grindr, Brett felt like maybe his concerns had been misplaced. Far from being an outlier, it seemed lots and lots of gay guys were looking to act out racial fetishization, and it forced Brett to question his motives. On one hand, maybe this was normal in this day and age; to look online to find custom mail order dick. But if he was put off by the white guys' messages and their clear objectification of black sexuality, he was more dismayed to see his own aims echoed graphically in the far less numerous black guys' profile descriptions.

"I'm gonna make u my little slave boi"
"Thug here to tear up your asspussy"
"Dom BBC hard for a little white bitch"

The idea of all these guys meeting up; acting this out, fucking each other day in and day out, made Brett feel queasy... but still aroused. He stayed off the app for a few days, somehow dissuaged by realizing how easy it would be to get a hotel room, message one of these guys, and act out this scene.

He had thought Grindr would be a little more like online dating, but realizing how much it was about casual sex, like anonymous digital cruising, made him question whether that's what he was looking for. What if he got addicted to it, became like Marco, like the guys posting, demanding a new partner to act out iterations of this obsessive fantasy over and over, never able to escape Jerry's mental hold on him until he slept with the wrong manslut one day and got HIV?

He thought about deleting the app. He felt like an alcoholic with a full bottle, afraid to open it, afraid of what it would do to him, what he would be able to justify doing with it. Brett's father had been a drinker, relapsing again and again, and Brett was well acquainted with the idea of a slippery slope, of not going where it's wet, not looking for trouble.

A week went by, and then, on Friday afternoon, realizing that he wanted more from his weekend than sangria night and a movie with the girls, he opened the app again and saw the profile.

"FIT mature tech exec whiteboi seeks Dom BBC to put him in his place"

* * * * *

Brett couldn't help himself. He was intrigued. He began to swipe through the body shots, and really liked what he saw. He wasn't sure if he'd be friends with the guy; his photos of mountain biking, ultramarathons, and rock climbing all seemed pretty intense, but he seemed healthy, fun, and like he had a lot going on in his life. His face wasn't clearly identifiable in the shots, but he had a great body, especially for a "fifty-something."

"Do you think he's bangable?" Brenda asked him in the Uber they shared to go meet up with Megan and Lindsi at The Garden, an outdoor bar that was quickly becoming their Sangria Night go-to.

"I... Uh... Yeah, I guess he fits what I'm

looking for."

"Say it. He's totally bangable."

"Ok, he's totally bangable."

"So have you messaged him yet?"

"No!"

"Brett," Brenda leaned over in the backseat, putting her hand on his shoulder. "I want you to be happy. And I've seen how much this shit with your ex has torn you up since you got here. You need a fresh start, someone to reset your internal balance. My breakup mix hasn't even cured you, and it's never failed before! You need to message him. You've been on this site for weeks and you haven't liked one guy until now."

Brett sighed. She was right. What was he afraid of, that the guy would remind him of Jerry? Jerry wouldn't be caught on a mountain bike in a million years.

"I like the mix," he said, "It just… reminds me of him, of what I'm moving on from.'

"The whole point of the mix is to jumpstart your new life without him! Have you tried listening to it while working out? That might help…" Brenda replied.

"Yeah, I'll give that a try. Thanks for burning it for me," Brett said. He continued, voicing his anxieties, "You don't think it's weird, that this white dude is looking for a black guy though? A… Uh… BBC?"

"Well, do you have one?"

"What?"

"A BBC… You know…" she leaned in further to whisper in his ear so the driver couldn't hear, "big black cock."

"God! I know what it stands for. That's not what I'm worried about. It's the... you know, the fetishization of it."

Brenda raised her eyebrows, leaning back in her seat and clapping her hands a few times. Brett rolled his eyes. He had never felt particularly insecure about his penis; it was a bit larger than average, and had served him well enough, but it was strange to feel reduced to it, as though the particular guy attached didn't matter.

"Everybody's looking for something," Brenda replied frankly. "It's a little weird, but I wouldn't beat yourself up over it. Although maybe he wants you to beat him up over it!"

She laughed.

They had arrived at The Garden, and they paid the driver and went in to find their friends at the table.

"Brett found a guy!" Brenda said immediately, as they sat down.

"He's not..." Brett began, but was drowned out by their affirmations.

"Tell us everything," said Lindsi.

She was already sipping a tumbler of sangria from their first bottomless pitcher of the night. Brett pulled out his phone, opened up the Grindr app, clicked on the guy's profile, and placed it in the middle of the table. "That's all there is to know."

"Tech exec, nice!" said Lindsi.

"Oh please, that could mean anything here," scoffed Megan.

"You don't think the race thing is weird?" asked Brett.

"I only fuck Asian guys online," said Brenda. "All the white guys on Tinder start saying racist shit at some point, about my sideways pussy or some other shit. I've learned to weed them out early and just go with Asian guys who can see me as a woman and not as a fetish."

"That's what I mean, this is totally a racial fetish!" said Brett.

"Yeah but it's your racial fetish," said Megan. "It's ok if it goes both ways. You're looking for a white Daddy to fuck, and he's looking for a hot black stud... which you totally are!"

Brenda continued, "It kind of sucks, though, because you know I'm more into white guys. I only dated white guys in college. Not on purpose; they're just my type. But it feels fucked up, because I'll meet up with these Asian guys and never want to see them again. It's just sex."

"Brett, didn't you used to only date black guys?" asked Megan.

"I guess," he said, "but it wasn't intentional!"

Megan clarified to the others, "That's how Brett and I met, in college. He was dating my friend Steven for like two years. Then my other friend, Paul. They're both black—and super cute! Everyone has a dating type, but now that we're adults, it's better to claim that you're just looking for sex and move on. It's just sex! That's the beauty of all this, you can find exactly what you're looking for, and then not be stuck married to it!"

"Yeah, but what if you want to find someone to date... or marry?" Brenda added. "No one's getting any younger here."

"Marriage is for gays now," Lindsi said. Her Eastern European accent had thickened after her first couple of drinks, and she continued, "The rest of us are born alone and die alone, and hopefully get a good fuck or two in between."

"Speaking of..." Megan picked up Brett's phone and began swiping through Tom's pictures.

"Don't!" Brett started.

Megan laughed, and said, "Have a drink, loosen up! Let's send him a message."

Brett felt a slight rush of panic. This was a real guy, not just a profile, and he could respond in any way...

"What should we say? What do you want to say, Brett? How do you usually flirt?"

"You're obviously interested; it's a sex app. You can keep it simple," said Megan. "What about just saying 'hey'?"

"That's good, keep it casual. He's looking for someone who knows how to take charge... Want to add something that communicates that? Like... bitch?"

"I was thinking a winky face," insisted Lindsi.

"Not 'hey bitch'!" Brett said, distressed that Megan was already drafting the message on the screen, ready to press send. "How about boi? Like, 'hey boi."

"I think you should add a winky face."

"Sure, add a winky face," said Brett.

Megan finished typing out the message:

"hey boi ;-)"

She showed it to Brett for his approval, and hit send.

"I need another drink," Brett said. He rose to top off all of their glasses from the pitcher in the middle of the table.

"He's typing!" Megan said, her voice almost a shriek of excitement.

"Give me that!" Brett responded. He snatched the phone.

He had been more worried about a response than about sending the message in the first place. This proved it was real, that this was something he was pursuing, even if he backed out.

"hey stud :-)" popped up on his screen in a little orange message box.

"He's typing something else!" A location tag popped up on the screen, showing a pinned intersection near the airport.

"He sent you his location! He wants to fuck!"

Was it really that easy? Brett thought. He still wasn't even sure he wanted to, although now that the mood of the night had taken hold, he had to admit that this could turn into a fun, sexy adventure, and that a large part of him wanted it to.

"let's get to know each other."

Another message came through.

"I'm at the regency. Meet me at the hotel bar for a drink, and if we hit it off..."

Brett dropped the phone, looking around at

the women.

"See? He didn't say anything weird... and that's a nice hotel!" said Brenda.

"He's hot, and he's ready to go. I say do it," added Lindsi.

"You want to, don't you?" asked Megan.

She could see the look of temptation in his eyes, the smile beginning to curl the corners of his mouth.

"Do it!" said Brenda. "Skip the movie, we'll go. And you can meet up with us later to debrief."

"If you're done by then! He's an ultra marathoner. I hope you've been up on your fitness," said Lindsi.

"Yeah, you should probably stop drinking," said Megan. She swiped Brett's glass since her own had run dry and their pitcher needed a refill.

Brett's mouth felt dry, a warm nervousness rolling in his stomach. He could go over there right now and just fuck this guy. Finally, after so many months of fantasy, he could act out his obsession.

"What should I say?" he asked.

"Say you're on your way! It's right down the street, you could get a cab and be there in five minutes."

Brett picked up the phone and typed out "*be there soon.*" He added a geo-tag confirming his location, and pressed send.

He could hear a dull pounding in his ears as he saw the words on his screen, black silhouetted in tangerine orange.

The guy was typing a response.

"I'm sitting at the bar wearing a grey suit."

It was really happening.

He was about to go fuck this stranger; well, at least to go flirt with this stranger. Brett was excited, his heart pounding. He hadn't been on a date in a long time, let alone had the potential of a sexual experience with a guy he was interested in.

"What are you waiting for? Go!" Lindsi urged him.

"Wait... do any of you have condoms? I wasn't planning on getting laid tonight!"

"Do you need, like, some special kind of gay condom?" asked Brenda.

"No! Just a condom, although Magnums are better."

"Gotta treat that BBC right," Brenda giggled. She was a little tipsy.

"I have some Magnums," said Lindsi. She pulled out her purse, and reached into a little pocket, taking out one, then two, then looking up at Brett and handing him a whole handful of them. "You have a lot of dicks between you," she explained.

Brett thought about giving some back, but he wasn't sure what they'd be doing, and thought some extra condoms could come in handy. He tucked them into his wallet.

"You have to give me your movie ticket though," Lindsi said. "I know you bought it in advance, and a pack of condoms is like $10 these days!"

"Sure, sure," said Brett. He forwarded her the confirmation email with his code to pick up the ticket. He could see Trainwreck another day, although he wasn't sure who else he'd go with.

"Text us to let us know how it's going," said Megan

"Don't go upstairs with him if you get bad vibes! Trust your gut!" added Brenda.

Brett said goodbye to the women, apologizing for bailing on them despite their protestations that they all wanted him to do what he needed to do to move on from Jerry, and that they could see a movie together anytime. He stood in front of the restaurant and flagged a cab, telling the driver the name of the hotel and climbing into the back.

His actions carried a note of the surreal. He was about to do this. He, Brett, was about to meet up with a man—an older white man—he'd found online for some anonymous casual sex on a Friday night in the Valley. Who had he become? Not only that, he was going to—This guy wanted him to top him, to "put him in his place," whatever that meant. Brett hoped he didn't want to be spanked. Too many of the guys on Grindr had been into that, had wanted a "big daddy to punish this naughty boy."

Brett just wanted to fuck, he wasn't really into all that, but then again, what did he want to do? He had thought about it for months, but not concretely. He probably wanted the guy to submit to him, to blow him, and to take him in his ass. To finally fuck someone after so long; to have a guy, a white guy, bent over, ready to let him fuck his ass... In his head, it would be passionate, satisfying, but in reality he feared it would be awkward, uncomfortable, even depressing and desperate.

What if the guy was unstable? Or wanted Brett to do shit that was too freaky? Or wanted Brett to be some racist caricature; an animal, a thug? What did it mean, that he was looking for a black guy, or at least a black guy's dick? How far would this go, with the parameters they had set? Would he, too, just end up seeing Brett as an available sexual object, this time one to be glorified rather than denigrated? Maybe it wasn't Jerry who had a problem, maybe it was all white guys, and Brett was the delusional one, expecting something else... Jerry hadn't been particularly mean to him; he just hadn't seen him, and hadn't cared. Why would things be different with yet another well-intentioned white guy with a fetish?

Brett's mind didn't have much time to wander, since before too long the cab was pulling up outside the Regency Suites. He got out of the cab, and looked around furtively, as though he wasn't supposed to be there.

Part Two

Brett walked into the hotel's chic lobby, seeing the lounge and bar to his right. He went to the bathroom, emptied his bladder, and tidied up; rinsing his face, tucking in and smoothing his shirt. He looked good. Any guy waiting to meet him in person should be pleasantly relieved, he thought. He was a catch, for the online hookup marketplace. He hoped the guy was too. God, he didn't even know his name. He was glad his friends knew where he was and who he was with.

Brett thought about chickening out, heading over to the theatre, seeing Amy Schumer's rom-com with the girls after all. No... he had come this far. What would he do if he bailed? Spend yet another night compulsively surfing Grindr profiles and jerking off to skeezy interracial internet porn? He shook his head and headed to the bar before he could further deliberate.

He saw the guy sitting at the bar, wearing a stylish grey suit with simple dark loafers and a navy blue skinny tie. He was... attractive, and not just for an older guy. He was cute. Really cute. He looked like he belonged in a Ralph Lauren ad. If Brett saw him in a bar, he would probably approach him. And indeed, he was about to.

He entered the bar and the guy looked up quizzically, then averted his eyes quickly. He looked again when Brett gave him a little wave, approaching slowly.

"Hi. I'm Brett," Brett said. He squared his

shoulders and held out his hand to shake.

"Wow! Glad you came. I can't wait to get to know you. I'm Tom!" The guy jumped to his feet, beaming, a little overenthusiastic in his welcome, taking Brett's hand and shaking it firmly.

"You have warm hands. You must have good blood circulation!" Tom continued, still holding Brett's hand.

Brett looked at him. He was older, definitely in his 50s, although he looked almost strangely youthful and "FIT," as his profile had described. He literally seemed to have a twinkle in his piercing blue eyes. He had dimples, a neat yet stylish cut to his salt-and-pepper hair. Tom pushed back another chair for Brett, and reclaimed his seat at the bar.

"What would you like to drink?" asked Tom.

"I'll have a Belvedere Cosmo," said Brett. He had planned on a girls' night, and didn't intend to have to over-assert his masculine side tonight. If Tom wanted him to be some alpha male thug, that was too bad.

Tom motioned to the bartender, and ordered the drink. He settled back in his chair, flashing Brett a nervous smile and flicking his eyes up and down Brett's form.

"So... You're clean, right?" asked Brett. He thought he might as well break the ice and get it out there. Clearing his throat, he added, "Like, sexually."

"Yeah, I'm negative across the board," said Tom, "When did you last get tested? Any risky sexual encounters since then?"

He was awfully forward, and specific, thought Brett, but he had brought up the topic for a reason, wanting to at least be responsible in his anonymous sex. He appreciated Tom's candor, but he was a bit disarmed.

"I got tested a few months ago after I ended things with my long-term partner. I haven't been with anyone since then," said Brett.

"I'm actually on PrEP," continued Tom. "Have you heard of that?"

Brett shook his head, hoping it wasn't some gross new STI or party drug.

"It's preventative. Pre-exposure prophylaxis. The drug is called Truvada. It blocks the enzyme, specifically the reverse transcriptase, that allows the HIV virus to replicate itself, so even if I did have a risky encounter with a positive mate, my chances of contracting the virus are, you know, infinitesimal."

Brett noted that Tom spoke quickly, and had a habit of saying you know frequently, even though already Brett hadn't the faintest idea what much of Tom's strange jargon was referencing.

"But I believe in safe sex." Tom continued. "I'm just a bit of a hypochondriac when it comes to my health, hence the PrEP. I... I've been around the block a few times, and I've seen too many young men die horrible deaths at the hands of that virus. I'm not particularly high risk, especially with the comparatively infrequent sexual encounters I have, but you know, HIV rates have been spiking locally in our subdemographic, and you don't want anything to damage your health like that, permanently, especially with how important t4 count, immunological competence, and mitochondrial regeneration are to a healthy extended life span."

"Healthy... extended life span?" Brett asked. He hadn't heard the term before. Perhaps it was a fitness world thing. Tom seemed like he worked out a lot. Brett was well built, but didn't frequent the gym. In fact, he hadn't even gotten a membership since moving west. He wouldn't mention that to Tom.

"You know, as long as your telomerase integrity isn't compromised and your DNA replication mechanisms aren't faulty, the human body can technically live much longer than most people do today. All this suffering, all this death, we see in our culture—is technically totally avoidable."

"What do you mean, death is totally avoidable?" Brett asked. He hoped Tom wasn't deranged. He seemed so professional, but you never could tell, especially with high functioning types like that. How had the conversation about safe sex spiraled to this point?

"Well, I wasn't going to bring this up... but now that you ask, that's actually what I do. I'm an entrepreneur. I used to be a doctor, a general practitioner back when that was still the thing to be, for 20 years and it just made me sick to see the same problems over and over—obesity, heart disease, cancer, you name it. Chronic disease. And of course, the angel of death herself: autoimmune deficiency syndrome. The incurables, we called them, back at San Francisco City Hospital where I used to be a GP. More like untouchables, with the kind of care they received—or didn't. A lot of ugly deaths. A lot of deaths that shouldn't have happened... Guys who shouldn't have died like that; all alone, so young. What a degenerative disease does to the body is truly spectral. You become a ghost, a living ghost, a shell of a person. And it's jarring to us when it happens to young people, but why do we accept that whether it's quick and untimely or after years of chronic illness and morbidity, that death is something that should happen to anyone?"

"Wait, what?" asked Brett. He had been with Tom, if a little sobered, up until the last comment.

"That's what I'm saying. Death is preventable. I'm a transhumanist, Brett. That means I'm a pro-evolutionary human who believes that we as a species are destined for more, destined for far greater things than mortality and materialism. There are quite a few of us out here."

"I'm new in town. I guess I haven't heard about that yet."

Tom continued his evangelization. "It means I believe in the evolutionary adaptation of humans through technological and spiritual means. And that I pursue both. I intend to live to 150 healthy years of age before uploading my consciousness to an alternative non organic life form base that can endure indefinitely, and I'm perfectly on track to do so, considering the anticipated breakthroughs in mitochondrial regeneration therapy, DNA synthase, and artificial intelligence are realized. Which they should be.

Brett said nothing, pursing his lips and taking another drink. What the fuck? he thought.

Tom continued, impassioned, "If a human consumes an optimal nutritional intake for their blood type and genotype, perfectly calibrated to their unique deficiencies and surpluses, their cells should be able to regenerate indefinitely. Technically. We haven't been able to prove this yet because of how toxic and unbalanced our current cultural nutritional intake is. Absolutely abhorrent. We're all poisoning ourselves, and for what? To subsidize an overblown and outdated agricultural system that is already tottering in its grave. America needs to embrace the future, embrace the promise of technology, and let go of our outdated prejudices and limitations if we have any hope of evolving."

Brett felt disoriented. Everything Tom was saying seemed like English and sounded technically correct. It just felt like he was talking to an alien, someone from a near yet adjacent reality to his.

"That's very interesting," Brett affirmed, unsure what else to say.

"So that's what my company does!" Tom exclaimed, "My company is Forever Fit. I don't know if you've heard of it. We just got picked up by a big VC firm, so we've been all over the media lately. Here's a business card. I'm the head honcho, that's my personal cell phone right there. I give that to all clients. I believe in radical accessibility."

Brett thought he recognized the logo at least

from a magazine he had leafed through at his office. Had it been an interview with Tom? He wracked his brain, trying to remember anything specific from the article.

"I think I've heard of it. What does it do again?"

He wasn't sure if he was missing something, but it didn't seem like Tom had explained the actual concept yet. He needed to work on his elevator pitch, thought Brett, but he was very compelling, whatever the fuck he was talking about, going on about extended human life and the angel of death.

"Forever Fit conducts specific genetic analyses of blood type, genotype, DNA, you name it, and we work with a team of nutritionists to custom design nutritional profiles for each client. We work with their unique tastes, preferences, restrictions, and so on to create the perfect diet, one that will allow each unique client to get and stay Forever Fit. I based the concept on the testing I started doing on myself after I found out I was adopted and wanted to learn more about my genetic predispositions to certain diseases. I've been doing the bio-regulated cycle diet for years. All my numbers are great, for a guy my age and going strong!"

"Wow," Brett didn't know what else to say. Tom sounded like the several pre med friends he'd had at UPenn, the ones he had fallen out of touch with after they went to medical school.

"What do you do?" Tom inquired.

"Oh, nothing that interesting. I'm a

development specialist at a nonpartisan immigration think tank. I basically translate the organization's story to potential funders, and secure financial support."

"Wow, that's great!" said Tom, nodding enthusiastically. "What's that like? Have you always been interested in immigration? I know that's another big problem, and I'm glad people like you are tackling it."

"Oh, I don't know about that," Brett said with a sigh, "I just started working there recently. It sounded like a great idea, but I didn't know too much about the issue before I was hired. Now I spend all my time talking to potential supporters, which basically involves fielding and deflecting all their potential objections to our theory of change. I can do it, I know the talking points, but I'm starting to have some doubts about the mission.

"A lot of people bring up the difference between H-1 skilled visas and H-2s, or the problem of asylum seekers and global migration; brain drain, you know, how we're siphoning off the rest of the world, especially the developing world's skilled labor force because they can individually find better economic opportunities here. But why is that? Because our foreign policies have devastated and suppressed their own economies and political systems. You talk to the immigrants, even the highly skilled ones, the 'ones we want,' and most of them would rather work and live in their own countries, if it were possible to do the work they wanted to there. So the message I'm pitching is, let's help all these immigrants find their American

Dream, but I can't help but wonder why that comes at the expense of the rest of the world?

"And that's the ones we want, the H-1s, the STEM graduates, the professionals. But we don't want to talk about H-2s, migrant guest workers, and how they're functionally enslaved, or undocumented immigrants and how they perform dirt cheap labor with no protections and none of the benefits we provide other workers, like social security, healthcare... and then asylum seekers, millions of them, trying to flee religious persecution, torture, civil and natural disasters, and we let in how many? 1%."

Brett realized he'd jumped onto a soapbox of his own, but Tom was paying rapt attention, and he continued, "This isn't the pitch I give to funders. Don't worry. I'm actually pretty good at my job, but I wonder if I should be? It's like the whole thing is centered around this fragile economy and us-vs-the world conception of border integrity. We focus on the H-1s because that helps the tech industry, and whenever anyone brings up the people who are actually suffering, even dying, by the millions, we start saying 'comprehensive immigration reform,' and 'border security,' and all those buzzwords, assuring them we'll get around to it, we're working on it, after we focus on the H-1s. But why would we? That's just placating people's actual concerns with our current band-aid, which happens to serve most of our funders anyway, since they want to hire more H-1s because the broken American educational system isn't churning out enough technically skilled graduates for them to hire, especially graduates who look like me."

Tom was nodding emphatically, and Brett continued, "So these immigrants, these professional H-1s are imported to mend the gap, and also serve the dual purpose of making this whole 'tech community' seem a hell of a lot more diverse than it really is. And I'm the go-between, passing these scripts around, getting buy in, and I talk a lot, but no one, not the funders, and certainly not my employer, wants to hear my take on it because I'm exactly the kind of person who highlights how flawed the whole set-up is, and who's not being served by it. And it makes me think that part of the reason I was hired is to have a nice, happy Black man making everyone feel more morally okay with what we're doing here, making it seem as though somehow this benefits everyone, benefits those black and brown American kids failed by our educational system who would love to have those skills, those jobs, or those kids all over the world who really do just want a shot at the American Dream and are willing to do whatever it takes to reach it—those are the ones we find dead at the borders. The ones shot by the police. The ones pushed out of this educational system.

"I just don't see that upward mobility being realized by anyone like me but me, and I went to Penn, you know? I'm not your average African American guy; that's not realistic or attainable for most people. More and more, the people being invited, being welcomed to the seats of power and to these high paying dream jobs are global elites, and that's what we're really trying to do with this talk about immigration reform; open the door for those people to attain global mobility and a global labor market without creating policies that work for the rest of the world, even the rest of America."

Brett sighed and took a drink. Tom was staring at him, wide-eyed, nodding slowly. He had really put it out there. Maybe he was inspired by Tom's verbosity, maybe he needed to get that off his chest, and maybe he wasn't willing to sit and nod and hold back what he thought as another white guy in a suit bragged about saving the world, especially a white guy who was there to be "put in his place."

Brett finished, "That's about it, I just moved out to the Valley recently. I was in politics before then, back east. Lot of need for fundraisers there. Kind of lost the heart of it though, lost that hope for change that pulled me into it back in 2008 after I graduated."

Tom continued to nod slowly for a moment, saying, "Wow. Wow. Wow." He continued, "That was like a TED talk, man! That was so powerful, and so important for me to hear. Thank you for telling me about that. You know, that happens so much around here, people claiming to be 'problem solvers' but wanting credit for solving the problem in the way they've defined it, not for comprehensively evaluating the underlying causalities, the reasons why we have these issues.

"All that, with the schools, and the police, and the borders… You're so right. I never thought about how that all fit together before. And that's why you're exactly the kind of voice that needs to be listened to in those conversations, not just brought to the table, not just a face in the room to make it look more diverse. I've noticed that in my own circles, that we welcome in some diverse faces—you're right, a lot of them are elite immigrants!—and then just expect them to acclimate to the way we're doing things, to pat us on the back for letting them join.

"But that's anti-evolution!" Tom continued, "The status quo only replicates itself unless it is exposed to and responsive to new perspectives and variables... Why do you think we've had all these problems for so long, for millennia? You're so right, we need to change the way we're defining the problem, and that means looking at it through new eyes, and listening to the perspectives of those who have been on the receiving end, taking the brunt of all these problems. Because it's not people like me! Hell, don't just listen to their perspective—let them call the shots!

Brett was slightly bemused by Tom's racial reparations plan, but he appreciated the sentiment.

Tom said, "Sometimes I think that's what it would take to change these systems, to evolve and realize the potential of humanity, is for those who have created, benefited from, and inherited these systems—I'm talking about white men—to step aside and let others take the lead. To really listen. To be open to seeing things from the other side. You know, that's why I'm here... why I wanted to meet you, or someone like you, but I couldn't even have imagined what we'd talk about, what you just told me! So I just wanted to say thank you, for being the first breath of fresh air I've had in a long time. Can I buy you another drink?"

Tom finished speaking, grinning widely.

"Sure," said Brett. He had just polished off his Cosmo and wouldn't mind another. Tom gestured to the bartender to fetch Brett another of the same.

"I just don't know how to examine my own privilege, when I can't see it because it exists in all my blind spots! It's so frustrating! I've been trying to educate myself, you know, to seek out different perspectives and read different things, but I don't think that will work without actually knowing a person who... isn't like me, who actually has that perspective, and like I said, there's just nobody I know like that who's willing to speak their mind, at least to me."

"Well, I'm not just here to educate you..." said Brett.

He felt bolder now, like he could say what he thought and Tom would applaud him for having the courage. But if Tom was seeking black affirmation and insight, wasn't Brett also guilty of seeking white affirmation and insight?

"Of course not!" said Tom, "I hope... I hope we can learn from each other, although I'm sure you've heard a lot from people like me."

This was turning into more of a first date than an anonymous hookup, thought Brett. "I'm not sure I've met anyone quite like you, man," he laughed.

* * * * *

Brett thought they'd better address the sexual elephant in the room before things progressed, as he knew a lot about Tom now, but not why he had turned to Grindr to help him with his predicament.

"So... What does all this say about why we're really here, though? You know, sexually?" He asked pointedly as the bartender placed his drink on the bar, clearing away the empty glass.

"Oh god," said Tom, looking mortified. "Well I guess that is why we're here! Well, I'm an entrepreneur, and for me, everything is about optimizing performance. And I've been off my game lately. All this stuff I've been thinking about has really gotten to me, really unsettled me. My company was just picked up by KPCB, they're my dream VC firm, and we're going through an international expansion this quarter. 150 new hires, offices in London and Tokyo, huge. And I just have this fetish, this obsession... I can't stop thinking about black cock!"

Brett sputtered into his drink a little, and Tom said, "Sorry, I hope that didn't make you uncomfortable."

"No, you're right, we both know why we're here," added Brett.

Tom took a deep breath and said, "Well, it all started with Kanye. It was back when my company was first launching, when I left Johns Hopkins—I was teaching there, back then—and moved back out here. I was keeping insane hours, and I started listening to Kanye to get me jazzed up, to keep me awake. At first it was just his popular tracks—Jesus Walks, All of the Lights, Stronger—but then I started, to get more interested, to look into the controversy around him. Why did so many people hate him? I wondered. And why did so many people love him? After looking into what he did at the VMAs and why, I thought, now that's someone willing to claim his power, opinion be damned. That's what my team was focusing on at the time; brand uniqueness, controversy, and the charismatic mission-driven founder. That was about the time Yeezus came out, and it was brilliant; so conceptual, so raw. I listened to his entire discography. I really followed the story of it. I learned how he remade himself, after the accident, how he was reborn, how he became something larger than himself. How he manifested his mission, his destiny, his purpose, you know?"

Brett was confused. Did Tom want him to pretend to be Kanye West? He thought the guy's music was pretty good, but he seemed like an asshole. Brett was more of a Nina Simone kind of guy, but he didn't care to share that with Tom, and let him continue.

"I was there in the office, alone at night after the rest of the team had gone home, keeping late hours... and I started jerking off to it, to his music. Listening to every album, I would come. 808s & Heartbreak. My Beautiful Dark Twisted Fantasy. Watch the Throne. Sometimes to songs that weren't even sexual. It was just the power in his voice, you know? It was so fucking sexy. And he knew people wouldn't like it, that he would have haters, that they would criticize him for saying the things he does, for claiming power, because he's, you know, a black man and people have a problem with that. People can't stand that. Well, white supremacists can't stand that, it makes them sick. And I grew up around a whole lot of people like that, people who didn't even realize they were white supremacists, but wouldn't stand to see a black man—a black person—speak their mind. Have you read James Baldwin? Notes of a Native Son?"

Brett shrugged. He thought he probably had in college, or high school maybe, but it wasn't a body of knowledge he actively dialogued with. Tom continued, taking his passive assent at face value.

"You know, he's talking about how black men—black people—haven't even been legally considered full persons for almost all of the time they've been here, since we brought them here. Speaking of immigration, they're—you're—the only forced immigrant population here in this land of immigrants! The rest of us chose to be here, at least our great-great grandparents did, but black people were kidnapped and brought here against their will, then seen as property, as less valuable than animals, sold, killed, you name it. Whatever the white people wanted, because they were the only ones seen as people."

Tom continued, "But what does that even mean? White isn't a thing, it doesn't pass the rule of a linguistic construct because what it is and what it isn't are not able to be clearly bounded, you know?

It changes over time. It's defined by its opposition to another, and that other is anyone and anything not considered to have power. It's a tautology. It's meaningless outside of the meaning we attach to it, which is that white is better than non-white."

"You know, I'm white, but the truth is, I had no idea where I came from, where I'm genetically linked to, because I was adopted. I was adopted by some well-meaning, God-fearing people in a little town outside of Milwaukee. They said they just wanted a child who looked like he was part of the family, but they never bargained on getting a gay son! So I made my own way, after they found out. It was the 80s, you know, there was the whole AIDS panic, and they said they wouldn't have me in the house, around my brother's kids with the way I was. They said I hadn't really ever been their son in the first place, and that they had always known there was something wrong with me from the day they got me, and they had tried to fix it, but if I was going to choose to spit in their faces and be gay after all they'd done to 'help' me, well, too bad."

Tom paused and took a drink, unable to hide the bitterness in his voice. Brett wondered where all this was leading.

Tom continued, "I don't know why I'm telling you all this. I guess four drinks is the magic number to open me up and I had a wet client meeting here before you came—but I had no idea where I was from until I started doing the genetic testing. It was way before 23andMe, and all that, but I found out that I'm 32% Eastern European, with a specific allele that has a 50% co-occurrence with Polish heritage, and 28% Scandinavian or Northern European descent. Isn't that interesting? That hints at a history, you know, that stretches back before this generation, before me. It means I'm not the first, that I came from somewhere. That my people came from somewhere."

"And I read that piece by Ta-Nehesi Coates in the Atlantic, about Jim Crow and economic disenfranchisement and all that, and I started to think about how much I've benefited every day of my life from the fact that this culture has decided that being 32% Eastern European and 28% Scandinavian makes me white. You know, my white privilege. And I started to feel really bad about it, really ashamed whenever I saw a black person, whenever they looked me in the eye, or talked to me. And it made me really aware of the fact that I don't even see that many black people here in the Valley, at least in my circles, the circles full of people who claim to be transforming the world, just like you were saying."

"And I was still jerking off to the Kanye albums. And about that time, last fall, I read 50 Cent's book The 50th Law. And I was like, this guy really fucking gets it. He's a genius. He sees how the system works, sees that it's stacked against him, and he develops the skills he needs to come out on top. It's surgical. It's precise. It's masterful. It's evolution. He's like a god. Everyone gets pissed off, about Kanye calling himself a god, and it's like, do you know what that means? To create something from nothing, to claim your fucking space in the universe. He is a god. We all live in his world. Did you see him on the cover of Time magazine, at the top of the Time 100 list?"

Tom didn't wait for an answer. He continued, "And that's why everyone got so worked up about the thing at the awards show, about Yeezus, about what he said about George Bush and Katrina and all that, because it's the fucking truth. I told you how I feel about technological evolution, but I really believe that black people in America have discovered what it means to evolve spiritually, because of what they've—you've—had to overcome, and what they've—you've—created. And the white people still just commodify it and claim it as their own, but most of them don't even understand what it's saying, what it means..."

Tom trailed off, realizing he had drifted from his point. He took a drink, and continued, "But then I started jerking off to 50 Cent's book too, just like, as I was reading a chapter on my damn kindle before going to sleep I'd be jerking off. And that's when I started really sexually fantasizing about black men, not just Kanye, but black men. How powerful you are. How much you've overcome. How fucking hot you are. And when I saw black guys, I would still be ashamed, but I'd also start to get hard. And it was really fucking inappropriate, and I had a really embarrassing situation at this angel investor meeting in Chicago last month."

"Ever since then, I've just been off my game. It's like my confidence is gone, like I just feel like I'll always be trapped in this white body, and it will never be ok for me to desire black men, and I just can't stop thinking about it. I know this has been a lot, and I hope I haven't offended you. I just wanted to tell you more about who I am and why I... posted what I did... And to tell you that I think you are so fucking hot and I would love to worship you and your gorgeous body if you're not totally weirded out by all the fucked up shit in my head."

Brett sipped his Cosmopolitan, enthralled. He felt like a priest, receiving Tom's confession. Now, finally, it was his turn to confess, to explain what it was he intended to do there. Tom had really gone deep, and Brett wasn't sure how to respond.

"Wow, man. I guess in a way that makes sense. I don't think you're fucked up, but I have to say, all that stuff you're saying, all those fantasies... That's not me. I mean, I am a black guy and I can relate to that, but you know, I'm Brett, not just another interchangeable 'big black dick.'"

"Of course! Of course! And that's why I want to get to know Brett!" Tom proclaimed.

He looked relieved by Brett's preliminary response to his divulgent monologue, sipping his own drink as Brett continued.

"I obviously have my own shit. I mean, I'm the one who messaged you. There's not much to it. I started seeing guys in college, mostly guys like me, black guys. I guess I didn't really think about it too much, they were just the guys I could relate to. I hooked up with some guys of other races, I guess, but it never lasted. There were a couple more serious things, but there's no ring on this finger, besides my class ring. And then I was with this white guy, a politician, back in DC, for four years. He was on the down low. Now that I'm looking back on it, I'm not sure he knew me, knew Brett, at all, and I'm not sure he cared. After all that time, he left me high and dry for his image, and for the wife he was with the whole time we were together."

Tom looked sympathetic, and curious; like he was trying to stop himself from asking the identity of the politician.

"I guess I just got a complex about it, about him not respecting me. I'm still not sure if it's because he's older than me, thought he was more powerful than me, or because of his race. It's all tied together. But I've developed a bit of a fetish as well, and I don't judge you."

They finished their drinks and shared a moment of silence.

"Should I have some champagne sent up to a room?" asked Tom pointedly.

"I'll get the room," said Brett. He didn't want to feel beholden to Tom in any way, like Tom was buying his favor or attention.

"It's really not a problem, I have a gold membership with this location..." said Tom, motioning to the receptionist across the lobby.

"Tom?" Brett prompted.

"Yes, Brett?"

"You're my bitch tonight. I'll get the room."

Brett got up and walked over to the desk, smiling at the receptionist and requesting an executive suite. He shot a glance back at Tom as she ran his card, and saw that Tom was staring at him. Brett smiled. Tom was odd, but cute. And he seemed ready to appreciate Brett for more than just his outward accomplishments and the accoutrements of success he had managed to acquire despite his identity. Brett motioned for Tom to come over, and they met at the elevator doors, both looking each other up and down.

Part Three

They stood side by side in the elevator, still shooting glances at each other. When it arrived at the sixth floor, Brett gestured for Tom to go before him, discreetly checking him out, and they made their way to room 646.

Brett slid the keycard into the lock. It flashed green, and he opened the door. The two entered, looking at each other expectantly for a moment.

"So... Whatever you want, I'd be happy to provide," Tom offered.

Brett wasn't necessarily turned on, but he felt excited, prickly sensations dancing over his skin. Truth be told, he felt a little nervous.

"You can start by taking off your shirt," Brett said.

He took a seat in the room's comfortable chair, watching. Tom took off his suit jacket, throwing it over the desk, and untied his knit skinny tie, letting it hang loose as he unbuttoned his shirt, starting from the top. He finished and pulled it off his arms, giving Brett a little smirk and flexing ironically, standing there in a slim fit white t-shirt that hugged his muscles. He really was fit, and not even just for an older guy. His pictures hadn't been misleading. Tom pulled off the t-shirt too, standing there bare-chested in front of Brett. He had a little tuft of silver chest hair, and great muscle definition.

"Take off my shoes," Brett continued.

He had thought of slipping them off himself, but was at a loss for what to command Tom to do, and realized that it would feel nice to be taken care of that way. For the first time since he had met Tom, his thoughts turned to memories of Jerry, and as Tom dropped to the floor, untying Brett's laces, a little smile flickered across his face. Jerry wouldn't have been caught dead undressing Brett, caressing him, serving him... Tom loosened and pulled off Brett's wingtips, and looked up at him.

"Rub my feet," Brett said, on a whim, and Tom responded, "Should I take off your socks so I can do it better? I can get some lotion from the bathroom..."

"Yeah, take off my socks and get some lotion," replied Brett.

He was starting to really appreciate his desires being respected. Tom pulled off Brett's black and grey micro-striped socks, and got up to go get the lotion from the bathroom. Brett wiped his feet on the carpet, a little self-conscious that they might smell bad—but then again, that was Tom's problem.

Tom returned and settled back onto the floor, cross-legged. Brett felt a little thrill seeing this older guy, this professional white man, sitting on the floor like a child ready to serve him. Tom seemed pretty happy himself as he squeezed out some of the lemon verbena artisanal lotion onto his hands, rubbing them together as a masseuse would to warm up the liquid.

"I took a class on acupressure meridians last

139

spring. I'm going to release your pressure points," said Tom, "It might be a little painful... and sexually stimulating. Most people don't know this, but a lot of the body's energy, especially sexual energy, is caught up in the feet."

He began to rub Brett's feet, and Brett sighed. Tom's hands kneaded, pressing along his soles, separating and gently pulling on his toes.

"I'm going to play some music," Brett said.

"Sorry, I should have thought of that," said Tom.

His hands were squeezing Brett's ankles.

"No, I got it. It's right on my phone. Keep rubbing my feet, that feels great."

Brett pulled out his iPhone and pulled up the Amy Winehouse playlist, pressing play. It wasn't the most obvious choice, but it was what relaxed him, what made him feel like he was in his own space. Tom was pulling on his feet now, teasing apart his metatarsals, draining away Brett's tension. Some of the spots were surprisingly sore; Brett hadn't had a good foot rub since god knows when, and he couldn't help but groan a little as Tom teased over them.

"Why don't you come on over, Valerie," played in the background, and Brett felt buoyant, even happy. How odd that it was with this peculiar man he had just met, but there was definitely something good between them.

Tom was working over Brett's feet with broad circular motions, and Brett finally stopped him, saying, "That's enough. I'm going to use the restroom. I want you to order me a snack from the room service menu while I'm gone. Surprise me."

"Sure, I'll get right on it," said Tom.

He ceased his efforts, wiping his hands together, and leaping to his feet. He certainly was spry, Brett thought, and remembered that he wanted to live to be 150. He laughed to himself a little as he rose, and went to take a leak. He could hear Tom's voice on the phone outside the door and smiled slightly. What would he have Tom do next?

Brett washed his hands and looked at himself in the bathroom mirror. He smiled. He felt good, and he was excited to see where the night went. Tom was good with his hands, and seemed earnest in his desire to please. Brett returned to the room, seeing Tom standing there next to the bed, shirtless. He felt a thrill of arousal as he imagined him on his knees, ready to satisfy Brett, to pleasure him however he wanted.

"Is there anything you'd like me to do?" Tom asked.

"Take off the rest of your clothes."

Tom stepped out of his shoes, and unbuckled his belt. He unbuttoned his pants and let them fall to his ankles. He was wearing light blue boxers, simple and a little charming for such a refined guy. He looked to Brett, and as Brett nodded, he pulled down his boxers too, letting them fall to the floor and stepping out of them and the pants. He stood there, naked, looking comfortable in his body but a little self-conscious, with his semi-erect penis exposed. He was a handsome guy with neatly trimmed body hair, and the muscle definition extended down through his hips and thighs. Jerry had been a very different sort of silver fox—handsome, but balding, and with a bit of a paunch. Tom looked like he belonged on the cover of Men's Health. Perhaps he had even been on the cover of a male fitness magazine, considering his industry and personal image. Leave it to Brett to find the older white guy who was also an actual male fitness model in a sea of desperately aging queens on his first dip into the online dating pool.

"Come undress me," Brett said.

Tom walked over, walking a bit crookedly, unable to conceal his erection.

"Take off my pants."

Wordlessly, Tom dropped to his knees, and reached up to unfasten Brett's belt. He unclasped it, and unbuttoned Brett's pants. He pulled down the zipper, clearly excited by how close he was to Brett, to Brett's dick. Brett could feel his own heart rate accelerate slightly, feeling Tom brush over him. Brett's pants fell to the floor but Tom stayed on his knees, looking up at Brett as though he wanted the go-ahead to remove his underwear too.

"Get up, I'm not ready for you to blow me yet," said Brett.

Tom looked slightly rebuffed by the answer to his unspoken question.

"Take off my shirt," Brett commanded.

Tom's fingers began to undo the buttons on his cheerily refined Ted Baker microfloral button up. It was Brett's favorite shirt of his new West Coast business casual wardrobe. Tom ran his fingers over Brett's chest gratuitously as he pulled the shirt open to reveal Brett's own slim fit undershirt, which hugged his relatively well-defined pecs and shoulders.

"You have a beautiful body," Tom said breathlessly.

Brett shrugged. His body was sturdy and well-formed, but by no means ripped, and he wouldn't necessarily think of it as "beautiful;" however, Tom stared at him in awe. As he pulled Brett's shirt from his shoulders, there was a knock at the door.

A voice chimed out, "Room service!"

"I'll get it," Brett said, "since you seem a bit indisposed."

His eyes flickered down to Tom's dick, now fully erect.

"While I'm gone, I want you to think of three things you want to happen tonight," said Brett, "If you please me, maybe you'll get to do them."

Tom nodded and a slight grin cracked his impassive visage. Brett went to the door, and was greeted by a chipper young bellhop with a basket of fruit and an ice bath containing a bottle of champagne perched on his service trolley.

"Great! You can just leave that here," he said.

He collected the goods and handed the boy a few crumpled ones he had pulled from his wallet. He returned, closing the door behind him and saw Tom emerging from the restroom, wiping his newly washed hands together; his erection had somewhat subsided.

"I hope you like what I picked out!" Tom said.

Brett replied inscrutably, "We'll see."

He set the ice bucket on the table next to the bed and climbed onto the center of the bed, placing the basket of fruit in front of him.

"Would you open the champagne?" He asked Tom.

He watched Tom dutifully uncork the champagne with a pop as Amy sang,

"You went back to what you knew
So far removed from all that we went through
And I tread a troubled track
You go back to her
And I go back to
Black."

He had gotten much more into Amy Winehouse after the break up, he acknowledged. Amy's dark and soulful tone had captured his mood for the last few months, but was beginning to sound a little morose. He pulled out his phone, swiped through his playlists, and with a shrug, pressed play on Brenda's Breakup Mix. Perhaps he was finally in the mood.

"I got the Dom Soliloquet. I had it at a launch party my friend threw and it blew my mind," said Tom, "I was stoked when I saw they carried it on the menu and I wanted you to try it. I hope you like it!"

He plucked two crystal flutes from on top of the mini bar and poured the champagne, handing one of the glasses to Brett as Nicki Minaj's "Boss

Ass Bitch" began to play. Brett smiled. Tom came and sat on the edge of the bed, raising his glass to clink against Brett's.

"Salud."

Brett took a sip, meeting Tom's eyes. The champagne was light, fragrant, definitely top shelf.

"Nice choice," Brett said.

Tom looked pleased with himself, downing his own glass, then setting it on the table. Brett took another sip, and reached to pick up a strawberry from the edible bouquet.

"Would you like me to feed you?" Tom asked.

"Is that one of the three things you'd like to do?" Brett replied.

Tom looked on the verge of blushing, and he replied, "Not quite..."

"Did you come up with three things?" Brett asked.

Tom nodded.

"What are they? You can go ahead and feed me some fruit."

Brett took another sip of his champagne, and Tom raised a strawberry to his lips. He took a bite, his lips brushing Tom's fingers.

"Well, I'd like to..." Tom began, then sputtered out.

It was clear that he wasn't the type of guy who often had trouble getting his words out, and it was endearing, even cute, to see him at a loss for words.

"Go on," said Brett.

"I'd like to suck your cock," Tom said, eyes

downcast.

"That's one," said Brett, smiling slightly.

"I want you to fuck me," said Tom.

He met Brett's eyes this time, holding a grape up to his lips.

Brett ate the grape, and replied, "So that's something you'd like me to do to you... What else?"

Tom took a deep breath and said, "I want to eat your ass."

Brett was a little taken aback. He had never had someone do that to him. Rimming, they called it, and he knew it was a common practice for many gay guys, but he had had a bit of a skewed sample and had never tried it. He wasn't opposed to it, he just... hadn't really thought of it as something he desired. Despite himself, he noticed that his dick was starting to get hard, pressing against the fabric of his boxers.

"We'll see about that," he told Tom.

Tom's eyes had drifted to the bulge growing below his hips, and he scooted a little closer on the bed, feeding Brett a slice of pineapple and gazing at him flirtatiously. Brett took the pineapple in his mouth, closing his lips over Tom's fingertips.

Tom smiled, and his hand dropped to caress Brett's thigh, stroking upward towards the hem of his boxers.

"Not yet," Brett said.

Tom withdrew his hand. He was clearly aroused, hoping he could begin to serve Brett in a more sexual nature soon. Tom fed Brett another strawberry, asking, "Is there anything I could do to please you? Or... make you more comfortable?"

Brett's erection was pulsing, and he had an idea. "You're doing a good job," he said, "I'm going to give you one of your three wishes."

He scooted up to lean against the headboard, pulling off his boxers with slight difficulty. Tom's eyes drew magnetically to his dick.

"Nice cock," Tom said. He gazed longingly at it as it lay long and hard against Brett's thigh.

"I'm going to let you blow me," said Brett, and Tom eagerly drew closer. "But there's a catch. You have to lie on your back, and I'm going to sit here."

"Ok..." said Tom. He lay down in a passive position, scooting himself closer until the top of his head was pressed against Brett's balls and Brett's dick lay over his face. It looked pretty big, the tip hovering just above Tom's chin.

"It's kind of like bobbing for apples, but in reverse," Brett chuckled. He had never done this before, but the guys in the sexy menlovingmen Tumblr posts he'd been using to jerk off lately were always doing playful things with their dicks and he thought Tom would find it exciting.

Tom opened his mouth and, reaching upwards, licked the underside of Brett's shaft. On a second attempt, he managed to nearly get the head into his mouth before it popped out again. Brett was rock hard, seeing Tom lying in front of him, totally naked, trying desperately to get his dick in his mouth from this impossible angle. Brett let Tom struggle for a while longer, licking him with greater and greater desperation as his own erection bobbed, reddening, over his thighs. He didn't want to give him a neck ache, and was ready for a real blowjob, so after a few moments of laughing and some groaning, he told Tom, "You can get up and continue."

Tom sprang up, turning to kneel and bend over, wrapping his lips around Brett's cock without any further instruction.

"Stop," Brett said.

Tom froze, slowly drawing back and looking up at Brett.

"Start with your hand," said Brett.

Tom reached out, stroking him, his light skin in sharp contrast with Brett's dark cock.

"You like that big black cock?" Brett asked, trying out the phrase.

"Yeah, I like it," said Tom, his voice a little hoarse. His fingers were trailing over Brett, his hand caressing him, gently pulling.

"What do you like?" asked Brett pointedly.

Tom replied, "Your big black cock."

Tom was close to him, sensually jerking him off, and the two began to passionately kiss, tongues winding together as Tom's motions grew stronger. The kiss ended, and Tom was breathless, clearly wanting to continue with his fantasy of blowing Brett.

"Now you can use your mouth," said Brett.

Tom eagerly complied, bending over and taking him into his mouth, his lips sliding up and down Brett's shaft as he tried to get more and more of it into his mouth. Brett groaned. It felt good to be taken care of sexually, and Tom certainly knew what he was doing, caressing Brett's balls, stroking the rest of the shaft with his hand. Brett relaxed for a moment, enjoying the sensation, before Tom lifted his mouth from the head of Brett's dick and moved it to his balls, tracing down with his tongue. Tom was trying to add in his other fantasy, of eating his ass, Brett realized. He put his hand in Tom's hair to pull his head back, saying "Not yet. But I'm going to give you your second wish. I'm ready to fuck you."

Tom sat up, adjusting his jaw, clearly excited.

"Do you have lube?" Brett asked, "I have condoms."

"We can use the lotion," said Tom. "It's hypoallergenic, non-oil based. I checked. Should be ok."

"Get the lotion, and get the condoms from my wallet," said Brett. He sat back and watched as Tom got up and retrieved the items from around the room.

He returned and climbed onto the bed, handing the bottle of lotion and a condom to Brett, a hint of nervousness perceptible through his smile.

"You ready to be my bitch?" Brett asked.

He felt inspired by the role-play Tom had said he was looking for; earlier, he had thought it would be uncomfortable, but now he too found it hot.

"Yeah, how do you want it?" replied Tom.

"Kneel on the edge of the bed and bend over," said Brett.

He climbed off the bed, his dick in his hand.

He felt confident, powerful. Maybe this was how Kanye felt, if people treated him this way all the time. He stood by the edge of the bed, opening a condom wrapper. Pausing, he said, "Actually, help me put this on."

Tom straightened up and turned, taking the condom from Brett and placing it over the head of his penis. It felt a little cold and slimy against Brett's dick and he shivered, before Tom placed his warm mouth over the rolled rubber and unfurled it over him, using first his lips, then his hands. He held Brett in his fist, sizing up his girth.

"You think it's gonna fit?" asked Brett.

He thought back to the last time he had been the active partner in anal sex, back with Robert, before Jerry. Robert was a big guy too, and had taken him like a champ, but Brett could acknowledge that he was a bit too large for comfortable anal with many guys. Unless they were guys who were looking for that, guys like Tom. But just because Tom fantasized about it didn't mean he had taken a dick like Brett's before. In fact, Brett had no idea what Tom's presumably long sexual history was like, save for his recent and derailing obsession with black power.

"You're gonna make it fit, and I'm gonna take it," said Tom.

Brett found Tom's ambition attractive.

"Put some lotion on me," said Brett.

Tom reached for the bottle, squeezing it into his hand and warming it up before massaging it over Brett's dick. It felt good, soothing against his aching hardness. Brett was getting excited thinking about pushing himself into Tom's ass, and once Tom had rubbed the lotion up and down, Brett said, "Ok, now bend over again, like before."

Tom followed instructions, turning around.

"Are you ready for this..." Brett sighed, then continued, "big black cock?"

He knew that the words excited Tom, and it excited him to be able to say them too, to claim the fetish. He looked down, seeing Tom kneeling, facing away from him, bent over, ass in the air.

"Do you think you've earned it?"

"Only if you want to give it to me," Tom said. He was breathing heavily, turned on, face pressed against the bed.

Brett reached forward, grabbing Tom's shoulder, and pressing his dick between Tom's ass cheeks. Tom moaned, and Brett began to rock his hips, pushing the tip of his erection into Tom's asshole with greater and greater friction until he felt Tom relax and he began to slide inside.

"Oh fuck," exclaimed Tom.

Brett groaned a little, feeling Tom's hot ass tightening around him.

"You like that? You want me to give you more?" Brett asked. He was half teasing Tom, but was also uncertain how quickly he should proceed.

"Fuck, yes. Please," said Tom, and Brett smiled.

He continued to lean forward, rocking his hips to the beat as Zebra Katz sang,

"Imma take that bitch to college,
Imma give that bitch some knowledge."

Tom was groaning as Brett sank deeper and

deeper into him, thrusting in and out. "Fuck yeah, man," he gasped out.

Brett was building momentum, getting more excited as he felt Tom wrapped around more and more of him.

"Yeah, take that cock," Brett said, adding, "bitch!" with a little thrill. He was really getting into it, moving his hands to grab Tom's hips and thrusting deeper as Tom's groaned rhythmically.

"It's gonna be cohesive,
It's gonna be my thesis"

Brett lost himself in the motion, pumping in and out, as his vision began to tunnel and his consciousness descended into awareness of his movements, his breathing, and Tom—receiving him, submitting to him, and getting off on it.

He pounded into Tom's ass, no longer as concerned with whether Tom could take him, but thinking more about the friction, the heat building between them. He could tell he was going to come soon, and he slowed down, reaming his full cock in and out of Tom several more times as Tom cried out, "Oh! My! Fucking! God!"

Brett's body started to seize and he grunted and pulled Tom's hips against him hard as he came. He felt great. Tom was hot, so much hotter than Jerry, and the sex had been so much better than Brett's fantasies of white male submission. Brett closed his eyes, feeling his release subside and his dick begin to soften in Tom's welcoming ass. He stayed still for a moment, his heart pounding, his breath coming in heaves, and he could hear Tom's own gasping breaths as he steadied himself. Brett slowly pulled out, and pulled off the condom, saying, "I'm going to go clean up."

He went into the bathroom, tossing the condom in the bathroom on the way, and washed the come off his penis in the sink. He finished by washing his hands, feeling pretty pleased with himself. He was a hot black stud, he thought, with a little smile. The girls were going to be so impressed with how he had pulled this off...

* * * * *

Brett returned to find Tom sitting on the bed, face flushed, with a massive boner.

"That was really hot, man," said Tom.

"For real," replied Brett. He opened a bottle of water from the minibar and drank some, standing there naked, Tom's eyes still on him.

Brett plopped down in the chair and said, "Well, I need a breather. I see you're excited and didn't get off. I want you to jerk off for me. I'm going to sit here and watch. Maybe have another glass of this champagne."

"Want me to pour you some?"

"Sure."

Tom got up, his boner protruding from his lap, and poured Brett another flute of champagne. He poured a glass for himself too, and toasted Brett, taking a sip, then asking, "So where do you want me to be? Want me to do anything special?"

"Why don't you stand right there in front of me, and think about how much you like it when I top you."

"No problem," said Tom. He squeezed a bit of lotion into his hand and massaged it over his own dick now, standing a few feet in front of where Brett sat, sipping champagne, in the chair.

"Oh, I, I think I'm into you
How much do you want it too?
What are you prepared to do?"

Tom groaned, and began to stroke himself. He closed his eyes and wrapped his hand around the base of his dick and started to squeeze, working his way towards the head. Brett was intrigued. It was always interesting to watch see how another guy got himself off. Tom had been hard for a while now, and his erection was dark, almost purplish at the end. He groaned, opening his eyes for a moment to look at Brett again, and Brett raised his eyebrow. Tom continued his rhythmic strokes, working with a slight twisting motion as he tugged on himself. Brett could see Tom's chest beginning to flush, and his breathing became more shallow as his strokes sped up.

Amused, Brett said, "Wait 'til I tell you to come."

Tom nodded, and slowed his strokes, writhing somewhat uncomfortably, trying to keep himself on the precipice. Brett noticed his own dick getting hard again as he watched Tom.

After a few seconds, Brett said, "Ok, I want you to come on yourself."

Tom began to rapidly jerk his hand, grunting as his muscles began to contract, directing his dick upwards towards his own chest. His mouth fell open as his balls finally spasmed and he ejaculated up in an arc over his shoulder.

Brett was enjoying the show. Tom gasped, shaking, his body contorting slightly as he stood there. Finally he opened his eyes and smiled at Brett. "Sorry, I missed," he said.

He gestured to the streak of come that had landed on the edge of the bed, and Brett laughed a little. "You tried your best."

Tom's eyes flicked down, seeing that Brett had another erection. "Anything I can do to help you with that?" he asked.

Brett's eyebrows raised. This guy really did go above and beyond. He remembered Lindsi's comment about ultra marathoning, and thought that she wouldn't be disappointed.

"You can blow me, if you're ready," said Brett.

Tom moved to kneel between Brett's knees, again perched in front of Brett as he sat in the chair.

"I want it to be special, though," said Brett, "I want you to give me the best blowjob of my life."

"I have some ideas," said Tom. He reached out to slide his hands up Brett's thighs, placing one hand on either side of Brett's junk and pressing gently.

Brett sighed, relaxing. So this was more of that acupressure stuff. It felt like his dick was growing harder, more blood flowing into it. Tom moved one hand below Brett's balls, cupping them gently, then pressing his thumb against Brett's perineum. His balls started to tingle and he let out a little moan. Tom smiled, and began to stroke Brett's shaft loosely with his other hand, massaging it. Brett groaned a little as Tom increased the pressure, squeezing the base and milking upwards as he had done to himself. When he got to the tip, he moved his mouth down to cover where his fist left off, enveloping the end of Brett's dick fully in his mouth and hand, gently teasing at his perineum still. Tom wasn't fucking around, thought Brett—or rather, he was an expert at it.

Tom started to gradually work up and down with his mouth and hand, taking more of the erection in his mouth, working his hand downwards towards the base. He was making sucking motions with his mouth as he gradually slipped more of Brett's length inside, and Brett began to breath deeply, feeling pleasure swirling all over and through him. Tom really knew how to handle a dick. He had several inches of Brett in his mouth, his jaw extended, when he began to slide upwards, bobbing up and down for a while as he jerked off Brett's entire length with his hand. He then slowly slid up to the tip and swirled his tongue around, sucking gently.

Brett closed his eyes, losing himself in the sensation. He almost didn't notice when Tom removed his mouth, continuing to massage with his hand, and was a little startled when he felt Tom's tongue begin to lick his balls. It felt good, and he relaxed, spreading his legs a little further to give Tom access. Tom closed his mouth over one of Brett's testicles, then the other, taking them gently between his lips.

Brett couldn't help but moan slightly. It felt more intimate than sucking on his dick, and more sensitive. Tom used the hand resting against his perineum to lift his balls, continuing to lick along their underside, back towards where his hand had been, back towards Brett's ass. Brett opened his eyes to see Tom looking up at him, slowly jerking him off, tongue lapping against the underside of his balls.

"Tom?" said Brett, his voice cracking slightly.

Tom nodded, raising his eyebrows inquisitively without stopping his movements.

"You can do that other thing you wanted to..." Brett said. He was curious, if a little squeamish, about the rimming. But if Tom wanted to...

Tom looked excited, from what Brett could tell. He moved his tongue to Brett's perineum, teasing it with firm and soft strokes, before licking lower, and lower... Brett was breathing steadily, until Tom's tongue found his asshole and he let out a gasp. Talk about sensitivity, he thought. Tom licked over it broadly, and Brett felt oddly vulnerable, as though this new act was somehow more explicit or compromising than anything they had already done. It felt as though he was letting Tom take this to a deeper level, that it was turning into more than a hookup. There was some powerful chemistry between them, sexual and otherwise.

Brett closed his eyes again, letting himself relax and give in to the feelings building in him. Jerry had loved to fuck him in the ass, but had never thought of doing this, of soothing and pleasuring Brett before he did it. And Tom wasn't even expecting to fuck him... He just wanted to do it, to be submissive to Brett because he thought he was "fucking hot" and wanted to "worship him," as he had said.

Brett's breath began to come in deep heaves. The waves building inside him felt very different from his earlier orgasm. Tom's wandering tongue felt like it was stimulating his prostate from the outside, as he continued to stroke Brett's shaft. His movements were gradual but insistent, and Brett felt himself slipping into a deeper and deeper state of relaxation and arousal. Tom lifted his head and asked, "Can I massage your prostate?"

Brett nodded. Tom pressed his finger against Brett's ass, lubricated by his spit, and slipped the first inch or so in. He began to twist the finger quickly against Brett's prostate, flicking his tongue all over Brett's balls. Brett shuddered, gripping the arms of the chair, his hips jerking, his thighs starting to convulse. Tom was just holding the base of his dick now, not stroking it, focusing his efforts instead on Brett's ass and balls.

Brett had had prostate orgasms infrequently throughout his years of homosexual activity and ass play, but he was familiar enough with the feeling to tell that the contractions beginning in his pelvis were a harbinger of something much bigger coming. "Uh! Uh!" he heard himself starting to groan.

Tom continued to masterfully tease at his prostate, flicking and tapping it as he continued to kiss his balls, before moving backwards to the perineum. Brett was scooted forward in the chair now, slouched so Tom could access his ass like this, and he felt his hips involuntarily thrusting in the air, bucking, as a full body orgasm began to spread through him. After so much sexual stimulation, so much arousal, and such new sensations, Brett felt himself descending to a deep and unfamiliar terrain of pleasure. His whole body was shaking now, his hands tightly gripping the chair as Tom continued to stimulate his prostate and perineum. What had he expected, asking this perfectionist and master of the human body to give him the "best blowjob of his life?"

Brett could hear himself moaning, and he thought that he sounded almost like a woman, albeit a woman with a deep voice. He didn't really care. He felt an urge to pee, but he knew that came before the prostate orgasm and he let it pass, relaxing into it and letting the convulsions intensify. His legs shook, and he felt as though he nearly blacked out for a moment, a mosaic of golden light bursting behind his closed eyelids as deeper and deeper waves of pleasure surged through his body for what must have been minutes until suddenly and without warning the sensation of having to pee returned, and he ejaculated a strangely large volume of come all over Tom's back. Tom groaned, feeling it land on him, letting it run down his back as he slowed his movements, continuing to gently lick and coax Brett's ass until Brett gasped, "That's enough, man. Shit!"

Tom withdrew, got up, and went into the bathroom, presumably to wipe the come off his back. Brett lay in the chair, sprawled out, stunned, his body totally limp. He heard the shower running, and closed his eyes, his body totally still, little spasms of muscle contraction still rippling through him.

His breathing returned to a regular tempo, and, hearing a familiar ping emanate from next to the bed, Brett got up to look at his phone. It wasn't that late, and he noticed several new texts in a group chat with Megan, Brenda, and Lindsi.

"How's it going??"

"Hot or not?"

"Movie's out! #hilarious"

"Are you going to meet up with us to debrief?"

Another message came through:

"Or are you still busy!?"

Brett typed out and sent:

"Meet you back at The Garden in 30m?"

"Ok!" came Brenda's quick response, with two thumbs up emojis from the others.

Brett began to pull on his clothes, shaking his head as he continued to experience what felt like tingles of electricity shooting through him. Tom returned from the bathroom, hair wet from the shower, a towel around his waist.

"I'm going to go meet up with my friends," Brett said.

"Yeah, I should get back to Mountain View. I have a retreat tomorrow," said Tom.

The two rummaged around the room, collecting their things and making small talk as they dressed. Finally they found themselves at the door, a tense energy between them, and with a jolt,

Brett thought, "What if this is the only time we ever meet?" Their interaction had begun as a mutual fetish, but he hoped Tom hadn't gotten it out of his system and was ready to move on, as he found himself quite interested in seeing Tom again.

Tom leaned forward, giving Brett a little kiss on the lips. He pulled back and said, "Well, I hope this was as good for you as it was for me. I have to say, I would love to see you again, and to get to know you, and to hear more of your fascinating thoughts on the world. I know you might just be looking for something casual and I don't want to put you on the spot and make you feel pressured to say yes, so don't say anything now! You have my card, and you can contact me anytime if you'd like to take me on a date. I'd be happy to hear from you, and I'll leave it at that."

"I'll think about it," Brett said impassively. He gave Tom a little smile, adding, "I had a good time too. You're an interesting guy."

They went down to the lobby, and each hailed a cab, driving in opposite directions off into the night. Sitting in the cab's back seat on the way back to The Garden, Brett pulled Tom's card from his pocket and ran his finger over it.

He knew he would call before the week was out.

4: JAIME

Trauma

Trigger Warning: Graphic Sexual Violence, Rape

Part One

Jaime turned her truck off I-43 and onto the gravel road that led to Ian's house, headlights sweeping the rural Colorado road. Kenny Chesney sang, "*Everything gets hotter when the sun goes down,*" on the radio and she rolled her eyes. Was she really doing this again? Why did she keep getting together with Ian?

She thought of the last time they had seen each other, the awkward blowjob, swallowing his jizz after looking around for a trashcan, then deciding that she didn't want to run to the bathroom and make a scene. Feeling a thrill of success at having gotten him off so easily. Then, his even more awkward attempts to reciprocate, licking her roughly with his broad tongue, his stubble scratching at her own sensitive shaved skin. It felt painful, invasive, but there was some pleasure to it, and she had been excited by the idea, hadn't imagined they would do this together, that he would do this to her—and so she hadn't stopped him, breathing steadily, until his sucking on her clit and attempts to penetrate her with his tongue grew more uncomfortable than intriguing and she put her hand in his shaggy hair and said, "Hey, you can stop. That felt good."

He had looked up from between her legs, wiping his mouth, grinning sheepishly, clearly a bit uncomfortable himself. He had certainly tried to make her feel good, but it hadn't seemed like it was for her, but rather to prove he could make a girl come by going down on her, and so her body's failure to respond with any resemblance to pleasure seemed to have struck a direct blow to his confidence and self-esteem. Far from the intended effect of oral sex, but why hadn't he started more gently, building into it? She had done that for him, kissing his abdomen, then the sides of his penis, stroking it before putting her mouth over the tip and gently sucking, her fingers trailing up and down it until he came seconds later. She might have liked it better if it had been more like that, but then again, maybe he had done everything right and she was just so uncomfortable with him looking at her down there that her body had betrayed her, shutting down before it could get any further.

But why was she going back, why had she texted him, "*Hey, do you want to hang out?* :-)" this late on a Thursday night?

Was it just to get back at Adam? Not that Adam had wanted to fuck her anyway, he probably wouldn't even care if he found out that she had fucked his Call of Duty buddy the week after she'd dumped him.

He was such a loser, and probably gay anyway.

He probably wanted to blow Ian, and would be jealous of that, not of Ian for getting to fuck her—besides, she didn't want him to find out. She certainly wasn't going to tell him.

Ian knew, of course, but he had been discreet about everything that had happened between them since that first drunken make-out two years ago at his brother's party. But was she going to fuck Ian then, finally? Going to let him fuck her?

It seemed like Ian wanted to, of course; last time they had gotten together he had mentioned fucking his ex, and her trying to hook up with him again, implying that he could be getting pussy if he wanted it. She, Jaime, was the perfectionist, the good girl, and if she wasn't with him, the stoner, the burnout, for weed and sex, then what was she doing? Just looking for some rebellion while still coloring neatly between the lines? But when he mentioned having sex with Jessica, Jaime's first thought had been, how did she fit his massive penis inside her, whoever she was?

This was the tension that had been developing throughout their hook-up buddy-ship, was what had stopped them from going further. His size hadn't been a problem when she had just been giving him hand jobs or grinding against him, and had been slightly uncomfortable when giving him the blowjob, but she hadn't put much of it into her mouth, wrapping the rest of it in her hands, and he hadn't seemed to mind. But she was still a virgin, which had been apparent each time he fingered her and she winced in pain, unclear whether it was from the roughness of his explorations or her tightness.

The things they had done so far hadn't been so painful that she couldn't manage and hide her discomfort, but if they had sex tonight, it would be a totally different matter. Would it feel good at all, or just be painful for her and pleasurable for him?

It seemed perverse that the tighter she was, the better it would feel for him, and the bigger he was, the more it would hurt for her. That's why guys got all excited about virginity (taking the virginity of girls anyway), and why girls feared it and felt as though they'd lost their value afterwards.

She was excited by Ian, his physical stature and strength as well as the size of his dick thrilled her, but she was also afraid of him, of how he could hurt her, at the same time, neither of which had been dynamics with her lanky, petite exes. The guy was supposed to pursue, to try to initiate, but Adam and Sean and James had all been weirdly shy sexually, she thought, seeming to have no interest in anything but making out, only fingering her or even touching her boobs after they'd been drinking, which had caused a lot of insecurity for Jaime. After all, her girlfriends all complained about how their boyfriends wanted to go too far too fast, but then boasted about how exciting every milestone was. Jaime didn't feel like her boyfriends had even wanted to be with her at all, not physically anyway. James was a Christian, and they'd dated in junior high, so that made sense, and Sean had his own sexual guilt as a Catholic, and had always wanted to get drunk before they did anything, like that one time when he'd asked her to touch his penis then said "Never mind" as she felt it. And Adam was just a punk, drinking Mountain Dew and role-playing with other geeks on the internet, calling her a bitch—he was a terrible kisser, too.

But still, she was 17 and her longest and most mature sexual relationship had been as Ian's on and off hook-up buddy. She hadn't intended to lose her virginity to him, but she was attracted to him, and he made her feel more validated sexually than anyone else had, so maybe it made sense after all. She'd rather do it with him than with some stranger at college, and her other high school prospects seemed less and less likely or desirable as graduation approached.

She'd hoped to lose her virginity to someone else, someone she had more of a friendship with maybe, someone who wasn't so physically imposing, someone with a normal sized dick at least. But Ian was her friend with benefits, and she had a crush on him, and was attracted to him sexually, and so it would maybe be a good choice after all. Wouldn't she be nervous no matter who it was with? And she was a grade older, and she was the one who texted him, and kept texting him after each encounter, and so maybe it was fitting that she have this experience with him. What was he thinking, sitting up in his room, waiting for her to arrive? He probably thought he was going to get laid, expected to fuck her, considering that now they'd done everything else and she was still coming back for more.

"*No shoes, no shirt, no problem*," played on the radio now. God, why did this station have nothing but upbeat redneck Chesney songs about being laid back and having sex on tonight?

She pulled up in front of Ian's house—well, his parents' house—but she never saw them around, and his older siblings were gone and moved out so it seemed like his house, out here in the middle of nowhere, just down the road from her backwoods church. The gravel crunched under her tires as her little Chevy slowed to a halt.

Her heart was pounding, nervousness surging in her stomach as she texted him, *"I'm here."*

He responded, *"K,"* almost immediately, and after a couple minutes opened the front door and walked out to meet her.

She climbed down from the cab, and he smiled at her, saying, "Hey," as he pulled her into a hug.

She wrapped her arms around him, smelling his musk, feeling his t-shirt against her cheek, his muscles hard under the soft fabric. She felt a rush of—was it desire? Anticipation? What was going to happen tonight?

"Come on in," Ian said, heading back towards the front door. She followed. It was so different to see him outside of school, at ease on his own front porch. He seemed out of his element in school, smart but an underachiever at best; except in the band, where he acted the fool with the rest of the drums section, across the room from her and the other brass players. There he radiated confidence and self-assurance, just as he did now at his house, although he did seem a little nervous around her; the upperclassman, the valedictorian, the good Christian girl who drank too much at parties.

"You want a beer?" he asked as they walked through the kitchen, and she stammered, "Uh, sure. Yeah. Thanks," as he pulled two Coors Lights from the refrigerator and continued upstairs.

She walked behind him, noting his posture, the torn sagging jeans, the zebra print boxers that climbed to his hips, his broad shoulders. He was 16, but he had seemed like such a man even the first time they had kissed, when he was 14 and she was 15, and he had unfastened her bra through her shirt to everyone's drunken amusement at his older brother's party. His brother had taught him the trick, and had kept him hooked up with weed and beer ever since. They reached the landing, and he pushed open the door to his bedroom, covered by curling Nirvana and Bob Marley posters. We're both such caricatures of ourselves, Jaime thought.

The stale smell of weed wafted from the room as she leaned in the doorway, attempting nonchalance.

Ian sunk into a chair, and asked, "Want to watch a movie and blaze?"

"Sounds good."

She felt awkward standing in the door and went to sit on the edge of the bed. She remembered him unfastening her bra, sliding his hands up under her shirt the last time they had watched a movie, his warm rough hands squeezing her breasts. She swallowed, and opened her beer, sipping it so as to have something to do with her hands and to make her more comfortable, less uptight.

They attempted casual conversation, but it was clear that while they were attracted to each other, they were not the types of people who naturally enjoyed each other's company. The conversation settled on booze, weed, and partying, discussing several of their acquaintances' recent exploits, as well as the particular attributes of the strain of weed that Ian was grinding up and packing into his bong. Maybe she should buy some of it to smoke alone behind her garage. It was unreasonable to come out here and hang out with Ian every time she wanted an excuse to relax. He popped a DVD of Wedding Crashers into the TV, cutting short their conversation.

"You seen this?"

"Yeah, it's hilarious."

God, could she manage to get through one sentence without using a word longer than three syllables? She rolled her eyes at herself as he picked up the bong and came to sit on the bed as well, leaning against the headboard, leaving plenty of space between them. Piles of dirty boxers and t-shirts littered the floor, next to empty beer cans and straight up trash, with a giant glass bong visible in the corner. This looked like a dorm room, not a 16 year old's bedroom, at least to her. She couldn't imagine his parents leaving him at such ease, but they must.

"Oh they don't care, they've been through all that with my brother and sister," he'd said when she mentioned it to him before, but it was still shocking to her.

Her own parents didn't seem to care what she did out of the house, as long as it didn't get back to them, but were rigidly controlling and judgmental of everything she said or did within the house. What if she just started drinking beer in her room, or smoking weed?

Ian had come over to her house once, a couple months ago while her parents were out, and they had smoked weed under the stars and eaten the remnants of her chocolate birthday cake, and kissed, and he had fingered her on the couch while she gave him a hand job—but then they had heard her parents car in the driveway and he had leapt over the back of the couch and hidden under the foosball table as she pretended to be sleeping, until her parents went to bed, ruining whatever moment there had been. Perhaps the sneaking around had added to whatever thrill or attraction he felt towards her, she granted.

He began to hit the bong, and passed it to her still glowing.

She coached herself, "inhale slowly, take out the thing, breathe in, try not to cough," hoping not to make a fool of herself as she took a small hit and held it in for a respectable 10 seconds or so before letting out a few coughs.

Ian smiled at her, slightly patronizing, and she laughed sheepishly, handing the bong back to him.

She noted the distance between them on the bed, them sitting so close to where she had blown him last weekend, where he had seen her vagina... She remembered her earlier nervousness about their sexual relationship and how it might develop tonight, and moved to sit next to him, leaning against the headboard. She put her hand on his knee, not looking at him, and he slid his hand over hers briefly before taking another hit and passing the bong back to her. They laughed at the movie for awhile, feeling each other's heat inches away, before he slid his hand over her ass, then up the back of her shirt, unfastening her bra. They didn't kiss much, and Jaime was ambivalent about whether she wanted to kiss him more, although she sort of liked hooking up with him. His mouth had a metallic taste to it and seemed oddly wet, his tongue too probing. She didn't want to sit here passively again though, like some prude, so when Ian set aside the bong, she set down her beer can and turned and climbed into his lap, straddling him.

"Alright!" he said, pulling off her shirt and putting his mouth over her nipple, grabbing her other breast in his hand. She was pinned against his lap, legs spread, and already she could feel him growing hard against her. She squirmed against him, then tried to sit still, as she didn't want to make it seem like she wanted things to go even faster. This was already going awfully fast, but maybe that's just what happened. She wanted to have sex with him, didn't she? She was ready. They had done everything else. Ian had stopped paying attention to the movie and was holding her hips against his crotch, kissing and licking her breasts.

"You have a great body," he murmured, looking up at her, then sloppily kissing her on the lips.

Jaime ran her hands over his chest, before sliding them down to his waist and up under his shirt, stroking his bare abdomen and chest, his skin hot and strangely firm against her fingertips. She pulled his shirt up and he lifted his arms, letting her tug it over his head. He grabbed her again, roughly, urgently, his hands at her breasts, her hips, and as he pressed her against him, he whispered in her ear, "You want me to fuck you?"

A shudder ran through her, of shock, of fear, of anticipation, and she said, 'Yeah."

It wasn't until he threw her onto her back and was pulling off her jeans, and had stood up to unbutton his own and let them fall to the floor that she added, nervously, "You know, I've never done this before."

Part Two

She already felt vulnerable and exposed, lying there, wearing nothing but her thin cotton underwear, his eyes devouring her hungrily, standing over her. Now that his pants were off, she could see the outline of his massive hard-on through his boxers, and she thought, "What the hell have you gotten yourself into?"

"That's ok, it'll feel good," he said.

"For whom?" she asked herself, but didn't say it out loud.

Ian crawled between her legs and pulled down her underwear. Jaime closed her eyes. The movie's laugh track played in the background, punchy banter droning on. Now she was completely naked. It was really happening, and things had already gone so much faster and further than ever before. She had shaved most of her vagina, and she felt Ian began to stroke her over the now-smooth areas. Before she opened her eyes, she felt him pushing a finger into her, and cried out in surprise. She felt too tight, or maybe just insufficiently aroused, that even his one finger felt like it was stretching her—or was it two? No, just one, she realized as he immediately began to maneuver a second finger into her. She kept her eyes closed, trying to acclimate to this penetration, trying to find the pleasure in it. She was excited, maybe it would feel good if she could just relax.

Ian knelt over her, pushing his two fingers in and out of her. He leaned over to lick and suck on her breasts again, then her neck, and she moaned in pleasure, feeling her body start to let go. She ran her hands over his chest, through his hair and across his back, feeling him over her, strong and powerful, masculine and assertive. She slid her hands to his hips and tentatively brushed across the front of his boxers, caressing his erection, feeling another rush of fear when she realized that it was still too big for her one hand to close around it. She hadn't been exaggerating it in her mind, and had even minimized how large it really was.

"You want that fat cock, don't you, virgin," he whispered, and she swallowed, at a loss for words, excitement—or was it fear—shooting through her stomach.

"I'm gonna give it to you," he said, reaching down and pulling it out of the slit in his boxers with some difficulty, then tearing open a condom wrapper with his teeth and rolling it over the shaft in one quick movement.

Jaime was starting to feel some panic—it looked much too big, and she wasn't even sure she was turned on yet. He didn't seem very able to listen to her body, or even interested in doing so, and she let herself acknowledge that she was afraid of him, that he could hurt her—and that maybe he wanted to. This was a conquest to him. He was obviously more excited by the fact that she had given him clearance to go all the way, that this teasing and sex play was going to end in fucking, than he was about her comfort or pleasure.

He positioned himself over her, between her legs, his penis lying against her stomach with a heaviness and hardness all its own. She felt sick as she thought about him shoving it into her, tearing her open so it could lie like that inside her. She looked down at it and it seemed as big around as her wrist, and as long as her forearm. He kissed her again, pinned beneath him, his cock pushing into her abdomen uncomfortably as he began to hump against her slightly.

"Fuck, I need to be inside of you. You ready?"

Jaime's mind was shouting, "No! No! No!" but she couldn't back out now—what was she going to tell him, that she needed more foreplay? That just seemed to turn her off. Of course she was nervous; it was her first time. Of course it would hurt, but only for a while, and this was the guy she was into. So what if they weren't dating, they had been hooking up for a long time and the chemistry was better than with any other guy.

"Ok," she murmured shakily, and he pushed her thighs further open with his knees, moving his hips to position the head of his penis against her.

"Relax, relax, relax," she told herself as he said, "Ok, it'll hurt for a little bit but then it'll feel good so you just gotta stay chill, ok?"

She nodded slightly, eyes closed and felt the massive bulb pressed against her begin to thrust. Immediately she felt tearing, burning—it was much too big, and she wasn't sure how wet she had gotten. Instinctively her thighs tried to close against him and her hands went to his chest to push him off.

"It's too big," she gasped.

She looked at his face finally, seeing annoyance there as he replied, "Hey, we haven't even gotten started yet. You won't know if you like it until you try it; you're a virgin. Of course it hurts at the beginning."

She relaxed again slightly, and he used this momentary lack of struggle to grab her wrists, pinning them against the bed on either side of her shoulders and pushing her thighs further open with his knees.

"Ian... what are you...?" she began, but he replied, "You'll thank me for this," and her fear blossomed into a full out panic.

So he was going to do it, whether she wanted it or not. He was going to rape her. Was it rape, though? She had come over, she had straddled him, taken off his shirt, told him she wanted him to fuck her, told him yes over and over... But now she was fighting against him, and he was holding her down, and she was afraid and all she knew was that she didn't want him to hurt her like this, that she didn't want him to put it inside her like this, and that he was going to. She could feel him pushing it against her, trying to find the entrance to her vagina, his hands holding her wrists, and she started to cry.

"Ian, please, not like this... I'll do it, just... not like this, ok?"

"Shut up, this is how you wanted it and this is how it's going to happen. Now are you going to be good or are you going to scream like a bitch? Do I have to put something in your mouth?"

"No, no, I'll be quiet," Jaime said shakily. She felt trapped, defeated, helpless.

"Good girl."

His penis found her entrance, and he groaned as it began to press inside. Jaime whimpered, turning her head from him and closing her eyes, her wrists pinned, her legs held open, unable to move, feeling him begin to force himself inside her.

"Oh, you're so tight. It's gonna feel so good to split you open," he groaned.

She began to cry again, whimpering at the pain.

"That's right, you're all mine, bitch. That's what you want, isn't it?"

He had been pushing into her slowly, letting the head of his penis sink into her as she squirmed against him, but now he thrust firmly at least a couple more inches into her and she felt something inside her give way with a rush of pain and warmth. Was that her virginity? She let out a little scream. In one fluid movement, Ian let go of her wrist and slapped her across the cheek.

She was so shocked that she didn't move, just looked up at him, stunned, as he said, "I thought I told you to be quiet,"

"It... it hurts..." she stammered.

He leaned over and picked up a rolled up pair of socks from the corner of the bed. She prayed they were clean as he commanded, "Open your mouth," and shoved them into it to muffle her cries.

He pinned her wrist again, and she wondered if she should have used that opportunity to fight him off. What was the use? He was so much stronger than her, and he was clearly willing to hurt her—the best option seemed to be to give him what he wanted. His penis felt impossibly large, and she knew that he had only put the tip in so far. How long would he last, she wondered—would he get it all in?

He drew back and pushed in another inch or so, and Jaime screamed into the socks, biting down, her body attempting to fight him off but pinned helplessly. He was grunting, clearly turned on by her struggle, thrusting deeper into her with each thrust. It felt like he was ripping her open as he started to lose control, driving it in further and further as he began to shake and collapsed against her with a series of grunting moans.

It would be over soon, Jaime told herself, lying frozen beneath him, gritting her teeth against the balled up socks. She tried to stifle her cries, not wanting to give him the satisfaction of hurting her more than he already had. She had hoped he wouldn't last long, but what would happen now? Should she yell at him, storm out? Did he think this was normal? She hadn't told him to stop, hadn't said no outright, and hadn't said the word rape out loud... Would he say she was making a fuss over nothing, that she had wanted it? What had she thought it would be like? What had she expected? Had he just been talking dirty? Like in one of the porn clips they had watched together that time... But he had slapped her, had pinned her down...

Her cheek burned, and her wrists were still held tightly in his fists.

He lay on top of her, his penis still inside her, softening, as she waited for him to release her, to pull out, to get off her, to let her go. She didn't want to move, to upset him. If this was just kinky sex, why was she afraid of him? Why was she trying to plan an escape? He was her friend. She had felt safe in his arms while they had watched movies, and cuddled... Well, not safe, maybe. He had always seemed dangerous, her bad boy, and she had been attracted to him for this reason. He almost felt nice inside her now, smaller, still, although everywhere between her legs felt sore.

She spit out the ball of socks and took in a full breath, feeling pain shoot through her abdomen. Her heart was pounding. He still lay motionless atop her, his face buried in the pillow next to her and she wondered what was going on. Was he ashamed to look at her? His hips jerked suddenly, and with horror she realized that his dick was starting to grow hard again. She remembered him saying he practiced jerking off over and over, trying to beat his brother, his friends in consecutive orgasms.

"No, no, no more; Ian, please—" she whispered in his ear. His face was still turned from her. He began to pull out, slowly, and to lift himself up off her.

"Ok, ok, thank you," she said as his penis slid from her.

He still hadn't released her wrists, though, and as he raised himself onto his knees, he lunged forward, jerking her wrist across her body, flipping her onto her side, then pinning her face down with his forearms and knees.

"Ian! Ian, please, what are you doing? Please just let me go, we already did it," she pleaded quietly.

He responded, "I told you this was going to feel good, didn't I? The first part is supposed to hurt. If we stop now, you'll never want to do it again. We're just getting started."

At this, Jaime began to struggle wildly again, attempting to push herself up, to flip herself over, but her legs were pinned under his, and his forearm was pinned across her upper back, hard, making her feel claustrophobic, panicky with the pressure on her chest and lungs.

She went still and tried to focus on breathing, and he said, "That's it," removing the arm from her back and sliding his hand roughly up her neck to grab her by the hair at the nape of her neck, pulling back her head.

She whimpered and lamely tried to reach her arms back to push him off her. She heard him laugh and then settle forward so that he was sitting on her thighs, his thick hardening dick resting between her ass cheeks.

"You can fight a little, I don't mind," he chuckled and she started to cry again, burying her face in the pillow. She heard rustling, and could tell that he was pulling off the old condom. Her arms lay uselessly at her sides. When she tried to push against Ian's knees, he grabbed both wrists again, and folded her arms behind her back. He was holding her forearms together over her lower back, and rubbing his dick against her as she tried vainly to escape. Tears wet her cheeks as she cried, noiselessly.

"Lift your ass up," he said, and she shook her head but he pulled back on her hair and her arms to lift her hips in the air as he rose to his knees.

He pushed her face back into the pillow, muttering, "That's better," spreading her knees with his own, and repositioning his cock at the entrance to her vagina.

She stiffened, whimpering, bracing herself for him to thrust deep into her, but instead he gently pushed at her, rubbing the head up and down, not pushing hard enough to enter her until, to her shame and some relief, she felt herself growing wet. He continued rubbing against her, then slowly pushing back into her with little thrusts as she gasped into the pillow. It still hurt as he pulsed into her but more in a burning than a tearing way.

She was starting to moan, to her embarrassment, as he slid smoothly in and out of her, stretching her further and further. Ian laughed and said, "That's right, you like that, don't you, bitch."

With a nauseous jolt, she realized that he hadn't put on a new condom. What if she got a disease? Or got pregnant? Fear twisted inside her. It felt like he was growing harder, and suddenly he released her hair and gripped her just above the elbows with both of his hands.

"Put your face in the pillow," he commanded, and began to thrust into her deep and hard.

With each thrust, it felt like he was tearing her open, and each seemed to have more momentum than the last. She was screaming, silently, into the pillow, terrified he would break something inside of her, waiting for it to be over. How had this turned into such a nightmare?

It felt like he was acting out a porn with her, one that she hadn't agreed to appear in. Her arms were twisted painfully and there was uncomfortable pressure on her neck, but this was overshadowed by the assault between her legs as he shoved himself roughly into her, his hips finally slapping against her as his cock fully sheathed itself within her. There was some sharp pain at the deepest point of his thrust, and she twisted to try to change the angle somehow as he picked up speed. How had his parents heard nothing? Did they ever check on what was going on with him? Or had this whole scene played out at a lower decibel than the film still playing in the background?

"Yeah, take that cock, bitch," he said, as he thrust it roughly into her, holding her arms. He suddenly released her and she clutched at the bed, falling forward as he pushed her flat onto her stomach. She considered trying to push him off but didn't want to further upset him at this point, as he had just used that as an excuse for further violence, which he seemed to enjoy. She clenched her ass and thighs, trying to stop him from reentering her, and felt a sharp slap as he struck her across the ass, saying, "Spread your legs, I'm not finished."

She whimpered but relaxed and he pushed her ass cheeks apart, groaning, sliding his cock between them. She felt sheer panic—he wasn't going to force her that way too, was he? They had watched a porn clip about anal sex once that had made her uncomfortably turned on, and it was obviously something he thought about.

Wasn't it enough to take her virginity? She realized with sinking horror that if he wanted to do that too, there wasn't much she could do to stop him.

She heard him spit and felt a wet splat above her ass, which he began to rub into her asshole with his fingers. Face buried in the pillow that she was clutching at with her hands, she began to moan, "No, no, no, no, no," almost imperceptibly, knowing it didn't matter to him but unable to stop herself.

"I'm going to come in your ass," Ian said, and she didn't move, lying there stiffly, still crying quietly.

He began to push himself against her again, grinding his penis against her asshole, but she couldn't make herself relax, even when he slapped her on the ass again, and again. He continued to shove at her, and eventually she felt something give as the head slid into her with a sharp burst of pain. Her cries grew louder, buried in the pillow, but she didn't bother trying to resist, just to pray that it would be over soon and that he would let her go.

Ian was breathing heavily, grunting, and she could tell that he was trying not to come. She hoped he did. She clenched her ass, trying to prevent him from entering further, and they struggled against each other for a few frantic seconds until he let out a groan and pushed into her a desperate last few times, coming at least partially inside her. She could feel his cum inside her, she realized with a wave of disgust. He stilled, then pulled his cock out of her with an aching squelch. She stayed still, crying quietly, not wanting to look at him or even to move.

Part Three

Why did it have to be like that? Why did he have to do that too? Why twice? Why did he do this to me? Jaime asked herself. Loops of panicked thoughts spiraled in her mind. Her body felt both numb and aching, frozen in shock. Ian climbed off the bed, and she thought she could hear him putting his pants on, picking up the beer can, taking a drink.

"Hey, Jaime, get dressed," she heard him say as if from a far distance, her own name jarring to her. She flinched, pulling her legs together, wiping her face on the pillow. She slowly, tentatively pushed herself up onto her knees. There was blood on the blanket, blood on the used condom lying there, dried blood between her thighs. She couldn't believe how naked she was, couldn't believe what had happened, although the swiftly forming bruises from where he had grabbed her, the blood, the pain in her vagina and ass reassured her that it had all been real. Ian sat there, in the chair, pants on, shirtless, drinking a beer, staring at her expectantly.

"Do you need anything?" he asked.

"I... I have to go to the bathroom," she stammered. Why did you do this to me? Why did you do this to me? echoed in her head, unspoken.

He picked up a towel from the floor and stood up halfway, tossing it onto the bed. She flinched, then grabbed it and wrapped it around herself. She collected her jeans, underwear, bra, and t-shirt in a bundle and shakily climbed off the bed.

In the bathroom, she looked at herself in the mirror. Her eyes looked hollow, empty. Her face was pale, tearstained; redness on one cheek where he had slapped her. Her hair was a mess. She ran her fingers limply through it a few times, realizing that somehow they hurt too. There was a dull buzz in her head, and everything looked greenish, eerie under the bathroom's fluorescent light bulb.

She let the towel drop and looked again at her body. It seemed completely different from when she had gotten out of the shower that morning. It felt alien, violated, used. She didn't feel like Jaime anymore. It was hard to tell what part of it was losing her virginity, and what part of it was the... rape. She stumbled over the word even in her mind. Rape, rape, rape, rape, rape. She had been raped. He had raped her.

She started to feel lightheaded and realized she had stopped breathing. She gasped and her breath started to come in panicky gasps. Hyperventilating. You're hyperventilating, she told herself. You need to calm down. You need to clean yourself. You need to get out of here before he does it again. She felt a sob welling, but told herself to keep calm. You have to get out of here.

She looked again at her bloodied thighs, and numbly took some toilet tissue, wet it, and began to clean herself with little circular movements. She couldn't believe this had happened to her. But what did she expect? What did she expect? She had never been able to picture a pleasurable sexual experience between her and Ian, between her and anyone.

Jaime started to cry softly as she finished cleaning the blood. She threw the tissue in the toilet, more and more of it gathering into what looked like a filthy broken pink heart. She felt cramping in her abdomen; it had been building since he had violated her anally, and with another sob of humiliation she sank onto the toilet and released her bowels. It burned, and fear knotted in her stomach... Fear that he had broken something, that she would have to go to the doctor, explain what happened... Except she would just say, "I had sex... I had anal sex, I lost my virginity," and they would just think she was a slut.

Who would believe her if she said it was rape? Her friends would blame her for hooking up with a deadbeat, her parents would blame her for having sex... and she had contacted him, she had driven over here, she had said yes, she had literally asked him for it. Asking for it, asking for it—she pictured the faces of her friends, her parents, the doctor echoing this internal refrain.

She wiped herself gently, and put on her underwear—a flash of Ian pulling them off, sitting on her, holding her down burst into her head and she cringed. The same thing happened as she pulled on her jeans, fastened her bra, pulled on her t-shirt. She washed her hands, rinsed her face, smoothed her hair and looked at herself in the mirror. She looked more like Jaime, more like herself, and she gave herself a little smile. You're ok, she reassured herself. She had all her things, she just needed to get her keys. She would just tell him she was leaving and go.

She opened the door, took the several steps to his doorway and froze. She stood there for long seconds that turned into minutes, rocking gently on her heels. She didn't want to see him. She didn't want to go back inside. What would she say to him? What would he say to her? She had to get her keys from the table to get out of here, she had to see him to get out of here, and so without further hesitation she turned the doorknob and opened the door.

Ian had put his shirt back on and was playing Call of Duty, turned away from the door. A wild thought raced through her head as she wished she had a knife and could stab him before he noticed she was there. Who was she now? She had never wanted to attack anyone unprovoked before... but it wasn't unprovoked. She hated him, sitting there as though nothing had happened. She wouldn't give him the satisfaction of seeing how much he had hurt her. She cleared her throat, standing in the door and he turned.

"Oh, hey. You were gone a while."

"Yeah," she said flatly.

Why did you do that to me? echoed in her head. She refused to let it past her lips.

"Sorry, the first time can be a little rough," he said dismissively.

She imagined cutting his throat. No, cutting off his stupid dick, that would be better.

She didn't respond. Keep it together, Jaime, she told herself.

"It's getting late. I'm going to head home." she said.

She saw her keys on the table next to the bed, next to her nearly untouched Coors Light tall boy. She strode over and picked up the keys, holding them between her knuckles in case he tried to attack her again and she had to gouge out his eyes, as they'd said to do in her health class. She paused, then picked up the beer can and took one long chug. Ian watched, still expectant, still waiting to see how she would respond.

"Can I have some weed?" she asked. It was more of a statement than a question.

"You... You wanna smoke another bowl?" he said blankly.

"No... A baggie. To go," she replied.

"Oh, um... yeah, sure, I guess..." he started. He rose slowly from the chair and retrieved a jar from the closet, his back to her. She heard him rustling around, putting a few buds into a Ziploc, then he turned to show her, "That good?"

"A little more, thanks. And I don't have any money on me," her tone matter of fact, cutting. It scared her.

"That's... that's ok." He seemed a little nervous now, wanting her to leave.

He closed the jar, returning it to the closet, and held out the baggie. He was extending his arm fully, not meeting her eyes, not getting too close. She took it, and pocketed it.

"Ok, see you around," she said flatly, turning to the door. "I'll show myself out."

190

She walked down the stairs slowly, afraid he might say something else, might follow her. No, she was free, she was getting out of here. As she passed the fridge, an impulse to take another beer arose, and with a shrug, she opened the door and grabbed two cans for good measure. She felt better already about her small attempts to balance to scales, to take something from him, even if it was just a fraction of what he had taken from her.

She opened the front door, strode out into the moonlight and took a deep breath. She felt disconnected from what had happened inside, from who she had been before, but she felt the cool air on her skin, her head spinning slightly from the beer she had just chugged, and she felt alive. Wounded, hardened, but alive.

She felt the baggie of weed in her back pocket as she sat down in the cab of her truck, and she thought, maybe I'll smoke a bowl when I get home. She started the ignition and the radio flickered back to life. This time it was Shania Twain, singing *"That don't impress me much."*

The flicker of a smile danced across Jaime's face as she pulled out of the driveway, gravel crackling under her tires in the cool spring night air.

5: MICHAEL

Intimacy

Trigger Warning: Discussion of Sexual Exploitation & Violence

Part One

"We haven't had sex in six years."

Miriam's— Professor Lenard's —face crumpled, and her hand rose to her brow. "I shouldn't be telling you this."

Michael took a deep breath, blinking several times. His head spun. He was Professor Lenard's doctoral student now; after two years of papers, of testing, of reading other people's research (largely hers), he was beginning his own Philosophy dissertation, and she had agreed to be his advisor! She didn't take many students, but Michael had been diligent his last two years; his clear goal, if he was to find the answers he sought at Blakeley, had been to secure her as an advisor, and his long hours studying, taking her classes, understanding her theorems in and out had paid off. Now, here he was, at 8 PM on a Tuesday evening, in her office for their second formal advising meeting, and she was telling him about not only her personal life, but her sex life!

This was the sort of intimacy Michael had sought with her, to go beyond her groundbreaking philosophical work in the field of symbolic interpersonal ethics and to understand what was really going on in her head that allowed her to see the world in the way she did, to open all the doors of meaning that so many other philosophers had found closed. Michael felt trusted, seen as an adult, a peer in their intellectual pursuit to understand the ontology of desire in a hegemonic value system.

He also felt a little uncomfortable. To acknowledge his subjectivity would be to claim that he, too, hadn't had sex in years... with another person, anyway. Four years to be specific; ever since he had begun his thesis as an undergrad and had told Astrid he needed to be focused on his work and didn't have time to see her socially anymore.

Michael finally responded to her admission, "No, it's ok. You're right, we have to acknowledge our bias, and... you can confide in me. We are researchers, yes? Everything is on the table for us, you always say." He paused, then added, conversationally, "How are things with your... wife?" He was looking to break the ice and to give her an opportunity to tell him first-hand what he had heard so much interdepartmental gossip about for the past few months.

Over the summer, Miriam's spouse, a celebrated, tenured professor of biochemistry and genetics at Blakeley long known as Dr. Lloyd Lenard, had made a dramatic and highly public transition to become Linda Lenard. The Lenards were staples of the Blakeley faculty, and although the community had rallied around them, that hadn't stopped the gossip. After all, Dr. L. Lenard, man or woman, working solo from Blakeley's little biogenetics lab, had transposed healthy codons in vivo to heal cancerous tumors in mice shortly after arriving at the school from the more prestigious and well-funded Texas A&M, making the most promising breakthrough in curing cancer of any major research hospital in the last three years, and winning the MacArthur Genius Grant. The entire community, faculty, and administration had rallied to support the work, and had used the ensuing media storm generated by her coming out as transgender to proclaim the merits of Blakeley's gender diversity policies, launching the transBlakeley campaign and even using the transition of such a renowned academic figure at the school as a marketing point to attract gender non-conforming and trans* prospective students.

Michael, however, was yet more impressed by the work of "the other Dr. Lenard," formerly known as "the woman Dr. Lenard;" Miriam. Michael didn't see her as derivative in any way. To him, she was Miriam Lenard, the most important phenomenological post-structuralist philosopher since Merleau-Ponty or… Kierkegaard—maybe the most important American philosopher—no, philosopher—of the 21st century, and if the rest of Blakeley disregarded the importance of her work, at least in comparison to her husband's— now her wife's—they were just… obtuse.

Michael had heard the gossip, of course, beginning last spring when Professor Linda Lenard had sent out a letter to the entire academic community and issued a national press release announcing her transition. His first thought, and his ensuing pattern of thought as the story unfolded in the media and throughout the Blakeley community, was: how is Miriam making sense of this? Seeing her standing there by Linda's side at the press conference, holding Linda's hand during the CNN interview, sitting with their little daughter at graduation while Linda made a speech, all he wondered was: What's going on in her head? How will this influence the work?

And now their work together had officially begun. It was a partnership that would span at least 5 years. Michael was giddy. He had thought about how he would have this conversation with her, rereading her work on the construction of the social meaning of gender, watching Trans 101 videos on YouTube, practicing switching pronouns. It felt like a gradute-level module of the English classes he had taken with his brother and sister after they moved from Taiwan when he was nine.

"She underwent a gender transition and is now socially a woman. She underwent a sex change and now identifies as female," Michael had practiced saying. He was stuck on the distinction between a gender transition and a sex transition for two weeks of July, but when he finally understood, it lent a completely new dimension to his understanding of Miriam's work, and he had re-read everything she had ever written about gender, sex, the phenomenology of the human body, and gendered perception.

Michael didn't know how to continue the conversation about sex without admitting his own embarrassing bias, since Miriam clearly found years of sexual dormancy exceptional and intolerable. Michael didn't mind too much; he made do with porn and the Tenga egg he used to masturbate. It felt as good as Astrid's vagina had, if a little clammy, and didn't come with any of the headache and social obligations. When it came to sex, Michael was a utilitarian, but Miriam clearly had a more emotional relationship to the topic. He supposed it was different in a marriage, different for a woman, certainly different with a transgendered partner! Perhaps this was one of the areas in which Miriam would expand his intellectual horizons. Michael noticed that Miriam seemed to be getting emotional thinking about Linda.

"So... your wife is always a woman on the inside, though?" Michael continued. He was trying to prove his competency in the topic, to get her to continue to open up to him.

Miriam appeared on the verge of tears as she said, "She was my husband for 16 years... I... didn't know. I knew she wasn't happy. I just thought she was obsessed with her work, with finding the cure..."

There was a note of bitterness as the word "cure" passed her lips.

"You know, I had a crush on a girl once, who turned into a boy," Michael began, thinking of his ambiguously gendered childhood friend, Lin. He hadn't planned on saying anything, but he hoped opening up would ease Miriam's distress. "Well, I think he identifies as a boy now. We're still close online, but we haven't actually talked about it. She—he—was always a tomboy, but never tried to hide it, always wearing his brother's clothes, playing video games. Sometimes girls dress like boys, though, and it's not as strange—well, not strange! It's fine either way!— as a boy dressing like a girl. Lin and I talked a lot through high school, and I started to think of her as my girlfriend, actually, since we were so close and I didn't have any other female friends like that, but we never really talked about gender. I got over the crush when I went to college, and I saw that he went by male pronouns online so I just switched how I referred to him without mentioning it, and we're still friends. Lin and Linda, it's an interesting coincidence, you know? But for him, it wasn't really social, or anything he announced outside of the Internet, even though he makes more sense as a guy, really. Lin's not a very social person, though, and I don't think his family in Taiwan would understand. It was more of a personal, and even online transition, since that's where he's himself after all... But with Linda... it was a secret all those years, and now she is a woman—How does that affect you?"

Miriam smiled slightly, and said, "That's interesting... to think about public versus personal and private gender identities, and how that manifests in the digital space... Thanks for sharing." She sighed deeply before responding to his question, "You know, no one asks me that. Everyone asks about how Linda's doing, how it's affected our daughter, even how it's affected our marriage. I usually just say, I guess I'm a lesbian now!" She laughed slightly, but Michael wasn't sure how to respond. Could someone really just become a lesbian? How did it affect one's sexuality when one's partner transitioned gender? Hadn't Miriam said that she and Linda didn't have sex, at least not anymore? Fortunately, Miriam continued,

" I hope Lisa—my daughter—knows both her parents will always love her, but I suppose this is all about how the transition affects my family system. How does it affect me?"

"Yes..." Michael leaned forward, enthralled.

Miriam said, "I've been seeing a psychoanalyst to help me make sense of it all. You know, it's a loss, it really is. Not that I'm not happy for Linda, and proud of Linda, but I married Lloyd—and he hasn't been here for years. I didn't know why, but now I do, and I need to grieve all those lost assumptions, the falling through of the meaning I'd made of my own life. That's what my psychoanalyst thinks, and I'm inclined to agree. I need to do the internal work to shift my perceptions to reflect this new understanding of myself so I can mend this trauma, this break in my narrative and self-conception."

"So how do you do that internal work?" Michael asked.

"Well that's the million dollar question, isn't it?" Miriam laughed. "Right now it tends to be going to yoga classes. It helps me think, gives me space to connect to myself. I used to go to spinning with some other humanities women, but now Linda goes to the class, and they're all so happy to see her there, who am I to stop her? It used to be my space to process what was going on in my marriage, though, so now I go to yoga by myself, lately, almost every day. But that's enough about me. I want to hear how your research is progressing. What have you done this week?"

The conversation turned to matters of a less

personal and more technical nature, and Michael detailed his progress and his lines of inquiry for her. Her words echoed in his head—yoga every day, yoga every day. She looked flexible, and Michael couldn't help but fantasize about her stretching, bending over, as they analyzed his literature review. He tried to keep his mind focused, telling himself that it was not only inappropriate, it was disrespectful to think of her in that way, but it didn't help. The evening passed, and before long, they realized it was nearly 10 PM.

"Goodness!" exclaimed Miriam, "I need to get home and tuck my daughter in. I've been so busy lately, but she needs some consistency in her life. I want her to at least see me before she goes to bed, even if I'm not her only mother anymore!" Miriam began to clear her desk, collecting her things into a side bag, and Michael followed suit, preparing to leave.

"Oh, you're helping with the Symposium this weekend, right?" Miriam said.

Michael hurriedly responded, "Yes!" He appreciated the opportunity to seem relevant and helpful to the department, to be part of the groundbreaking film and dialogue event they were co-hosting with the Feminist Studies and Black Studies departments.

He added, "Mary asked me to meet the guest speaker from Cedar Rapids when she arrives and show her around, help her with whatever she needs to set up. I'll be there all day on Saturday to help as needed."

"Perfect," said Miriam, "I think it's going to

be a very important conversation. I'll be there too; they put me on the panel."

Miriam locked the door to her office, and they set off down the dimly lit hallway, talking about the logistics and aims of the Symposium before parting ways outside the ivy-covered doors of Philosophy Hall.

* * * * *

Michael returned to his room, sitting down and placing his head in his hands before finally letting his fantasies take hold. Miriam had such a grasp on him—on his mind, and now, although he had tried to fight and repress it, on his desire, on his body. He thought about the two of them, lecturing at some conference and then rushing back to a hotel room to pull off each other's clothes, to make love, to consummate their intellectual union... His penis was hard, and he pulled it out and began to stroke it.

His fantasies of her seemed laughable, shameful, impossible; even insulting, and he began to lose his erection. With a second thought, he opened his browser to an amateur porn website and typed in "yoga." Disappointed to see that the women in the video stills all seemed young, girlish, he added "MILF" to his search. He had been more drawn to porn of mature women lately; their confidence and experience aroused him, although he hadn't linked the fetish directly to his crush on Miriam until now.

He clicked on a still of a woman who

looked like she was in her forties, in downward dog with her young male yoga instructor correcting her posture. The woman looked a little like Miriam, and he began to grow hard again, pressing play on the clip and turning down the volume. He opened the desk drawer and pulled out his Tenga egg, squeezing a little lube into it from a small bottle, and slipping it over the head of his penis. "Uhhh," he groaned.

What if Miriam wanted him too, like he wanted her? The sexual frustration and disappointment in her voice had been clear as they discussed her marriage. Who was she interested in being intimate with, if not Linda? Michael thought of the moments of questionable intimacy that had transpired between them, the way her hand had brushed his as they graded papers, how she had bent over to look at his abstract, showing him her silhouette as he sat at her desk. She was an adult, too; a woman, with fantasies and desires of her own. What if she, too, wanted something more between them, as he now finally allowed himself to acknowledge he did?

He was sliding his hand up and down slowly, imagining what it would feel like to be inside her, for her to want him to pleasure and satisfy her. The woman on his screen was bending her legs, moaning as the man began to fuck her, and Michael sped up his motions, his breath quickening. He thought of Miriam at her yoga class, flexible and contemplative, sexually frustrated and alone— maybe even thinking of him sometimes!— and he came quickly, a burst of energy shooting from the base of his penis up his spine as his head fell back. He lay there for a moment, sprawled in the chair, enraptured by the fantasy he had created, until the come-filled egg began to feel unpleasantly sticky and wet and he went to the sink to clean up.

Thoughts of her swarmed through his head as he returned to the desk, closing the window of porn and opening his word processor and Adobe Reader, ready to review yet another of Miriam's manuscripts.

* * * * *

The week passed both quickly and slowly, time feeling as though it were jumping and starting as Michael prepared for their next meeting, for the symposium. He was the TA for Miriam's "Ideology and Id" seminar on Thursday, and was uncomfortably—and pleasantly—surprised to note that she had worn her yoga pants to the informal class, coming straight from the studio to teach. While she didn't have any time to speak with him before or after class, he was grateful just to be in her presence, to hear every brilliant word that came out of her mouth in response to even the simplest of students' questions.

Friday found Michael with an anxious knot in his stomach. He spent most of the day in the library, then in his room, working through a stack of papers and sketching out the abstract for his thesis. "Desire transforms that which it encounters..." he started, his sentence sputtering off as he reflected on how hypocritical, how ironic it was that he, Michael, was pontificating on the topic as he descended further into the clutches of desire's hold on him. His desire, intellectually, emotionally, sexually, to know Miriam, to understand her, to share consciousness with her if only for the briefest moments eclipsed all other motivations. It seemed to invalidate his whole hypothesis that desire is that which gives humans motivation yet is always subsumed by free will and therefore it is the free will to adhere to one's desire in an unethical way that links desire to unethicality, not desire itself. It was the work of an intellectually tormented non-practicing Buddhist, he granted.

Michael wished to prove that desire was a positive force in the universe, one that linked subjects to their pursuit of meaning and happiness, but now his own desire threatened to sabotage not only his hypothesis, but also his relationship with the one person who could guide him in his work. All it would take was one misstep, one misplaced divulgence, one unwelcome disclosure, and she could find him prurient, immature; another sexually objectifying, disrespectful male student with a crush on his teacher... and yet all they talked about was desire! Tomorrow's symposium was set to address the epidemic of sexual violence and how it affected young people's sexualities and identities, and Michael was nervous about what would be uncovered about desire; about male desire, and about his own.

Part Two

Saturday morning, Michael awoke to his screeching alarm clock at 7 AM. The day was upon him. He prepared himself quickly, in a daze, his mind elsewhere as he showered, pulled on some slacks and a polo shirt, brushed his teeth, and smoothed his short hair. He boiled some water in his hot pot, mixed in a pinch of instant coffee powder, and poured himself a bowl of Cheerios, using the dregs of the pint of milk in his fridge. He would have to remember to stop by the convenience store on the way home, he thought, before returning to his contemplations.

Michael cleared the papers stacked on the table, pushing them to one side, and sat down to quickly eat. He checked his phone, and noticed a text message from his father asking him to call that weekend. With a little laugh, he thought about how he would have to repackage his week, including the symposium, to assuage his father's concerns that all he was doing with his Philosophy degree was prying around and musing about things that made everyone uncomfortable. His sister, with her high-paying consulting job in Boston, would tell the family about all the accounts she was managing, all the clients she was serving, and Michael's father would always manage to turn it into some dig towards Michael, towards his impracticality and selfishness. Michael pressed ok, hiding the message. He'd worry about that later.

He checked the time. Noticing that it was almost 7:45, he grabbed his backpack in case he had any time to work during the day, and headed for the door. He locked it behind him, hearing the birds chirping and feeling the morning sun hot on his back. He wasn't a morning person, but couldn't deny that the bright energy of the early day charged him with a buoyant energy, even an excitement, as he walked the several blocks from his apartment to the front of College Hall where he was to meet Lolo Larson from Cedar Rapids.

As he approached the college's central building, Michael saw a pink VW Beetle with several bumper stickers parked in front. That must be Lolo, he thought. There were no other cars in the vicinity. He hadn't met her yet, but was already surprised and filled with anticipation to meet this regional expert.

Michael walked up to the passenger side of the car and saw that the blonde woman inside was preoccupied with her iPhone's glowing screen. After his small wave failed to catch her attention, he tapped softly on the window.

Lolo jumped, dropping her phone and looking wildly in both directions before her eyes fixed on Michael, standing there with a nervous smile outside her window. She reached over and pressed the button to open the window, pressing one hand against her chest, and exclaiming, "Oh my good Lord, you startled me! I've got post-traumatic stress disorder and I'm a woman of a certain age, sweetie! You can't be sneaking up on me like that!"

Michael immediately recoiled in shame, apologizing profusely, but Lolo spoke over his consolations, continuing with, "Are you the person who's gonna show me around? Help me get settled in?"

"Yes, yes!" said Michael. "I'm Michael Cheng, and I'm a PhD candidate with the Philosophy department. It's an honor to meet you! I'm so sorry to have scared you."

"Ooh, smartypants! Maybe you can teach me something. Get in!" said Lolo.

Michael heard the doors click unlocked, and he grabbed the fluorescently pink door handle, pulling it open and climbing inside.

"Oh boy, did I have a night!" said Lolo, placing her hand against her forehead. "My nerves are shot! I stayed up in Cedar Rapids last night because we had an all-day family retreat at the clinic yesterday, dontcha know, then a graduation party for one of our clients, and I got a few hours of shut-eye before getting in gear around three this morning and driving over! Thank God for coffee!"

Michael looked at her, and then looked a bit closer. She had angular features, and a platinum blonde bob. She was tall, he could tell, even sitting down, and her eyes were bloodshot from the long drive. There was something about her that caught his eye. She looked, he thought, a bit like Linda. Was she... a trans woman?

He kicked himself for not having clicked the link on the intradepartmental memo about each panelist's expertise and background. He remembered reading about Lolo's clinic; about the national award it had won for its rehabilitative success with previously incurable complex post-traumatic stress disorder cases. He wracked his brain. Her clinic helped survivors of sex work and the pornography industry, he remembered, and... LGBT youth struggling with homelessness. He had skimmed the blurb about her work, and it hadn't mentioned anything about her being a trans person herself. Did it matter? Michael chided himself. Why should he be surprised? Why shouldn't she be a trans woman?

Lolo was taking a sip from a large Caribou Coffee cup, and turned to look over at Michael, eyebrows raised. "Alrighty!" she said, "Where are we going?"

He replied, "We can drive by the Humanities complex first so I can show you the location of the Symposium—it starts in about two hours—and then I'll show you where the Inn is so you can get all your things settled. The other guest speaker arrived last night."

Michael pointed to direct Lolo as she put the Beetle in drive and began to roll forward. He continued, "I apologize again for sneaking up on you. It's wonderful to meet you in person! I read about your clinic and its' success. It really is an honor to have someone working in the field come to the Symposium."

"Oh, please!" Lolo exclaimed, "It's only a few hours away. I wouldn't miss it! It knocked my socks off to be invited, especially to a school like Blakeley. I've been a fan ever since it opened! It's just what this area needed, and I can tell by the kinds of conversations you're having. No one wanted to talk about sexual trauma and rehabilitation ten, twenty years ago, but here we are today. I'm tickled pink!"

"It's an important conversation," said Michael, "I know the whole Philosophy department is excited. I'm sure you speak at things like this all the time though…"

Lolo laughed. "Not really," she said, "More now, especially after the award and the article in the New York Times, but believe it or not, most people don't want to hear what a trans woman with a mental illness and no medical degree who used to turn tricks has to say about healing traumatized kids, dontcha know! Uffda! But they're starting to listen. Our program speaks for itself, and, well, the ones who need our help know to come asking. More and more people want to support the work, and to know how they could set up a program like it, but there will never be anything else truly like it, ya know? It's my baby, the clinic; where I help all my babies—ya know; most of my clients are over age 18, but they are so young and sometimes it just slips out. My babies! They've been through so much, it feels nice to appreciate that they're just kids—but I don't call them that to their faces, because I want to model respect for their independence and maturity. That's what we're trying to teach them, ya know, although sometimes I don't know if I should be teaching anyone anything! Then again, that's why I'm here, isn't it?"

They rolled up in front of the Humanities complex and Michael described briefly the structure of the day, where Lolo should register, and how the panel would work, before they continued on to the Inn.

Lolo continued, "As I was saying, it really means a lot to me to be here having this conversation. To have people want to listen to what someone like me has to say. All my life, people have tried to ignore my voice, to ignore what I have to say, and sometimes even to pretend I don't exist at all! My family's favorite trick is to make me disappear. Poof! No more Lolo, everything's fine!"

Michael laughed slightly, then caught himself, unsure whether her dark humor merited mirth or sympathy. Lolo chuckled herself, putting him at ease, and continued, "I grew up around here, actually! People don't usually talk about things like this around here, or about people like me, but this is where I'm from. The thing about not talking about something is that it doesn't go away, ya know? I suppose I did, for a while at least. I lived out on the coast for a long time, back when I was doing sex work, after I ran away, but I came back. I've been living back here since I opened the clinic, since I committed myself to the issue of helping trans* and gay kids heal from the traumatic childhood experiences they've had to become strong, healthy, resilient adults! Of course, the mission expanded when I learned about other traumatized and homeless young people and didn't want to shut the door on them. That's when we drifted more into healing sexual trauma."

Lolo paused, waiting at an intersection, and Michael nodded in affirmation, intrigued by her story, by her self-reflection. She continued, "A lot of people wonder why I came back here to open my clinic, why I didn't do it out in San Diego, or Los Angeles, where there are so many homeless youth, but I thought about my experience here, about how I disappeared when I was about that age, and how I kept on existing; about what happened to me and how I survived, and I thought, Lord, this is what I'm called to do! I know this is going on; I cannot deny it, and I know these kids' families aren't talking about it, and even if they want to, don't know how to help them. At the end of the day, these kids' families don't know how to talk about what's happened to them, what they're experiencing, but most of my clients come to me—or are brought to me—after a suicide attempt, after a parent sees the impact of trying to erase who their child is, or what they've experienced.

"Shame is a powerful force," she continued, "and it causes us to push things we find shameful away from us, to hide them in our shadows and to claim, 'I'm not like that; that's not me!' That's what parents say around here; it's what my parents said when I came out, and it's what my clients' parents say: 'This isn't the child I raised! This isn't me!' I've heard it so many times, and I just laugh, and then they get upset, and say, 'What's so funny? We're suffering here!' and I tell them, 'Well, I guess when you weren't watching, another independent, creative, beautiful, sensitive, loving being crawled into this child that God blessed you with, and you can be thankful that they're not merely the child you raised or a copy of yourself, but that this child has something to teach you about yourself and about the self you never allowed yourself to become!'

Michael was nodding, vigorously now, and he chimed in, "That's exactly what I wish I could tell my dad! I mean, I'm not homeless, or traumatized or anything, and I don't want to make light of that, but my dad is still ashamed of me and how I'm not like him. I just want to tell him that I don't have to become him because he already is! And that it's ok that I'm interested in different things..."

"Ain't that the truth? We're all interested in different things, and our parents are all ashamed of one thing or another!" Lolo laughed.

They had arrived at the front of the Inn, and Michael pointed to it and motioned for Lolo to stop the car. He explained, "Well, your room is reserved, and we asked for an early check in—I confirmed yesterday. Would you like to stay here, or do you want to head back to the Symposium? I'm going over there to set up."

"Oh, I need to take a shower, wake myself up, and put my face on before I see anyone else!" exclaimed Lolo.

"Ok, well I'll just leave you here, then—I'll give you my number in case you need anything!" said Michael. He was eager to return to work on setting up the sound system

"Are—Did you—What name is the hotel room under, sweetie?" asked Lolo.

Michael replied, "Lolo Larson, just like in the paperwork!"

"Uh-oh. You're gonna have to come in with

me in case we have a problem. Dontcha know, my Iowa ID still says Lawrence!" Lolo said, her tone a bit self-conscious, trying to make a joke of it.

Michael could tell she felt embarrassed, and he said, "Of course! I'm so sorry, ma'am, I didn't think of that," reaffirming that he saw her as a woman even though she had told him her "dead name," something he had heard was an existential no-no for many trans* people.

They parked the car, and as they waited for the desk clerk to check Lolo in, Michael gave her his phone number. There was no problem with the mismatched identification, since the school had paid for the room in advance, but Lolo gave Michael a grateful smile anyway. The two shook hands, and reaffirmed what a pleasure it had been to make each other's acquaintance, before Lolo removed herself to her hotel room and Michael walked out of the hotel lobby into the morning sun, shaking his head and reflecting on his conversation with Lolo.

What she said about shame and projection had really struck a chord with him, and he mused over what implications this held for the subject and its objects of desire as he walked the several blocks back to the Humanities complex, which was, confusingly enough, called Humanitas. It made for a lot of typos and misdelivered mail.

* * * * *

Michael entered the central hall, and noticed that it was empty, save for a couple of event and tech assistants who had already started to set up the registration table and sound equipment. His assigned task was to make sure the techs got in alright and were able to set up, so after he asked each person what they were setting up and cross-checked it with the event binder the administrative assistant, Mary, had given him, he sat down at the registration table with his tablet and began to skim his reading for the day, McKenna's "Violence and Difference." How prescient, he noted, chuckling to himself.

Time passed, and early-comers began to fill the hall. It was past 9, Michael noted, and he put away his reading. He looked around, and noticed two women approaching his table.

One of them was young, her dark hair pulled back in a ponytail. She said, "Hi! We're panelists; are you doing registration?"

Before Michael could respond, the other woman, who Michael thought he recognized as a professor, said, "You're Miriam's grad student, aren't you? What's your name again?"

Michael said, "I'm Michael Cheng; yes, I'm working with Dr. Lenard, and I can get you your packets if you remind me of your names! I should know, I did read the email…" he trailed off.

"I'm Adelaide Nkrumah," said the professor with a warm smile, reaching out to shake Michael's hand. "It's great to finally meet you, Michael. I've heard so much about you from Miriam. She and I are friends; you don't have to 'Dr. Lenard' with me! Call me Adelaide, please. You know, Miriam didn't think she was going to take on a PhD candidate this year, with all she's been going through, but she was so impressed by your work, she decided to anyway!"

Adelaide withdrew her hand. Michael was thrilled. She had said that Miriam had spoken about him to her; that Miriam was impressed with his work; that she had made an exception to her plans to work with him! He cast his eyes over Adelaide, taking her in. She was dressed elegantly, professionally, and had lovely dark skin and twisted braids piled atop her head. She was beautiful, he thought, and worried for a moment that he was really developing a thing for mature women...

Adelaide continued, "Maybe I shouldn't have said anything, but I think it's important for grad students to be affirmed in their pursuits, and to know that we are glad that you're here, joining us in the academy, even if we are often the harshest critics of your work. Especially for people of color, joining the sphere of cultural analysis and production is a powerful act and we need to support each other!"

"Of course," Michael affirmed. He rolled the words 'people of color' and 'like us' around in his head. He supposed he and Adelaide were both people of color, but looking at her, thinking of her perception and experience of the world and his own, he marveled at the weak logicality of oppositionally-defined, race-based identity signifiers. 'People of color' was the identity category opposite whiteness, and yet it was so much more varied than the construct of whiteness.

Indeed, it encompassed everything else! You might as well categorize animals by calling one species—perhaps his favorite, cats—by name, and calling all the others 'not-cats' or 'animals of non-catness.'

Yet Michael had already felt the ominous presence of whiteness at the philosophy conventions he had attended; had noticed that during his undergraduate studies at Highland the philosophy classes were all centered around male Euro-American theorists by default, and tended to mark every other kind of theorizing by every other type of person with their identity signifier; deeming philosophy by women 'feminist philosophy;' philosophy by people of color 'non-Western philosophy' and so on… He worried how his and Miriam's identities would affect the legitimacy with which their work was seen. Perhaps it would be siloed, deemed 'special interest' and relegated to the heaps of unread "me-ses" littering the floors of humanities departments around the world. Michael thought their work belonged at the center of the curriculum, and not just for philosophy courses; then again, that depended on what they were able to find…

Michael's introspection was cut short as the girl held out her hand as well. "I'm Charlie. I'm a student activist. Nice to meet you. I took Dr. Lenard's class last spring; she's great!"

Michael handed the panelists their materials, as well as their nametags, and a brochure about the symposium. They discussed the order of the films and the panel briefly, before Adelaide and Charlie went into the auditorium to take their seats.

Michael registered the small gathering crowds of attendees, and Emily, a grad student from the Feminist Studies department joined him at the table to help.

Michael and Emily were in the same 'PhD Pod' and were friendly. He was happy to see her. She reminded him of a girl he'd been friends with at Highland, another white girl named Emily (who Michael had incidentally had a huge crush on during his time as an undergrad). Awkwardly enough, she had been his girlfriend Astrid's roommate, and was indeed the person who had introduced Astrid to him! Michael had struggled with his preexistent and ongoing crush on Emily throughout his relationship with Astrid, unfortunately. Looking at this Emily, who bore some physical resemblance to the other Emily, Michael observed that he really did just think of this Emily as a friend, and reflected on how much his type had changed over the years. In high school, he had fantasized about Lin; in college, about Emily (and Astrid, of course!); and now, Miriam…

His stomach leapt slightly when he looked up and saw Miriam standing in front of the table.

"Good morning, Michael!" she said with a smile.

"M-Miriam! Welcome! Hi!" he said, a little ruffled. He rummaged for her materials and nametag, and handed them to her.

"I'll save you a seat in the reserved Phil section," she said, "Thanks again for helping out with the event!"

"See you inside," Michael returned, stammering slightly.

"Are you ok?" Emily asked, looking a little concerned.

"Yeah, I'm just tired," he responded.

Emily told him about the hours she'd been keeping to submit a conference proposal by deadline, and Michael listened, nodding sympathetically as the two continued to sign in attendees.

Lolo arrived, wearing a trim pant suit and a fresh coat of red lipstick, and Michael handed her a small stack of the materials, inquired about the rest of her morning, and enlisted one of the Feminist students standing around; a girl, Erin, to show her to her seat in the auditorium. Other professors and students he knew filtered by, and Michael was briefly introduced to the other guest speaker, Marsha Grossman, a legal expert and activist involved in one of the films who had flown in from Boston the day before. She was curt, professional, and her hand felt cold in Michael's. It didn't quite seem like she met his eyes.

Ten-o'clock drew nearer, and finally came to pass, and the doors to the auditorium were closed. It was nearly a full house, Michael noted, which meant it already met the criteria of a successful community extracurricular academic event, at least in the eyes of the hosting departments.

Michael and Emily stayed at the table until 10:15, registering stragglers and missing the opening remarks by Professor Annie Thanh, the head of the Feminist Studies department. They could hear trails of her remarks through the door, and Michael leafed through the brochure again, cringing slightly at the recurrence of the words 'rape,' 'porn,' 'violence,' 'sex,' and 'trauma' throughout the leaflet.

"It's gonna be a heavy day," said Emily, "I'm excited to see the films, especially *The Hunting Ground*. I've heard a lot about it. It's limited release, but we get to see it because we got the funding for a screening. Finally people care about sexual assault!" She threw up her hands in exasperation.

"Let's go inside," suggested Michael. The auditorium was nearly full, and there hadn't been any newcomers for several minutes.

"Ok," agreed Emily.

* * * * *

The two quietly entered the darkened room, and made their way to the front, where they crept in to set next to their respective departments. Michael noticed that Miriam had placed her purse in the seat next to her to save it for him, and he felt a fluttering of gratitude, of specialness just below his diaphragm as he took his seat, returning her friendly smile.

Professor Thanh finished her remarks with a theatrical flair, and the audience burst into applause. Michael was afraid he had quite missed the point, and he was jarred when a student speaker took the podium to introduce the first film with a trigger warning: "The film you are about to watch contains graphic material regarding the sexual exploitation of minors, the adult film and pornography industry, sexual violence, and depictions of female genital modification."

Michael checked the brochure again, skimming the film's description. *Sexy Baby,* it was called. He slouched in his seat, and crossed his arms over his chest, acutely aware of Miriam's arm draped over the armrest.

The film began to play, and graphic images rolled across the screen. What if he got turned on, and Miriam noticed, and thought he was a pervert? Michael wondered frantically, but the subject material was grim and gratuitous to the degree that his fear was unwarranted; indeed, he felt more nauseated than aroused. He was uncomfortable for most of the film, and, looking to see her reactions, Michael noticed Miriam shaking her head throughout the film, and covering her mouth at the depiction of surgical aesthetic genital reconstruction.

The film's points about the intensification of the sexual culture, especially for children of the digital age, due to the influence of extreme and highly accessible sexual material online were well received, although Michael noticed some active murmurs of dissent to some of the film's implications from different subsets of the audience. The cohort from the Black Studies department seemed particularly disgruntled, and Michael acknowledged that it was unlikely that the film's three white protagonists could represent the full scope of impact of this digitized sexualization.

The film finished, and Miriam clucked her tongue. "It's hard to see that with a twelve-year-old daughter," she said. "I try to give her freedom and respect her privacy, but it's a different world these days… It's hard to know how to balance that with keeping her safe."

"I can only imagine," Michael said, shaking his head. Miriam got up to go speak with another professor, and Michael sat there for a moment, thinking.

He had started to look at porn around that age, he acknowledged, since that was about the time he and his siblings had gotten their own computer and he had learned how to clear the browser history. He and his brother had looked at pornographic cartoons, hentai, in addition to the other comics and cartoons they liked. Throughout his teenage years, it had developed as a private interest into animated hentai clips, then into other free online content of "real people;" photos and videos, first of Taiwanese people, then mostly whites. It seemed like ever since he could remember, in Taiwan and in America, people had been talking about sex, even before he knew what that really meant. When his family moved to Florida, he remembered thinking "sex" was some combination of the images of nearly—naked women in advertisements, magazines, and store windows that his mother told him not to stare at, and what 'older kids' and adults did in private together. In middle school, everyone talked about sex, but he was unsure who was having it besides the kids who already liked to party with alcohol and drugs. In high school, it seemed like more and more of his peers developed some experience with elements of it, even though any physical intimacy with a girl had eluded Michael until college.

He had never thought of himself as having a porn addiction; his viewing stayed neatly conscripted to the part of his life that he allowed sex to fill—but certainly the videos, the pictures he had seen had affected him, influenced his perception, caused him to view women and himself differently… Like the girl in the film, he had been so young when he had started to see himself as a sexual being, in private, and yet so little of that had seemed to have much of an impact on the rest of his life—indeed, ten years passed before he became 'sexually active.' Sex had all been very mysterious, and frustrating, until he had started having it and had somewhat wondered what all the fuss was about, before concluding that perhaps he and Astrid just didn't have "chemistry," whatever that was. Michael still longed for "chemistry" with a woman, for the intangible intertwinings of desire, not simply shared mutual interest in each other's company.

How had he taken all this for granted, chalked it up as "normal' in his self-analysis and introspection? Perhaps, as Lolo had said, he had just seen all that as 'not him,' and pushed it away. It was akin to what McKenna said of violence, he thought… it began as "une division de soi"—the difference of the self from itself within itself, a division to which his parents had contributed, no doubt, with their urgings that he go into a more practical, a more employable field, and a division to which his desires were also undoubtedly linked…

Michael got up, and checked in with the techs as they set up the next film. His mind was reeling, and he braced himself for what he was in store for with the upcoming feature, *Hot Girls Wanted*. The lights flickered and attendees returned to their seats, he and Miriam settling in next to each other again. Another student took the podium to declare, "This is a trigger warning. The film we are about to view contains disturbing footage discussing sexual exploitation, coercive sex, rape, and violent sexual assault, as well as some graphic pornographic material. If you find yourself in need of a therapist or just an open ear to help you process your reaction to the film, you can find our crisis counselors in blue t-shirts in the back row. Feel free to step out if you need to."

Michael noted the counselors waving. He gulped as the film began to play. Immediately, he felt like he was watching a mix between a horror flick, a documentary, and an amateur porn film. It was deeply unsettling, and he recoiled in disgust as the film detailed how young women, often simultaneously sexually inexperienced and looking to cash in on their objectified position within the culture, were recruited unwittingly to "paid work" and "modeling jobs" in Southern Florida and pressured and coerced into participating in increasingly extreme amateur pornography.

Michael's head spun. He remembered himself, skimming over tens, hundreds, maybe thousands of video stills on youporn.com, on pornhub, on xtube... He wasn't attracted to the clips of girls being hurt, but they were there, undeniably numerous and banal, and the film's assessment suggested that it was the same girls who started out in more tame, sensual, even affirming videos, and as their shelf-life and novelty waned, were pressured into ever more extreme, degrading, and traumatizing work.

He felt sick. He had gotten off to this, been a part of directing traffic to these sites, generating demand, consuming this content for free... Miriam looked abhorred, a grimace of disgust plastered across her face, and Michael wondered what she would think if she knew he watched porn on sites like these. She probably assumed he did, but what did that say about how she viewed him, about her respect for him as a man?—being part of something like this, sexualizing this, let alone the fact that he got off to videos of women that reminded him of her! His balls contracted and it felt as though his penis itself was shrinking in shame.

Surfing through this content, anaesthetized to it from the time he was a boy, he had not once stopped to ponder the ethicality of his desire for porn and the manifestations of desire captured in the content. He agonized over his own shame regarding his sexual interests, his embarrassing fantasies and unfortunately-timed hard-ons, but he had assumed all guys watched porn, and that it made the most sense to get it for free online, without any magazines, DVDs, or even digital payments to incriminate him in his consumption of the content. The oversight seemed egregious. He, the self-analytical philosopher of desire, had taken for granted the functioning and ethics of his culture's sexual mores, simply because he had been socialized within them and was implicated in them himself.

The film finished, and as the credits rolled, Miriam said to him, "You know, my mother was a big feminist in the seventies, and she was quite the anti-porn activist. One time she and her friends looted an adult video store and burned the content in the street! I thought she was quite the moralizing prude at the time; that if people were having sex, it wasn't any worse to depict it—even considering the patriarchal dynamics of the industry!—but I don't think I realized how extreme all this has gotten with the internet."

Michael shook his head, intrigued by how different her background was from his own, but still wracked with self-deprecating guilt. "Yeah, it's odd to realize how extreme and ubiquitous it is, and yet no one discusses it…" he said blandly.

Professor Thanh returned to the podium to announce instructions for the luncheon, and the audience filtered out of the auditorium to the main hall. Michael had been asked to begin setting up for the panel over the lunch break, and he was relieved to have an excuse to avoid dialogue for now. He grabbed a turkey sandwich from the end of the banquet table in the hall, and returned to eat it in the auditorium.

He was still so internally conflicted over what he had learned that he felt self-conscious about processing it with any of the largely female audience in attendance. He worried they would turn to him as a male and ask why guys would consume content like this. He feared the answer to his own internal question, as it seemed to be, "desire." Was it insatiable, uncontrollable, demonic desire that drove this whole industry of exploitation and objectification?

Michael returned to the same problem he always did. How could desire be ethical within a system where certain actors possessed the privilege to superimpose their desires over those of others? Was not desire then that which drove people to exploit, to abuse, to enact their perception of reality over that of the other? That which selfishly blinded each actor to realizing the ethical impact of their actions on the whole? How had his desire for Miriam, which seemed so affirmative, caused him to participate further in this matrix of unethicality? Would he be powerless to stop it from sabotaging his partnership with her and his work itself?

He felt panicky, constricted. This was what he got for always asking another question, he thought, always trying to peer deeper into the webs of causality... Of course he would find himself at the center, implicated in his own perceptions.

* * * * *

Michael finished his lunch, threw away the paper plate, and began to assist the technician who was wiring up all the microphones for the panel. They erected several long tables at the front of the auditorium, draped them, and set up placards for each speaker. Michael tarried briefly as he placed the final paper, his fingers lingering over the printed, embossed words: Dr. Miriam Lenard—Philosophy.

He was nervous for the next film, which was about sexual violence on college campuses, and anxious over the upcoming panel. He was glad he wouldn't have to make any public statements analyzing what they had watched, although he hoped he would feel comfortable doing so by the time he finished his degree, since it was, after all, his professional aspiration to lecture to people about his insights into the nature of desire—once he had acquired these insights, whatever they would prove to be.

The transition passed quickly, and by the time Michael finished his preparations for the panel, the audience had started to mill back in, and he took his seat. Miriam returned just as the film was about to begin. Michael had been half-worried that she had decided to leave, that something had come up and he would have to take her place on the panel... He was reassured and comforted by her presence as she settled in next to him, which was curious considering how vulnerable and self-conscious he felt about how he had sexualized her and how that linked to the material they had just watched.

"Trigger warning," yet another student began, "This film details many survivors of sexual violence recounting their experiences and contains graphic footage and victim-blaming remarks.

Please feel free to speak with one of the counselors available if you feel it would be helpful to you in digesting this material."

The Hunting Ground began to play, and Michael was disturbed to relate so closely to the young people, mostly women, profiled in their pursuit of higher education. As face after face described assault after assault, and the betrayal and retaliation that followed, Michael reflected on his own experience as an undergrad. Had his classmates had experiences like this at Highland? They must have, as Highland was one of the many schools now under investigation by the Department of Education... Why had he never heard of how common this was? If the women he knew had experienced this, why didn't he know about it?

The words "culture of silence" were repeated over and over, and Michael admitted that he had likely found himself on the side of complicity with this issue, selectively minimizing different headlines and stories he heard as stand-outs, and focusing instead on his own development as a student and a sexual being in a way that had been denied to so many of his peers.

He thought of the young women in the classes he taught; about whether they would feel comfortable coming to him for support if they were assaulted, and how he would respond. He was sure he would do a better job than many of the administrators described, as their tone-deaf, often condescending remarks were chillingly indifferent, verging on sociopathic as they performed logical and rhetorical cartwheels to absolve the institutions they were enlisted to represent at the expense of the brave, savvy, and sympathetic students attempting to receive the education they had been advertised and were paying for. It seemed glaringly myopic for these institutions to prioritize short-term branding over their own students, Michael thought, if only from a pragmatic and self-interested point of view. These things seemed to come out all the time; institutional scandals and cover-ups, and they not only revealed flaws, but deeply damaged communities' trust. What seemed frustratingly counterproductive was that the damage to the community's trust—which was, of course, the root of the institution's health and brand value—came usually as a result of the cover-up, not the scandal itself. How did these schools expect these students to speak of their experiences at the institution? To donate to them? To participate as alumni, to claim pride in an institution that had abandoned, even violated and betrayed them? It made little sense, and he assumed these administrators must be operating from a sort of bureaucratic blindness, oriented to entrenched interests within an outdated hierarchical status quo.

Michael had heard much more discussion of the issue at Blakeley, discussion that didn't frame the conversation around the survivors so much as the community. He had even participated in Blakeley's recent #shiftthescripts campaign to change the community's perception of the problem, which had been sponsored by the Feminist Studies and Sociology departments, and which the student activist he had met briefly was there to speak about today. He was grateful to now be in a more supportive campus environment, one that felt more ethical than the ones depicted on-screen, but he was still shaken, chilled by the sadism and calculation attributed to the young sexual predators that occupied these campuses, these 'hunting grounds,' and the wanton carelessness and indifference to human suffering depicted by so many institutional representatives that enabled their behavior.

There was a fundamental difference, he realized, between the passive way he had contributed to the amateur porn problem, and the way the sexual predators depicted in the movie chose to manifest their desires and the violence they had learned to sexualize. He had never considered that he, Michael, was entitled to enact his desires over another's; particularly not over those of a woman who wasn't interested in him, and he wondered how this mentality, this combination of entitlement and insecurity, privilege and shame that seemed to drive these young rapists developed...

He had been frustrated when Emily had "friendzoned" him back at Highland; when she had set him up with Astrid when he was clearly interested in her. Back then, he had thought a lot about being more assertive, about being respected as a man, and had visited several Pick Up Artist websites, thinking that if he weren't such a weak pushover, Emily would be interested in him. He had found the advice laughable, the allusions to gaining control of women sinister, and at the end of the day, hadn't had the heart or will to act out any of the "power plays" to "assert his dominance." Was it alpha masculinity that was behind this rape problem? he wondered. Or was it familiar masculine insecurity, echoed across many a chat board by sad, awkward, desperate guys who felt more and more enraged and entitled over being denied the affections and affirmation of the females of their choice?

Michael had thought a lot about his masculinity, about his internalized insecurity over rejection, when that half-Asian kid who was a fan of the PUA boards went off with a gun over at USC last year, raving about how the women who had rejected him owed him sex. Michael had identified with some of the shooter's frustrations, which had disturbed him, and had caused him to think much more critically about his own relationship to women and femininity, and to his own masculinity. After much soul-searching, he had concluded that much of his resentment came not from the few women who had rejected him, but from his resentment towards his mother for never standing up for herself to his father's cutting remarks, and how he feared her inability to stand up for herself had been passed on to him.

Michael hated and avoided conflict, and was one of those guys who had never been in a fight, save when he was being bullied in eighth grade and he had swung back, once. He immediately regretted it. But a lot of guys asserted their masculinity through aggression, through physically intimidating others, and it made sense that this would carry over to their treatment of women. Everyday violence and erasure, if even just in the tinges of sexism and condescension, the cutting remarks and glares of disapproval he had seen his father direct towards his mother, created an environment where every kind of behavior became more and more acceptable, even coerced sex.

How many guys did something like this because they thought they could get away with it? he wondered; because they, like the athletes and frat bros depicted in the film, knew they'd be protected by their teams, their institutions, their brotherhoods, and their family no matter what? And how many did it just to bolster their egos? To assuage a deep-seated insecurity about their inability to feel respected by other men, and particularly by women; lashing out and exerting power, especially sexual power over women. To what extent did this insecurity drive young guys to attempt to out-do each other's conquests within all-male social spaces, like these teams and frats? "Beta male" insecurity, they called on reddit and in the PUA chat rooms, and Michael suspected it might be more implicated in this rape phenomenon than the film had implied. Indeed, the PUA community's focus on "getting" women, "scoring," and "getting in" was all predicated on identifying a target, and dismantling any reason she might have to say 'no,' to assuage deep-seated beta male social anxiety over low social status and rejection through the conquest of women's bodies.

Although he had anxieties about approaching women sexually, Michael had wondered something different—he had wondered how you got a woman you had feelings for—not all women, not just any woman—to really see you, to like you, to want to be close to you, intimate with you; not just to let you have sex with her. How could you foster mutual respect and admiration, not use linguistic tricks to disarm her, and subtle disrespect to undermine her? He had seen that dynamic develop between his parents, and between some of his male gaming buddies and their girlfriends, and so he did not eroticize it, but rather feared it—feared ending up with a woman who was dependent on him, who deferred to him, who 'let him' do what he wanted, because he knew how much that could isolate two people, and saw how lonely each of his parents seemed, each sacrificing for, and blaming the other…

His desire, and indeed, male desire, did not need to be infused with violence and the need to control; yet clearly many men continued to fuse their boredom, their desire for power into fantasies of sex and violence, pornography and video games. Two of his own pastimes, yet pastimes he now acknowledged clearly had not held the power to make him, Michael, into a violent person, or a sexual predator, despite years of viewing, of playing. Nor had his own role models of masculinity convinced him to adopt their attitudes and tactics; instead, they (and particularly his father) had served as a deterrent, propelling

Michael towards his own understanding of masculinity, of interrelation, of intimacy. The media, the culture and its depictions did not need to control one's desires, but they could certainly guide one astray, he concluded.

The symposium attendees shuffled in uncomfortable silence as *The Hunting Ground's* credits began to roll. Several people were quietly crying, and there was a heavy and somber mood in the auditorium. The panelists filtered to the front, and Michael got up to change the audio equipment to connect to the microphones rather than the movie's sound, grateful for something to do with his restless energy.

Part Three

Professor Thanh opened the panel, saying, "On behalf of the Feminist Studies department and my colleagues in the Black Studies and Philosophy departments, thank you for coming today; for spending your Saturday with us and committing to learn more about the issue of sexual violence in our culture.

"We have received a lot of disturbing information from these films, and I'm sure many of us are dismayed at what this may say about the development of young people's sexualities and desires. I know others of us are disappointed at the stories that were *not* told here today, the stories which are often selectively edited from the media we consume.

"Since we have ended on the note of campus violence, I would first and foremost like to introduce our student panelist to talk about the situation at Blakeley as well as her nationally renowned #shiftthescripts campaign, which I'm sure needs little introduction! Charlie West will be representing the Feminist Studies department today; Charlie?"

The first panelist, the girl Michael had met earlier, scooted forward in her chair and pulled the mic a little closer. There was a screech of feedback, and the audience laughed nervously as she recoiled comically.

"My name is Charlie Little Wolf West, and I am a proud member of the Sovereign Cheyenne nation," she began. "I'll get to the campus question, but first, I want to begin by describing where I'm from, so you all have some context of how my perspective fits into all this. I was raised on a small reservation, in a relatively closed community, where everyone either knew each other, or knew someone who did—which in many ways reminds me of Blakeley.

"My home community, and indeed, many indigenous communities, find ourselves besieged by an epidemic of sexual and domestic violence, alongside epidemics of alcoholism and drug abuse. I would argue the same is true of many college campuses," There was some nervous laughter and appreciative snapping, and Charlie continued, "—but for my home nation, we find ourselves at a crisis point. The leaders are not sure how to prosecute these crimes internally. Many people are sexually abused by family members and do not want to betray them. Many people feel that it would tear the community apart to speak openly of these issues, and that we must try to pretend they don't exist, that sexual abuse does not affect nearly the majority of our women and children, and the cycle of violence, shame, and silence that has operated since our lands were colonized and our people were forcibly resettled continues."

Much of the crowd was shaking their heads sympathetically, and Michael marveled at the fact that this colonization in question had happened less than two hundred years ago on the very land they occupied! It was such recent history, nearly as recent as Japan's occupation of Taiwan—which no one expected the Taiwanese to forget!—and yet many, especially whites, seemed to think it was long bygone. This was one of the facets of American history Michael had become more informed about after enrolling at Blakeley, which was renowned for its commitment to post-colonial studies, decolonization, and the empowerment of indigenous students.

Charlie continued, "I felt this way, too, when I lived on the reservation as a child. My father was white, and he did not live with my mother and I. I don't know what happened between he and my mother, but I know she was afraid that he would return someday. My mother taught me to be very careful around men, to never let myself be alone with them, and to never let them touch me. She warned me of dating, and of letting myself end up with a man who would not treat me like the princess I was. I watched my actions, and lived in fear, and part of me blamed the women that 'bad things' happened to, the women who 'let themselves' be raped, 'let themselves' be abused; and worse, had children with those abusers to start the cycle again."

Michael shook his head. He didn't think his parents' relationship was 'abusive,' but he had blamed his mother for putting up with his father in those ways, for letting him get away with his pettiness and meanness, if nothing else.

Charlie continued speaking, "I felt this way, and in many ways I felt better than these women, and indeed, better than my tribe when I got out, when I came to Blakeley. I tell you this because it was at Blakeley, in my promised land, where I finally felt safe and protected, that I found myself in an abusive relationship. My guard was down. I thought I could trust my classmates, and part of me thought nothing bad could happen here, not to me anyway.

"I began to date my ex my freshman year. He was another Native American student, and we grew close over our shared mission to learn the tools of success and return with them to improve the quality of life on our respective reservations. He was my first boyfriend, and I had nothing to compare it to, so I mistook some of the warning signs as natural parts of an adult relationship.

"I must say, I am glad we watched this film, but I have reservations about its depictions of this problem because of what happened with me. Things did not become violent between my ex and I. He did not beat me, and I didn't think he had raped me until I realized how many times I had merely been expected to have sex with him, and had agreed because I thought that was how a relationship worked. I moved off campus to live with him my sophomore year, and that's when the relationship really began to take a toll on me. He was more and more controlling and critical of me, and I stopped spending as much time with my friends and started to only hang out with our shared friends from the Native American community, friends he liked, friends who didn't criticize him or the way he spoke to me. I still didn't realize there was anything wrong, because I hadn't really seen any healthy adult relationships around me as a child, and all our peers seemed to think it was normal, but my confidence began to plummet."

Michael thought about what he had realized about low self-esteem and masculine control. It seemed to map on to the experience Charlie was describing—and perhaps mapped more onto his parents' relationship than he had acknowledged. Around him, the audience was silent, intent, listening.

Charlie went on, "I found myself orienting everything to making him happy, and trying not to make any problems, until one day I went to dinner with an old friend from outside our circle after a meeting without telling him. I returned to the apartment we shared, and he locked the door and began to berate me, saying this was why he couldn't trust me, and that he thought I'd been cheating, and that I was stupid, and irresponsible, and didn't deserve him. It went on for hours, and it felt like a nightmare. I was afraid to say anything because anything I said only made him more angry. I got up to leave, and he blocked the door, saying we weren't finished, and it was only then that I realized I didn't have anywhere to go. I had pushed away my friends, and our shared friends would take his side. It was in that moment that I realized I had lost my own voice."

Charlie looked down, and her voice cracked slightly as she continued, "I felt like one of the women I had judged my whole life, and I felt so much shame and self-loathing to have found myself in that situation; to be afraid to say anything, afraid to leave, afraid to tell anyone or to tell him no because it would only make it worse. And we lived together! That night he raped me. I didn't know to call it that at the time; It was like any other night that he had expected sex from me and I had gone along with it to keep him happy, but that time, I knew I was afraid to say no, and I just lay there, and it was like he didn't even notice the difference, or notice there was anything wrong."

There was a chill, a stillness over the audience. Michael noticed some people shifting uncomfortably in their seats; others were nearly in tears.

Charlie said, "The next morning, while he was at class, I called the school crisis line, and they helped me move into temporary housing, and informed me of my options. It was when he realized I was gone that he really lost it. He began to send me messages over text, email, and Facebook that grew more and more threatening, saying we were meant to be together and that something bad would happen to me if I walked away from him, that no one would ever love me as he had. His friends and he would stare at me, in the cafeteria, walking across campus, in class, and then it turned to stalking, waiting outside my new dorm, my classes. I began to feel hopeless, to panic, and when I went to speak to a counselor, I realized that my symptoms were early signs of post-traumatic stress disorder, and that even though I didn't think things had been 'that bad,' so much violence had been done to my sense of self, to my ability to make sense of the world and my place in it, that I now was developing a mental illness! Like I said, I had been moved to a new dorm, and even though I was seeing a therapist and going to a support group, my mental health grew worse. I started missing class and wanting to hide inside all day to avoid his harassment and any potential confrontation, but I was also terrified just waiting inside, because I was afraid he would find out where I was staying and break in. I had nightmares every night, and developed insomnia."

Michael was sobered to realize that what Charlie was describing must be how it felt to be the recipient of someone's unwanted, unrequited desire. This was why it was so unethical to inflict your reality over another person's, to force them to embody the object of your desire. Miriam sat down the table from Charlie, nodding, jotting some notes on her pad.

Charlie looked at her watch briefly, checking how long she'd been speaking. She continued, "Finally, the therapist said to me, 'Charlie, it seems like things are getting worse for you. What's going on?' and I told her about the continued stalking, the harassment. She referred me to the school's Title IX coordinator, who told me that even though my ex had not physically attacked me or violently raped me, his ongoing actions were preventing my access to education, and that she would support me in filing disciplinary action against him, although it could be a long process. I was torn. I didn't want to punish him, even then, and I didn't want to get him kicked out of school, no matter what he'd done. I cared for him, still, and I knew that as a fellow Native student he was working just as I was to improve things not just for himself and his family, but for his community, and I didn't want to stand in the way! I didn't think he was a danger to anyone else; I thought that things had just gone too far between us.

"The coordinator told me that even if I didn't want to report officially and file charges, I could enter my experience into the campus Callisto database so it would be included in the data about Blakeley's campus climate, and so that I could get a ping if anyone else had reported an experience of sexual violence with him. I did it, anonymously, just because I wanted to have some documentation of what had happened, and to get it out there in case it happened to anyone else... but as I entered in the information, I got a notification right away. It turned out someone had already reported him! He was a year older than me, and he had raped another woman before I got to campus; another Native woman it turned out!

"I chose to send her a message, letting her know about my experience, and we met up. We discussed what had happened to us, and why we each hadn't formally reported. Just like me, she hadn't wanted to bar his access to education; we were both unsure whether our experiences would be understood by the judicial process, and we both knew that we'd be ostracized, even shunned by much of the Native community if we chose to turn on him, to use the punishing power of the school against one of our own.

"We each did it for the other, going in to report him, to file charges, and we went through the disciplinary process together. Blakeley flew out my family to support me in the process, and told my professors I was going through a personal crisis and needed some additional support. Meeting the other survivor, feeling like someone believed in me and thought what happened to me was wrong, and realizing I could use the system to advocate for myself all improved my mental health, but it was only once he was found guilty and expelled that I felt comfortable to be myself again—but there were repercussions, just as I had expected.

Charlie sighed deeply and looked around the auditorium before continuing, "It was once I started to experience victim blaming myself, from former friends saying that he was just in love with me, that I was weak, that I was a bitch, that I wanted to ruin his life, and that I had deserved what happened to me, that I realized that the problem was not my ex, or even the way he treated me. The problem is the way we talk about relationships, sexual violence and abuse. The problem is our limited scripts, scripts that cause people to respond in a way that is normative, disempowering, and minimizing when they hear about something like this. We hear about someone's suffering, and we want to make ourselves believe that something like that couldn't happen to us, because we are smarter, and make better choices, and don't deserve for something like that to happen to us!"

Michael noted that Charlie seemed to be

segueing from her personal experience to her theories on the topic, and he began to scribble some notes in the margins of his brochure as she went on, "People are trained to respond in this way, because it's how they see other people responding. We are social animals, and we learn through mirroring and oral tradition. But when this violence is occurring, what does it mean to distance ourselves from it, to fit it into a neat narrative and push it away from us? It means that the violence continues to operate unchecked against those this system has deemed it acceptable to abuse, to violate, to rape. As a Native American woman, that is concerning to me, because for much of this country's history, violence against women like me has been rampant and normalized at the hands of white masculinity, and even though we have attempted to tell our stories, to find justice and healing, many people's ears are closed to our suffering, because they see it as a regrettable but inevitable side effect of 'the way things are.'"

Charlie continued to speak, impassioned, "My people and I have not acclimated ourselves to 'the way things are,' and so I asked myself what I could do to make space for these stories, these truths in all their multiplicities to come forth and find the light of day, and ultimately, to shift the script of how these conversations unfold."

The crowd was engaged, listening raptly; some students had begun to snap affirmingly at Charlie's points.

She checked her watch again, and continued, speaking somewhat quickly, "The

#shiftyourscripts campaign actually started as a project for my Sociology of Violence class, with an idea I had that if people could work together to shift the scripts they use to blame victims, since those scripts are largely inaccurate misassumptions that map onto a limited set of key myths about sexual violence, that it might be possible to change the way we disempower and re-traumatize survivors through victim blaming and social erasure, at least at Blakeley, just by learning more about what sexual violence actually looks like, who is affected by it, and why.

"I started by doing a survey of my class, then of the campus, asking people to be honest about the victim blaming scripts they had internalized, and to identify different thoughts they had when confronted with micro case studies of sexual violence, even if they were things they knew not to say out loud. I conducted anonymous surveys about experiences students had with sexual violence and victim blaming, and I referenced my data with the campus's Callisto database and the Clery numbers to see how people's experiences related to who reported or told someone, and who didn't, and what that had to do with scripts and perceptions about 'people like them.'

"We started the hashtag #shiftyourscript, and we took to Twitter and other social media to ask people around campus, then around the world to contribute facts, stories, personal experiences about sexual violence. We got more and more data about people's key scripts, about what was really going on; more and more people joined in, and it really reached a tipping point, at least here at Blakeley."

The audience broke into applause. The campaign had been a wild success, and much of the campus—especially the contingent that was in attendance at the Symposium—including Michael, had engaged in the conversation across social media. He remembered being surprised to see that the kneejerk reactions of so many reddit and twitter trolls *did* map directly onto the five or six key myths the campaign had claimed, and it had caused a huge shift in his perception of free will, of autonomy and the social organism to come head-to-head with such blind groupthink spread out across the digital sphere, amongst people who hadn't even been socialized in the same ways! There was some larger element of 'culture' he concluded, that existed outside of the aggregation of individual perceptions, something that was larger than the sum of its social parts, that caused people to react in these ways, and was itself ever-changing and mutable.

Charlie continued, "I think we've changed the conversation here, and we're seeing that play out as the campaign goes national and is adopted by other campuses as well as in response to limiting media narratives about sexual violence online. I have to say, I am glad we are all here today to learn more about sexual violence, but I have some serious concerns about the way these documentaries present the most clear-cut and egregious examples of assault rather than the more nuanced and everyday examples that affect many, if not most, students, like me.

"As the film pointed out, young people are more likely to be raped if they attend college than if they do not. But which students are really at risk? Native American women are thirty-three times more likely to be sexually assaulted than white women. Black women are 7% of the population, but 27% of rape victims. Over 50% of convicted rapists are white. Queer women are three times more likely to be raped than straight women. Gay men are fifteen times more likely to be raped than straight men. And all the statistics we have can only suggest at what this problem truly looks like, because the best estimates are that anywhere from three to ten rapes are committed for every rape reported. Rapes by strangers are underreported, yes, but rapes by acquaintances are practically non-reported, for the very same reasons I was hesitant to report. And yet rape crisis center staff—and my data!—estimate that 70-80% of all rapes are acquaintance rapes!

"This film does not grapple with this reality, and indeed, I worry that this film reifies a rape myth that may disincentivize survivors of more 'everyday' violence from seeking help. One of the key scripts that disempowers survivors is that what happened to them was not that bad, that some people are experiencing worse, and when you see someone attacked, nearly killed by a stranger, and see that reinforced as the strongest example of violation despite its relative infrequence, it can't help but normalize and minimize more widespread forms of sexual coercion and abuse. The narrative presented in this film may be stirring, and may inspire moral indignation, but it is presented at the expense of depicting the real problem of sexual violence on our campuses and in our communities."

Charlie finished her points, and shot a sideways glance at the lawyer, who was fidgeting uncomfortably next to her. Adelaide, seated two seats over, on the other side of Ms. Grossman gave her an affirming nod and reached around the producer to place her hand on Charlie's shoulder. The two were obviously close.

There was a note of tension in the room, as people tried to reconcile their emotional catharsis to the film with Charlie's contextualization. Michael thought that what she had said made sense, and with how open and subjective she had been about her own experience, and how much data she had amassed, she indeed presented a strong case.

Professor Thanh leaned forward and spoke into her mic again. "Thank you, Charlie. We're happy to have you on the panel today. Thank you for sharing your story. We're all inspired by your scholarship and activism."

* * * * *

Professor Thanh looked to the next panelist with a broad smile, and said, "We are fortunate to have here with us here today, all the way from Boston, Marsha Grossman; a feminist legal expert

248

and activist who served as a consultant on *The Hunting Ground*![4] Here to speak to the current frontiers of the sexual assault movement and on her involvement with the film, let's welcome Ms. Marsha Grossman of Grossman Solutions!

The lawyer smiled, waving slightly, as applause spattered throughout the auditorium.

"Blakeley!" Marsha began, "It's an honor to speak at a school so celebrated for its impactful commitment to social justice, and to follow such a passionate and committed student activist! Let's hear another round of applause for Charlie, and her courage to share her story here with us today."

Charlie smiled wanly, and another, slightly louder roll of applause swept the audience.

"Well, the film has made many of the points I wanted to make about this issue," Marsha said, "so I'll keep my remarks relatively brief and leave space for more dialogue and perhaps some questions once everyone's said their piece.

She pursed her lips and said, "Just so you have some context for my issue and the project, I became interested in Title IX as a legal tool for fighting workplace sexual harassment rather early in my career as a lawyer. I left my corporate consulting firm to join a feminist civil rights firm, and after working with a female professor denied tenure several years ago, I became connected with my first student client, a young woman who had

---

[4] Marsha Grossman is a fictional character and is in no way representative of any real person associated with the film *The Hunting Ground*. All discussion of this film held within these pages is a hypothetical discussion of opinions held by fictional characters who are in no way based on any real person.

been forced out of her institution after experiencing rape. I first represented her in filing a Title IX lawsuit against the school, which was ultimately settled privately, and which I can't discuss here except to say that the survivor did eventually return to school.

"She began to connect with other survivors on campus, and connected them to me with the idea of filing a federal complaint to the Department of Education over the school's alleged noncompliance with Title IX. We had heard of other survivors, including the ones depicted in the film, beginning to file federal complaints against their institutions, and I helped them put together a federal complaint, which we submitted following a press conference with survivors from seven other schools who were also filing Title IX and Clery complaints against their institutions."

Most of the audience seemed intrigued, but less engaged than they had been during Charlie's monologue; however, some feminist students sitting near Michael were furiously live-tweeting the lawyer's remarks.

Marsha went on, "With that, the movement really began to snowball, and more and more survivors were referred to me to assist them in their cases against their schools and/or complaints to the Department of Education. There was so much demand that I split off from my former firm two years ago and launched my own sexual assault and harassment focused legal consultancy, Grossman Solutions. We have been instrumental in assisting many survivors in their pursuit of justice, and we see the impact of so much hard work and so much bravery on the part of these young activists realized in the successes this movement has only just begun to realize!"

There was a roll of applause throughout the auditorium.

Marsha continued, "We are at a turning point on this issue, I believe, with over one hundred institutions under federal investigation for alleged noncompliance with these statutes, and with the public beginning to have conversations about rape and victim blaming that would never have been possible before. Finally, after so many years, America is acknowledging that we have a rape problem and culture of sexual harassment on our college campuses that is barring so many young women from the education they deserve and damaging their ability to find professional success before their careers have even begun."

There was another roll of applause, centered from the Feminist contingent, Michael noted.

Marsha said, "It was in the spirit of bearing witness, and of honoring the stories of so many brave and brilliant survivors, as well as bringing my legal expertise on this issue to advise on how these allegations and institutions could be discussed on film, that I decided to sign on to consult on this project, which has been shown at many film festivals, has already screened at hundreds of campuses across the country, and aired on national television this fall. We have reached an audience I never dreamed was possible when I began work on this project, and it's been so moving to see people begin to change the way they talk about rape on campus, as you were saying," she noted, with a nod towards Charlie. "We're having conversations that would not have been possible even a year ago! I guess we're 'shifting the script,' as you call it here!" Marsha let out a small laugh. Michael noticed that Charlie seemed visibly irritated, as though she wanted to interrupt but had decided to hold her tongue.

Marsha went on, "In response to some of the comments made about the narrative and editing choices, I just wanted to say that we *did* make a concerted effort in the recruiting and interviewing stages of the project to solicit stories and experiences from survivors who had 'non-traditional' rape experiences, including same-sex rape, people of color, and domestic violence experiences, but just as you mentioned, many people with more complicated stories didn't want to share them on camera, or would only speak anonymously, or wouldn't speak candidly about their experiences... You do have to make some choices when you're in the editing room, and deciding on the clearest, strongest narrative that's going to connect with the viewer and really start a conversation about this issue can be very difficult, and necessitate some... shall we say, simplifications of how this may manifest for different students in different situations."

There were some disgruntled murmurs from the crowd.

Marsha said, "The key aim with this project

was to showcase the stories of survivors in their pursuit of justice, to uncover how even our leading academic institutions create environments that are breeding grounds for serial perpetrators, and to get a critical mass of Americans to change the way they personally relate to the issue of sexual assault. When you want to reach a critical mass with a major distributor, that does come with certain concessions and a need to simplify the narrative in the editing process for mass distribution and reception, and you end up moving away from stories that are more complicated and towards featuring bigger name, more shocking cases, such as the Florida State allegations, which as you may have heard, have gotten us into a little bit of hot water!"

Marsha shook her head, and continued, "We wanted to show how widespread this problem is; that what's going on is not just 'drunk college sex or 'he said/she said;' how serial perpetrators operate nearly unchecked on our college campuses, and how our institutions are abdicating their responsibilities to their students under the law! We tried to tell the best story we could with what we were able to find, and I hope many viewers take advantage of resources like the #shiftthescripts campaign to educate themselves even more about the rape epidemic and how it affects us all. Just like Charlie said, even the best research we have is limited and so it's so important to keep asking questions and learning more. I'm grateful to have had the opportunity to present the film here at Blakeley today, and I'd be happy to answer any questions you have during the Q & A!"

Marsha closed with a wide smile, her hands folded on the table in front of her. Applause, and some mutterings of dissatisfaction, swept through the hall.

Before Professor Thanh could return to the podium, Charlie leaned forward and said, rather abruptly, "I have a question, or perhaps more of a comment that I'd like to pose to your remarks about what I said and my campaign."

Marsha raised her eyebrows. She was leaning back in her chair, watching as Charlie continued to speak, "The everyday stories that I'm referring to are not 'more complicated' or 'non-traditional;' I have the data to show that they're not outliers, they're what the majority of survivors experience! Even if what happened to many people was closer to 'he said/she said,' whatever that means, or 'drunk college sex,' it's exactly those survivors who won't feel comfortable telling their stories because of your film and its impact."

Charlie shot another look, almost a glare, directly at Marsha, then looked out into the audience, saying, "*You're* working from the script we're trying to shift, even if you are at least trying to expand it. It's *not* making a stronger story to focus on only the cases that will translate to people who don't understand the issue. It's backing away from a fight, because you're conceding to victim-blamers that *some* rapes aren't as bad, and don't deserve to be talked about because they mess with a neat line drawn between good people and bad people in our society, and a lot of people try very hard to position themselves on the side that's trying to help those who are suffering, but in doing it for their own validation and enrichment end up making the whole problem worse!"

As Charlie finished, Marsha looked over to Professor Thanh, then Adelaide. It looked as though she was about to reply, when Professor Thanh butted in, "Let's keep to our agreed upon speaking order for now, and then perhaps we can field more questions and concerns about the film… and address those already posed… after all the panelists have had a chance to speak."

* * * * *

Marsha settled back in her chair again, looking aggrieved. Dr. Thanh continued, "Next we will hear from Dr. Adelaide Nkrumah from the Black Studies department. Professor Nkrumah is a distinguished scholar working at the intersections of race and gender in the African diaspora, and we are fortunate to have her here today to present her analysis of sexualities and desire to contextualize what we have learned today."

Adelaide gestured to the moderator, then leaned forward slightly, looking out into the audience. She began to speak. "Thank you to my dear colleague Professor Thanh! And the other hosting departments, thank you for affirming that a critical race analysis belongs at the center of this conversation about sexual violence in 'our' culture—just like I'm here, at the center of this table in front of you all today!—and for inviting me and the Black Studies department to be part of this conversation—even if it was a bit of a last minute decision!"

The audience, particularly the Black Studies contingent, clapped, and there were a few isolated whoops. Initially, the Symposium had been sponsored by only the Feminist Studies and Philosophy Departments, but when the Feminist professor asked to speak had given her spot to Charlie, and Charlie had refused to speak without a critical race analysis more prominently featured on the panel, the departments had hurriedly scrambled to invite and include Professor Nkrumah and the Black Studies department just two weeks before the event. Michael noted the tension of interdepartmental politics was highlighted by such an interdisciplinary event, although of course it was for exactly this reason, to put the disciplines in dialogue, that they all fell under the school of Humanitas. There was a lot of interdepartmental research at Blakeley, and collaborations within and between the institution's two schools, Humanitas and Physicus, were highly encouraged and sponsored by joint grants and appointments. It was one of the reasons Blakeley hummed with intellectual fervor, churning out the most cutting edge breakthroughs across the disciplines and indeed, throughout the culture, despite being founded as an experimental learning lab environment in the Midwest only ten years ago. "Tension fosters growth, so let us nurture tension in the hopes it shall bring forth new growth!" the College's president had said at Michael's matriculation, and the words had stuck with him, and had come to mind each time an intellectual or interpersonal conflict reared its head during his last two years at Blakeley.

Adelaide motioned with her hands for the audience to quiet. With a smile, she continued, "We are convened here today to digest information about and discuss a rape culture, and its traumatic effects on students, in ways both educational and personal. Charlie has, with her story, given us all a script to understand how these issues brought to light by the media we have consumed today have affected a member of our own community, and for that, we are all grateful. Stories should always be at the center of the quest for human understanding, and indeed, allow us to see realities we had not yet imagined possible. The power of empathizing with a story yet-untold is the power of new understanding, of gnostic insight, of 'being with' another, which is a profound and sacred experience."

Members of the audience were already nodding, snapping and murmuring in approval at her opening points.

Adelaide said, "The films we have watched together today also tell stories. They present to us theories of understanding, ways of knowing about the world we live in. Since this particular genre of, shall I say, docu-activism, strives to tell stories that help audiences understand the world we live in and inspire more conscious engagement, they provide the perfect content for us to analyze how themes and scripts of femininity, of masculinity, of sexuality, of power, of good and bad, innocence and violation, and all else we hold as the objects of our study within the departments brought together today, are digested and theorized as narratives within the culture.

"That's right!" cried out one student.

Adelaide smiled and went on, "There is certainly an ethical imperative to be questioned here, as Charlie has mentioned, in that by asserting a theory of the problem, these films also shape and mold public perception, and so there is an element of *meta*-ethicality and *meta*-coercion engaged in our discussion today.

"What is the reality of the situation? we may ask ourselves:

"Who is implicated within this?

"Who is affected by this, and in which ways?

"What then, shall we do?

"How shall we integrate this information?

"How shall we react?"

Michael scribbled notes on Adelaide's questions. Perhaps he should audit one of her classes, he thought. She seemed to have a lot of insights into how ethicality related to the culture, to identity, to the media...

She continued, "These are the endeavors of narrativising a social problem, to the end of transmitting that particular analysis through the available channels of distribution for the consumption by and absorption within the minds of viewers, who in return *create* the culture through the implementation of their perceptions. So we are right to ask questions on many levels, to engage with the slices of this problem, this analysis, this representation."

Michael was enthralled. She seemed to be getting at the mechanics, the specifics of how subjectively positioned actors consumed and created the culture—something that was only metaphysically analyzed within the discipline of philosophy.

Adelaide leaned forward, enunciating pointedly, "One 'slice' I would like to bring to bear with my space on this panel is what exactly we are talking about with the phrase 'non-traditional' rape.

Another student shouted out, "Yeah!"

"I'd like to break that down a little bit, look a little closer. If we consider *tradition* to be the blind adherence to that which has come before, and/or the inherited dynamics which have previously cohered our culture, there is nothing more *traditional* than rape, at least in the project of American imperialism we are currently embedded within."

Many members of the audience, especially the students of color, murmured in affirmation as she continued.

"This country was established on the genocide of native populations and the settler colonization of their land. For those who are unclear about the specifics of what that might look like in practice, let me assure you that it involves a lot of rape. Rape as an act of genocide, of erasure, of the assertion of *power* over the subjugated other, the indigenous body, and as Charlie alluded to, in particular the bodies of indigenous women. So that's *one* type of traditional rape. Let's carry on.

"Another type of traditional rape was the sexual enslavement and, indeed, forced breeding of enslaved African peoples brought to this continent to provide free labor for nearly 400 years of this country's history, in which it was assumed, *traditionally*, that a white man's ownership of black bodies extended to ownership of their sexual labor and the unchecked power to sexually exploit and rape them, which, in case you're not familiar with the historical specifics of the time period, I can assure you many took full advantage of. A *second* example of traditional rape; of the rape that built this country.

"A *third* type of traditional rape, which has been set forth at length today, is the male ownership, domination, and sexual exploitation of female bodies within a patriarchy, say, for example, the white patriarchy that has held power since this country's colonization. Throughout history, white women's labor, their autonomy, and their sexualities have been ensnared within this white patriarchal settler colonist project, and many women's attempts to break free of these dynamics, to claim their power, their autonomy, and their sexualities have been met by violence, and indeed, by rape. One more example of traditional rape."

The audience applauded, and Adelaide collected herself before circling her critique back to the film. She said, "The merits of this type of legal strategy set forth are severely impinged by, if they choose not to be informed by, a history of racial profiling and disenfranchisement within our legal and justice system. Indeed, the ability of indigenous women to testify against white perpetrators has only been guaranteed in the last several years, believe it or not, despite this prevalence of violence against them, or *perhaps* because of it. Studies have found that even when a woman of color does testify against an assailant, juries find the emotional damages and traumatic impact of the assault on the woman less severe than for white women. This is reflected in disparate sentencing that punishes assailants of women of color *less* severely, yet punishes male assailants of color *more* severely. This is deeply implicated in, and likely a result of how sexuality is depicted in the media, with women of color often being depicted promiscuously or in sexualized roles, and men of color often being depicted as sexually violent and dangerous. These narratives we consume cannot help but influence our perceptions, and the perceptions of law enforcement, judges, and juries as well.

"Some may say that media chooses to depict things as it will to capture attention, and may decry its biased sensationalism as an unfortunate byproduct of capitalism. Yet few realize that the bounds and norms of what our media is permitted to depict are shaped to this day by the legacy of the 1930 Hays code, a propagandistic law rigorously—but sporadically—enforced throughout the history of Hollywood which dictated specific moral norms and taboos that were to be depicted or forbidden on screen, so as to protect the *morality* of the American viewer. This meant that it was *illegal* to depict interracial relationships, *illegal* to depict whites in subservient positions to blacks, *illegal* to depict many forms of 'nonconformity,' including suggestions of homosexuality or gender deviance. Media was and has been therefore scripted into the propagandistic norms of early 20th century white patriarchal American imperialism, and tends to demonize any 'other' or 'deviance' to this day, while preserving the purity and morality of the white American heterosexual family, embodied through the inviolability of white femininity—except at the hands of white masculinity, of course. I'm sure students of feminist media studies here today are well-versed in the egregious nature of violence against women—as well as people of color—at the hands of white masculinity that has been depicted and normalized, even celebrated, in media, film, and advertising."

Adelaide sighed heavily, and continued, "Of course, within a broader context, it is the mythologized purity, chastity, and inviolability of white femininity that has been used by the same project to demonize and fearmonger scripts about the danger and threat of men of color and their sexualities to justify untold lynchings throughout this history. It is the *delicateness* and *sensitivity* of this mythologized white femininity that is defined oppositionally to—and set in contrast to— stereotypes and propaganda about women of color, justifying and normalizing *these* bodies as *acceptable* targets of sexual violence, as *unrapeable,* as *always already exploited*. And it is the *guilt*, the *shame*, the *complicity* of this implicated white femininity that has powered the 'soft arm' of colonization, the *civilizing forces*: the schools, the churches, and the charities that have metamorphosed into the charity industrial complex which upholds the legitimacy of the military industrial complex, the prison industrial complex, and the crisis of neoliberal global exploitation we see afflicting our world today."

Some members of the audience raised their eyebrows, looking to each other to affirm that Adelaide had taken this argument too far, or at least too far for the venue. Others continued to snap along enthusiastically. Michael was taken aback not by the political implications, but by Adelaide's interlinking of colonizing propaganda to scripts of gender and race; by how clear it seemed to him now.

Adelaide continued, "But I digress slightly. It is this branch of the neocolonial power infrastructure—the charity industrial complex— that brings to bear another topic I wanted to raise in light of these realizations about *traditional rape*, as well as the insights about pornography and exploitation that these films have raised for us today. How many of you here have heard the term 'disaster porn'?"

About half the audience raised their hands. Michael thought it had something to do with that Kony 2012 video he'd watched—he'd read an article on it—but he didn't quite remember.

Adelaide continued, "Ok, so disaster porn is produced media content that makes a spectacle of the suffering of others. You may remember commercials you've seen of suffering African children, or of the devastation of New Orleans or Haiti following their respective natural disasters. Disaster porn, like the charity industrial complex, often sets as its subjects the bodies of the dispossessed; black and brown people, women and children, depicted in moments of anguish or suffering for more privileged viewers. Disaster porn is often criticized as exploitative and voyeuristic. Disaster porn is often justified with the assertion that its distribution is meant to raise support, awareness, and compassion towards those who are depicted in their suffering—but since moments of direct human connection are not possible between the subject depicted and their viewer, all too often, the viewer uses the disturbing nature of the footage to distance themselves from it, to push it away, and to feel pity rather than compassion, to sympathize or 'feel for' rather than to empathize, or 'feel with.'"

The crowd had been snapping and emitting murmurs of agreement, of approval throughout Adelaide's speech, and these built to a small crescendo now. Michael thought about what a marvel of social interaction the Symposium was, almost like the Forums of ancient Greece, where orators held forth on their perspectives, and the demos, the crowd judged and expressed whether the speaker spoke for their perspective too.

Adelaide continued, "Can suffering be

depicted in a way that is humanizing, that leads viewers to root for the individuals depicted, to broaden their understanding of what it means to be human, and shape the way they interact with the world? I believe so.

"I believe in the power of storytelling, of narrative, and in the medium of film as one of the most powerful ways in which to convey that message. I believe that, in watching these films—and all films which claim to depict the real lived experiences of humans—we must turn to *context* and our own subjectivity to analyze whether the cultural work has achieved its goal of bringing us *closer* to the subjects depicted, to putting us into their shoes and inviting our empathy, and inquisitive support, or to *distancing* us from the subjects, from their *abjection*, their *distress*, their *suffering*, and their perceived *difference* from 'us' and our own experiences."

Michael remembered what Lolo had said about pushing things away; what he had read that morning about shame and the other, and thought that perhaps Adelaide was referring to the same phenomenon. What an interesting synchronicity, he thought.

Adelaide carried on, "Another question to ask is, is this film situated within a reality that allows for the existence of other narratives, or is it speaking from a 'false universal,' a meta-narrative which claims to be definitive and exclusionary, offered at the expense of another?

"The final question to explore is: what historical reality is this set within? Is it operating from the assumptions of dominant white hegemony and contributing to the ongoing propagandistic neocolonial project?

"Is this ideologically motivated?

"By whose ideology?

"Against whose?

Adelaide had really gotten into flow, thought Michael, as she continued, "As I have highlighted with my three examples of traditional rape, there is a broader historical context against which white feminist ideological propaganda—such as the films we saw today—are set forth. Unfortunately, I find that all the content we have viewed today shares the same historical shortsightedness and the somewhat myopic lens of exclusionary white feminism, which impinges on its educational merits and its ability to achieve its identified aims of 'setting forth the problem and inspiring action,' as all such inspiration is constricted within the scope of the ideology offered, and therefore implicated within a broader context of white supremacist imperialism."

Michael noted, with some humor, Marsha's double take at the words, "white supremacist."

Adelaide continued, "That is not to say that the narratives of the protagonists we have followed within these films are not valuable and enlightening and inspirational on their own merits! But to discuss them within a commercialized narrative such as the ones set forth today *does* introduce such questions, and in the dismissal and marginalization of experiences perceived as 'non-traditional' from all of these narratives, without providing context for such a biased representation, the films have implicated themselves in an exclusionary white feminist ideology that sets forth the third type of 'traditional rape' at the expense of the exclusion of the other two, for the reason that dominant (white) culture operates off of these exclusions, and therefore does not deem these experiences important, worth listening to, or even of note, despite their prevalence!"

The audience continued to snap, and some students cried out in indignant affirmation, as Adelaide continued her powerful oration, "Indeed, it is the third type of traditional rape, the violation of white femininity, that has given moral weight to policies that dehumanize and criminalize masculinities of color, and particularly Black masculinity, which I feel I *must* acknowledge given the current crisis over the criminalization of blackness, and the last film's choice to depict a violent black male rapist so prominently. Yes, this story is 'shocking,' given the nature of the alleged crime—and the alleged perpetrator's cultural prominence as the top NFL draft pick presents a powerful indictment of toxic masculinity and entitlement within our commercialized athletic culture—but it *does* make me wonder whether there were other reasons why this story made the 'strongest case' to 'mainstream' America about the nature of this 'rape problem.'

"This narrative choice pins the root of the college rape problem on one of the few pathways of upward mobility available to African American men; college athletics and the scholarships they provide to young people, who in return give their bodies and their talent to their institutions, which benefit economically. This economic benefit provides the institution's justification for the 'protection' of these young men, regardless of academic performance or even, clearly, alleged criminal behavior. These policies and practices are *likewise* benefiting the institution, and not necessarily serving this population of athletes, whose education and health are often also disregarded by the same institutions that fail to serve survivors of violence on campus."

Several feminists in the room looked deeply uncomfortable, but much of the audience seemed receptive to and affirming of the connections Adelaide was making.

Adelaide took a deep breath. It seemed like she was about to wrap up her remarks. She said emphatically, "It is my wish that long-overdue discussion about rape, sexual abuse and violation of women not happen at the exclusion of those women most affected, and that it not inspire increased targeting of those long at the receiving end of perceived punitive 'justice' in our society, whether that 'justice' be found in a courtroom with disparate sentencing, in the back of a police car, in the street in broad daylight, in a gated community, or at the hands of any other type of lynch mob 'standing their ground' against the presence of black life in America."

The crowd broke into thunderous applause, many students whistling and rising in their chairs. One student stood up on a chair and yelled "Black

Lives Matter," and the chant was taken up as a booming call and response by most of the audience for what felt like several minutes to Michael, who joined in, albeit quietly. He agreed with the sentiment, but making overt displays of his political inclinations always made him uncomfortable. With the mood of the crowd, it was only the staunchest defenders of (what had been revealed to be) exclusionary white feminism who pointedly abstained, as well as some older community members who seemed somewhat confused. Professor Nkrumah sat quietly, hands folded. Her eyes were crinkled in an unmistakable, but weary, smile.

Professor Thanh returned to the podium, and smiled indulgently as the crowd quieted. She said, "Thank you, Professor Nkrumah, for your incisive critique. You have such a gift for turning moments of tension to growth. It's always my pleasure to have you at the table, and much of the audience seems to agree!"

Part Four

Professor Thanh said, "Next, I am pleased to introduce another expert; this time one from a little closer to home. We are fortunate to have with us today Ms. Lolo Larson, a renowned businesswoman-turned-healer who operates a cutting edge, nationally recognized trauma rehabilitation center in the area.

"Ms. Larson's facility, Lavender House, serves sexually traumatized youth at risk of suicide and homelessness, specializing in care for survivors of sexual violence, former participants in the sex work and pornography industries, as well as LGBT youth. Ms. Larson, thank you for being here today to share your perspective on the impact of the sexual culture on our most vulnerable young people."

Lolo shifted forward in her seat, pursing her bright red lips and pushing her blonde bob behind her ears. "Oh-kay!" she began, her Iowan accent coming through loud and clear. Michael had just recently learned to differentiate between the Minnesotan, Iowan, and Wisconsonite interpretations of the English language, making him eminently more well-liked by his Midwestern colleagues and peers.

"Wow!" Lolo continued, responding directly to Adelaide, "I'm glad you went in on all that, Professor! I'm gonna put on my LinkedIn that I took a class at Blakeley, because you just took me to school!"

The audience laughed. They, like Michael,

were put at ease by Lolo's friendly, even folksy charm.

She continued, "You are a tough bunch to follow! I have to acknowledge, I've seen the film about amateur sex work before. Several of my friends and former colleagues were interviewed for the project and were… somewhat displeased with its depiction of the realities of our lives, I'm sorry to say. Just making my own personal bias clear here!"

Michael thought he saw Ms. Grossman mouth the words, "Aren't we all."

He chuckled slightly under his breath at how palpably the tension between race and gender always seemed to loom in interdepartmental events such as this one. It all seemed so counterintuitive to Michael, since they all seemed to be making perfectly complementary arguments, and since the very nature of the feminist perspective each of these women claimed to espouse was subjective multi-polarity! There was nothing about Charlie's experience or Adelaide's perspective that was inherently in contradiction with Marsha's argument, save that, as Adelaide had said, Marsha was choosing a strategy that didn't seem to take their realities into account, and they were asking not to be excluded. If anything, Marsha seemed somewhat unwilling to expand her reality to make space for the possibility of theirs, which is what they were alleging, after all. Who in this situation had the power to make their perspective prevail? Michael wondered. Where would Lolo take this? What would Miriam say?

"So I'm Lolo!" Lolo continued

effervescently. "How many of you have met a former sex worker before? Show of hands!"

Michael looked to his left and right. Members of the audience were shifting nervously, looking around. No one's hand was raised but Lolo's.

"Well! Aren't you tamer than a Lutheran ladies' luncheon!" Lolo laughed. "Let's try again— How many of you have met a transgender person?"

Michael raised his hand quickly, and nearly the entire audience followed suit.

"My goodness, transBlakeley indeed!" said Lolo. "Well, now that I'm here, you've all met a transgender woman *and* a former sex worker. Come on, don't be shy—say, 'Hi, Lolo!'"

"Hi, Lolo!" echoed much of the audience.

"Hi, Blakeley!" Lolo responded, batting her eyelashes and primping her hair.

"I'd like to tell you a story too," she continued. "I don't tell this story too often these days, but these films, and being here at a school really got me thinking about my experiences as a young person; how I began to have sex, and how I became a sex worker. We've certainly had a long day here, and I know I'm not the last person to speak so I'll be as brief as I can, but I do love to talk, and I do so appreciate how open and welcoming you all have been throughout the day."

Michael could have sworn she gave him a little smile, before she continued, "My story begins back in the late 80s, in a small town in Iowa, where a girly boy who everyone—except my father!—

called Lolo went to high school. As a young person, I didn't realize I was a woman for quite some time, because I had never heard of any boys who grew up to be women, and I'm afraid it was outside the reaches of my imagination that I could ever express myself and be comfortable in my skin as the lovely lady I knew I was even then, at least on some level. I tried to hide the ways I felt different, but that was quite impossible once I discovered my sister's closet and realized that I could fit into her clothes!"

The audience laughed along with Lolo, seeming more and more comfortable as the tensions of the earlier conflict dissipated. She was clearly adept at working a crowd, Michael thought.

Lolo went on, "My father found me sitting in her room one day, while she was out with her friends. I was wearing a darling denim miniskirt and a charming little blouse, and I'm sorry to say he was quite displeased. He tore off the clothes, and he beat me, and he told me that if he ever found me dressed up like a girl again, that I'd be out the door. Wouldn't you know, I was back in her closet before the week was out, and when he found me again, he made good on his promise. He threw me out of the house, and locked the door behind me. It was a cold evening in November, and I was still in Kelly's—my sister's—clothes. I didn't know where to go or who to turn to for help, and so I waited in the bushes until they were all asleep, and I snuck in my window, packed a duffel bag, stole some money, I'm sorry to say, from Kelly and from my mother's purse, and set out on foot. I was 16; it was two weeks before my 17th birthday, and I knew that if I wanted to be myself in this world, I would have to make it on my own."

Again, as during Charlie's story, the audience was quiet, intent.

Lolo said, "I walked to the bus station, and after a long cold night, I got a one-way ticket to the furthest, warmest destination I could afford; San Diego! I saved five dollars—that went a bit further in those days, ya know— to get myself food along the way, and spent the rest on the ticket.

"This is the first past of my story, of how I became homeless as a young trans person. The second part, which follows quite naturally in my story and in the stories of many of those I know, is how I became a sex worker to survive.

"I remain a bit put off by the narrative offered within *Hot Girls Wanted*, which suggested that many or most amateur sex workers do so for attention or to make fast money, because while that certainly is the case for some, especially those who make a choice to go into sex work after weighing other options, most of the young sex workers and amateur sex performers I know found themselves with a very different choice. Often the choice is, perform sex work or sleep on the streets. Perform sex work or starve. Perform sex work because when all else has fallen away, all you have is your body, and it is a pragmatic choice for survival to go into sex work, a choice many sex workers find simultaneously empowering, in the sense of knowing that they can do what it takes to survive, and degrading, in the sense of finding themselves in a situation so desperate that sex work seems like the only option. For some, it is merely an option, and one they choose to take of their own free will, and those people don't deserve our judgment either."

Lolo looked around the room, and smiled warmly at the audience. She continued, "I can see some of you are uncomfortable with the term sex work, and this brings me to a point I like to make about the sex culture. There are many ways of relating to the sex culture, and many of them do not fall under the umbrella of sex work, yet because of our Puritanical, anti-sex culture's shame over sex, almost anything having to do with sex is labeled as 'bad,' and pushed into the shadows, so it can be difficult to make these distinctions.

"There are many forms of sex work, and many reasons why someone would come to engage in it. Some people enjoy it! Some, especially those who consider themselves sex-positive performers and escorts, see it as a way to get paid to do what they like, to rebel against sex-negativity, to express themselves, and, when it comes to porn, to create representations of people like them engaging in pleasurable sexual activity. I don't think there's anything wrong with that. The porn industry has been skewed towards representations of straight white people engaging in acts largely centered around male pleasure, created by male producers for male viewers, and there are a lot of independent queer and female-centered porn production studios doing great work to change these perceptions, and I, for one, am cheering them on! But I'll get into that later... Like Professor Nkrumah mentioned, the media in general is very limited in the sexual content it depicts. Europeans can't believe that we'll show thousands of murders on TV every year, but flash a nipple, and all hell breaks loose!"

Lolo had a gift for putting people at ease over the topics they ordinarily preferred to avoid, thought Michael, as he found even himself smiling at her light banter over such heavy and shame-laden themes.

She continued, "This also means that the lives and sexualities of queer folks haven't been depicted in the media until very recently, and puts everything related to queerness, queer life and queer love into this sexual shadow along with everything from burlesque to human trafficking. It creates an umbrella of unmentionables, and makes everything that has to do with sex bad, whether we're talking about Janet Jackson's nipple, American Apparel models, trans equality, or child sex slaves. Let me tell you, there's not a lotta overlap!

"What all this *does* have in common is that it has to do with sex, and that the people who find themselves associated with this stigmatized sexual culture, whether that's just by dressing in a revealing manner, by being part of a sexual subculture, or by having sex for money, become stigmatized themselves, undeserving of protection and support—unless it's the kind of condescending support of saying, 'we won't listen to a single thing you say, but will try to outlaw your industry because we don't want it—or you—to exist,."

Lolo had drifted on a bit of an aside, railing

against recent celebrity feminist comments about criminalizing sex work. She took a breath, and continued, looking out into the audience, "Do any of you know how many trans women are raped every day? How many strippers and sex workers? I don't know. Nobody knows. The best numbers we have suggest that many, if not most, of these populations experience sexual harassment, sexual assault, and rape on an ongoing basis. And I'm here to tell you that it's not a secret, and that very few people care because of what our culture says about people who are 'sexually immoral.' Being associated with the sexual culture in any way makes you 'unrapeable,' because who gets believed and supported as rape survivors are the people who 'didn't deserve' for it to happen to them—but the people many sexual predators target are the people associated with the sexual culture for this exact reason; nobody would believe them, or nobody would care. So when these people are raped, they just try to keep on living their lives—if they can, making sense of it as best they can. I'm glad you folks are talking about rape, but please don't forget those who don't tell their story, who don't ask for help, because they don't think anyone gives a damn."

Lolo had become gravely serious for a moment, and much of the audience seemed deeply affected by her words. She carried on, her tone light and conversational again, saying, "Anyway, I found myself entering the culture of sex work when I arrived in San Diego. The first thing I did when I arrived was to change into some of Kelly's clothes and put on some makeup. Believe it or not, I felt happier than I'd felt in my whole life, to be dressed as a girl, out in California, on my own. Finally, I was the blonde bombshell I'd imagined myself to be, and nobody knew me, the old me, to say any different!

"I walked around the streets, getting to know the city, sleeping in parks, avoiding the police who I worried would have their eyes out for an underage runaway. There were lots of us, thousands of homeless people, and I got to know the lay of the land by talking to some who seemed friendly. They all had a lot to say. I couldn't stay in a shelter because I was under 18 and I didn't want to be reported to child protective services, and the trans women I talked to all had terrible stories of how they'd been treated in the male shelter dormitories they were housed in.

"The trans women had their own network, and I worked my way into it and was taken under the wing of some of the older girls. They supported themselves, buying food and clothes and the hormones and drugs they used to enable their transitions and self-medicate by performing sex work for the upstanding gentlemen of San Diego. I was young, and could nearly pass as a girl, and men would approach me, but the older girls were protective, and would shoo them off, saying I was just a child. For a while, they took care of me, feeding me and giving me a safe place to sleep near them. We'd all look out for each other, keep track of each other; keep an eye out for trouble. I felt bad, taking their food, their money that they'd sold themselves to earn, being a burden on the group—especially when some of them had started doing the work when they were younger than me—and one day I decided I would start to do it too. I wanted to be able to take care of myself, and I was no better than any of them, although I worried they were stronger, braver than I could ever be—but if they could do it, I could. They tried to talk me out of it, but eventually supported my decision, and gave me advice on what to do, how to talk to clients, how to stay safe. Of course, a lot of it I'd picked up from watching them, from hearing their stories. I'll always remember my first client; because it was also the first time I had sex. Once I'd done it, it seemed like I was in a different world. I knew I could survive on my own, if I was willing to do what it took. Of course, I thought about other jobs I could find, but who would hire me as an underage pre-transition woman?"

Michael felt deeply sobered. He really liked Lolo, and it affected him to hear how difficult her life had been, to think about what he had been going though at that age, and how she must have developed her dark sense of humor, as well as her faith and optimism in order to survive.

Lolo said, "I buckled down, and set myself to earning enough money to complete my transition so I could get a 'real job' and get off the streets. It took four years, especially since there are a lot of setbacks on the street, and during that time, I met some of the most courageous, funny, creative, and hard-working women I've ever known. I have so much respect for the people I lived and worked beside during that time, the other sex workers of San Diego, and for their bravery, tenacity, and love for each other. I had been so sheltered in Iowa, and I learned so much about the world just by listening to their stories, to where they had come from, how they had found themselves on the streets, and how they had decided to engage in sex work.

"I got off the street, once I could pass as a woman, and with the help of a local agency, found a job as a receptionist. Not all of my street family were so lucky, and I think I have to give a lot of the credit to my middle-class background and the color of my skin for getting me out of that situation, as well as my own hard work and the support of a very dear social worker. I will always be thankful that I could imagine a pathway out of that life, as around the time I got off the streets, my best friend, Cherise, was attacked and raped by a client. She couldn't imagine continuing to do the work after that, and couldn't imagine a pathway out, and she—she killed herself. That was the only other option she could see for an undocumented Latina trans woman who couldn't do sex work anymore."

Lolo was getting emotional, Michael noticed, as were many members of the crowd; indeed, he felt a lump in his own throat.

Lolo continued, speaking powerfully, "I got out. Cherise died. I've done my best to stay in touch over the years with people I knew from those days. Some of them got out too. Some shifted into working in pornography. Others are in prison. Others died... of AIDS, of hate crimes, of addiction, or at their own hands. Some of them are still working the streets today. I wouldn't judge a single one of them for any of the choices they've made, because heaven knows they've thought about every single one, and made their peace with it somehow. I respect each and every one of them.

"These are the stories that I carry with me every day, the stories that motivate me to do the work I do to help young people heal from the sexual trauma they've experienced, because I don't want any young person who finds themselves in that life to feel like they have no pathway out, to feel that what has happened to them, what they've done, makes them any less worthy of love, support, and happiness!"

At this, the audience broke into a spontaneous round of applause. Lolo looked a little taken aback, then pleased. Many people were clearly moved, even crying. It had been an extremely emotionally cathartic day, thought Michael.

Lolo continued, "The *Hot Girls Wanted* movie depicted a typical media narrative of exploitation, of unwitting young people coerced into doing things naively. I am here today to tell you that most sex workers enter into the work of their own volition, under their own assessment of the situation, having been disenfranchised by our society enough to perceive few or no other options for survival—not at the hands of some pimp, some manager, some producer, some big bad exploiter!—but out of an awareness that society has left them to fall through the cracks. This is why I am such an advocate for the decriminalization of sex work, because criminalization does not protect the vulnerable from being exploited, it merely pushes the entire sex work industry into the shadow, and channels money into an unregulated system, just like the war on drugs."

Many audience members snapped in agreement.

Lolo said, "My friends in the professional pornography industry would want me to point out that the type of amateur sex work depicted in the documentary is far from the industry standard, and these practices are criticized as unethical within the industry as well. Ethical sex work—which I believe is possible!—must be transparent, regulated, and not coercive. Amateur porn, which has really taken off with the accessibility of digital content, avoids these industry standards and regulations to produce dirt-cheap content that they can put up on free online sites, and treats its performers as disposable amateurs to use and pass over. The dreams these young women had in the film, of becoming 'porn stars,' is only possible within a regulated professionalized porn industry—which does exist!

"It just means paying for your porn, if you want it to meet certain ethical standards and to support the work of the performers, not to exploit them and their labor. Maybe we can start a hashtag—#payforporn! How about it, Blakeley? I know we all want to save money, but if someone is doing the service of taking off their clothes and performing kinky things and you'd like to partake, may I suggest that this isn't the place to cut a few dollars from your budget? Uffda! Think of it like a business—if you're the customer, and you're not paying anything, how are the performers likely being treated and compensated? Are they valued, or disposable?

"You can do your own research, on ethical porn, in which performers are fairly paid, can choose safer sex practices, and have some creative control in the content they are creating. Learn more about the standards in the industry, and go from there. Just know that getting off doesn't need to be unethical, or exploitative, and that there are ways to feel good about feeling good, if you know what I mean!"

People, including Michael, were laughing, but he, for one, knew he'd look into this next time he felt like watching porn. He was relieved to hear from someone with more moral expertise on the topic that porn wasn't *necessarily* unethical. He had felt guilty about his viewing, after all, but hadn't yet committed to swearing it off entirely.

Lolo said, "That brings me all the way round to what I do these days, and why I was asked to be on this panel, I'm sure! Short story is, I run a clinic out of Cedar Rapids. Long story is, I set up a social enterprise called the Cherise Lavender LaPaz and Ricky Anderson Memorial Healing House, or Lavender House for short, with my dear friend Richard Anderson, a professor of business and social entrepreneurship up at the University of Iowa over in that neck of the woods. Richard lost a loved one to suicide too; his son, Ricky, who took his life 14 years ago at the age of thirteen after being bullied and harassed about his gender identity and sexuality at the middle school he attended. It was a strange twist of fate, how I met Richard; I had been working as a receptionist for nearly ten years and was doing a lot of volunteer work to support the homeless LGBT and sex worker populations of San Diego, trying to be there for them like my social worker had been there for me, but it took a lot out of me, especially to do it on the side, as my passion while focusing on my full-time job as well. I was really starting to think about my mission and purpose in life, dontcha know? I had found my faith again, and had really started asking what God's plan was for me, why I had faced the things I'd faced, seen the things I'd seen, lived through what I'd lived through. I was nearly 30; that's when you really start to think about those things. When you're a young person, in school, or, in my case, as you're giving handies off Crescent Avenue, you ask yourself, who am I and what in the blazes am I going to do with my life?! And then, after a few years you start to really look for the next layer, for the underlying purpose. Although it sure seems kids are smarter these days because it seems like that's what you're doing here at Blakeley! Maybe it's the Internet... It's what we try to do at our clinic too, to ask the deeper questions, the questions that enable people to move on with their lives after experiencing trauma, after experiencing things that make you want to end it all, how do you keep going? What's the next part of the story?"

Lolo looked down at her notes, and said,

"I'm sorry, what a little tangent I went on! I met Richard about that time, in 2002, after my father died, not long after his son Ricky had passed. I went to Iowa for my father's funeral. It was tough—you remember, we had difficulties—but I loved him, even if we weren't ever close as adults. I met Richard at a local support group for the bereaved that I dropped in on after the funeral. He'd been going on and off since his son's passing, and we got to talking about how I had felt kind of like his son must have felt as a queer little boy in rural Iowa; that what had happened to me, to Ricky, to Cherise wasn't right, but that it was such a blessing that I had survived, that I had made it out and through.

"I told him about the work I'd been doing with the homeless and queer people in San Diego, that I had a lot of ideas about how people could heal if they really decided to, made a space for it, and had the resources and, if possible, the support of their families. Richard had been volunteering too, with PFLAG, with the Trevor Project, and as a business professor and social entrepreneur, he had a lot of ideas too, about connecting kids who felt isolated to each other and to places where they could get help, so they didn't end up on the street, so they didn't feel so hopeless.

"That put a real bee in my bonnet, and when I got back to San Diego, I couldn't stop thinking about all of those kids in the middle of the country with no one to turn to for help, just some idea that somehow, someday, it will get better. How? If they leave their families, their communities and all they've ever known behind? If they stop being themselves? If they manage to survive? And what then? They're traumatized for life! Trying to accumulate enough resources, enough stability and affection around them to hide their insecurity about being rejected, about never being good enough, about not growing up to be what society told them to be."

Michael thought about how much one's identity could shape one's experiences, about how, as a Taiwanese American immigrant, he could certainly relate to feeling like an outsider, feeling restricted by other people's perceptions and stereotypes about 'people like him,' but his experiences had held such a different tone than the stories of the women he had heard today, such a different context from the experiences of LGBT people, and even from other people of color, such as Adelaide or Charlie. Yet they could all relate to feeling 'othered,' feeling like there was something wrong with them, something somehow lacking, something that limited their ability to be fully seen. What linked all their experiences was the perpetuity of the construct Adelaide had so damningly critiqued, rather than any tangible similarity between any of them. He would definitely have to audit one of Adelaide's classes, Michael decided.

Lolo continued, "I heard about this grant through the grapevine in the social services center I was volunteering at, about grants from the National Gay and Lesbian Task Force to support rural populations, LGBT youth, mental health, and sexual health—and didn't I have a wild idea that fit the whole bunch! In a way, it all just came to me. I saw the kind of clinic we could set up in Cedar Rapids, as a satellite facility for the entire region. Young people and families who found us online or were referred to us after a suicide attempt, as well as sex workers deciding to leave the industry, or homeless youth could come to stay at the residential facility, stay there until they were ready for the next phase of their life, and have a safe space away from the environment that had triggered their suicide attempt or current instability to come to terms with who they were, what they wanted from life, what had led them to attempt to take their life, and how they could imagine a happy and fulfilling life for themselves! I called Richard, and he helped me apply for the grant—which we won!—and put together a whole business plan, a budget, and all that jazz.

"It began as a nonprofit, supported by local and crowdsourced fundraising and the national grant, and things were good! Well, I mean, it was difficult, but it was successful, and I loved doing it. We found clients immediately. There was a real need, since no one else in the whole region was doing that work, and people—parents, and youth—in that situation are desperate for anyone who can help. Since we were funded, we could help even clients who couldn't afford to pay us anything, which was real important for me in serving former sex workers, homeless people, and LGBT youth populations; people who don't have a whole lotta resources. That's why they need support in the first place, even if their parents have come round now, dontcha know!"

Professor Thanh caught Lolo's eye and pointed to her watch. She had been speaking for quite some time, Michael thought, even though no one seemed to mind. Lolo sped up the pace of her speech, saying, "After the grant ran out, we were in a bit of a pickle. It took too much time and energy to focus on fundraising, when we wanted all our energy to go towards the mission, and we really didn't want to go down the river of exploiting our clients—making 'disaster porn,' as you called it, Professor!—about the kids' sad stories and all that, boo hoo, give us $5."

Some people laughed, but many, who were supporters of more conventional charity efforts, looked uncomfortable.

Lolo said, "Richard heard about this fellowship called Echoing Green that supports social entrepreneurs tackling cultural problems with innovative solutions, and he helped me apply as the founder of our program to be in the fellowship for two years, to get paid and get all the support I'd need to take it to the next level. Richard's got a full time job over at the university, the center is more of a side passion for him and he doesn't need to get paid or anything, he's doing all right, so he didn't apply, even though we're co-founders, really. Wouldn't you know, we won! He's a real smart guy, Richard—and I have a knack for knowing what people need to heal.

"The idea we came up with was to make our clinic into a social enterprise, what's called a

'L3C' for all you business geeks out there; something that funded itself and was internally sustainable so we wouldn't have to orient our work around our funders as seems to be the case in so much of this 'save-the-world' work, including the documentary world it seems, so we could be true to our mission and not have to orient around what people wanted to hear, what would make our funders happy.

"We split the clinic into two branches: one, a for-profit rehab facility for LGBT youth and young former sex workers who have attempted suicide and whose families are willing and able to pay for a residential rehabilitation program; the other, a no-strings-attached drop-in program for young people who are not supported by their families. You'll notice I keep switching between LGBT youth, former sex workers, homeless youth, and survivors of attempted suicide, and this might be a little confusing, but all of these categories tend to overlap and blur within our client base under the category of 'traumatized and vulnerable youth' and since we're running our own ship, we get to define who our target population is, and that's anyone whose needs are suited to what we can offer! Each client is unique, and we can usually tell if they're a good fit. The main distinction is family support, and resources, and those who can pay, usually are happy to, and those who can't stay without a fee. The programs balance each other out budget wise if you add in the donations we still get from people who have heard of us and want to support our mission.

"Things have really taken off since we got the fellowship; Echoing Green, and we currently house and serve approximately eighty clients at any given time, with a much larger pool of program alumni who we follow up with regularly. We have great social workers, and counselors who have joined on to the team over the years, and it's turned into a real family, and I won't brag about it here, but you just need to Google 'Lavender House' and you can learn about the kinds of success we're finding at arguably treating complex PTSD—or at least reducing symptoms to the point that the person afflicted can live a happy, healthy, post-trauma life."

Professor Thanh looked at her watch again pointedly, clearing her throat. Lolo's allotted twenty minutes had passed; it was nearly six and Miriam hadn't yet spoken!

Lolo wrapped up, "I've certainly taken up enough of your time, jawing away up here! It's really been such an honor to come join you for this Symposium today, Blakeley, and to share my experience and my passion with you today. I think we'll have some time for questions, otherwise feel free to come say hi if you'd like to know about resources or anything else! Thank you, dolls!"

Lolo ended, waving with both hands, beaming at the crowd, which applauded enthusiastically.

* * * * *

Professor Thanh returned to her mic, thanking Lolo, introducing 'the illustrious Dr. Lenard' all in a blur, and finally it was Miriam's turn to speak. Michael felt a bit nauseous. He was sure she knew what to say, how to make sense of all this, but it was beyond the reaches of his own imaginary, and so he worried; not for her, but for himself, for what he was about to hear.

"Consent is never – and can never be—carte blanche," she began. "Consent can be given under neither duress nor coercion. We all feel sick at the amount of coercion, and duress, that has been attached to sexual intimacy within these films we have seen today; and indeed, within our culture. These *misinterpretations*, shall we say, have reduced intimacy to a series of nonconsensual sexual acts. We see today, finally, perhaps for the first time for many of us, what a rape culture is and how it operates.

"A rape culture is a culture in which there is such an imbalance of power distribution that it is possible for a privileged subset of the population to violate another subset with what appears to be legal and social impunity. We must accept that this is the society we currently live in; indeed, we have heard and seen so much suffering today that how can any of us deny it?

"We tell ourselves that this is wrong; that now we will be less apt to blame the victim; that we will recognize when this manifests in our own life, whether it be to a friend, a family member, or ourselves. But we are each ourselves powerless to stop this epidemic, powerless to help any of the girls, the young women we saw on this screen today, or the one in six boys who are a victim of sexual abuse, or the millions of people—young and old—trapped within abusive relationships., or the victims of ideologically-motivated sexual violence.

Miriam continued, "When looking at such an ethical Gordian knot—a seemingly unsolvable problem—we look to causality, and we look to impact. The causality, the first film asserts, is a hyper-sexualized and violent media culture, and the ready access to extreme and graphic sexual material online for our society's young people, for our children, boys and girls—and anyone else. This content, as my colleague has pointed out, is informed by legacies of centuries, millennia of exploitation and dehumanization of women, of people of color, of any dispossessed other in a 'winner take all' system. The source of this content, we learned from the second film, is a second layer of exploitation and sexual violence, transpiring under the illusion of consent.

"The illusion presented in this second film, *Hot Girls Wanted,* that an 18-year-old girl with little sexual education or experience, under financial pressure, and with limited perception of other available options to support herself and gain independence can sign a paper, a contract to engage in agreed-upon sex acts carte blanche is, to me, the major premise of the rape culture. It is a fundamental misinterpretation of the idea of a contract, and is, indeed, the *misinterpretation* that has allowed so many violations to proceed unchecked in our society.

"We can see a contract as an agreement entered into by two actors under neither duress nor coercion. But what does that mean, ethically speaking? How can we practice sexual ethics in a society with an unethical distribution of power? It can never be ethical to use one's power to coerce another to agree to something they would otherwise have never consented to, to create a contract that does not take both parties' interests into account, which one party upholds at the other's expense, and which one party perceives as impossible or disadvantageous to opt out of or even to question.

"We see the *misinterpretation* of consent that has pervaded our society and been the source, the justification of breaches of ethicality that have endured for decades, centuries, millennia in these films. We see the objectification of the other in the eyes of producers and directors who hunt for interchangeable young bodies to populate their screens. We see the imbalance of power through the eyes of young girls who have never been told they are valuable, and have never been offered $5000 before in their lives. Girls who have been taught to believe that sex is bad and not for them to enjoy, but rather for them to tolerate at the hands of a male for his pleasure. We see duress and coercion leading to these girls being recruited, selected, and brought out to Miami without knowing what they are going to be 'asked' to do. And finally, we see the impossibility of ethical consent under these circumstances when the girls sign on the dotted line to get their money and are pressured to engage in acts that many of them find distasteful and unpleasant under the auspices that they have already furnished consent.

"'I didn't know if I could say no,' is the line that reverberates in my head. This is consent in a rape culture. I didn't know if I could say no. This is the crux of the rape culture, that actors, adult agents are engaging in sexual activity with such a fundamental misunderstanding of consent, that often, the partner who has less power, less agency, less sense of their own personal value has gotten such extreme and mixed messages from our society that they don't know if it is possible, advantageous, or dangerous to dissent.

"Consent and dissent. Power and coercion. These are the ethical forces at play when we see value-neutral actors engaging in the sexual culture. Children watching porn, sexualizing the dynamics they see, learning how to treat a partner. Producers and directors creating what the market wants. *Hot Girls* and *Sexy Babies* acting out these dynamics whether on screen or in privacy with sexual partners without perceiving any alternative. The sex work industry, where those who have money exchange it with those who seek it to perform the same acts. And finally, *The Hunting Ground* that these dynamics have turned our colleges and universities into.

"Our schools. The places where young people are handed the tools of our society and asked to create their own. To see the reality that our young people exist within, are socialized within is an indictment of us all. An indictment of our sexual education system, of our own silences, and of the discomfort many of us share around the topic of sex; legacies of past generations of shame and sex-negativity.

"But we must acknowledge it now. If we take nothing else from these films, from this Symposium, let us now acknowledge that we live in a society with long historical roots and an imbalance of power that has robbed not only women, but also people of color and sexual minorities of the ability to consent for millennia. A culture in which their sexual, emotional, and physical labor was taken nonconsensually every day for hundreds, and thousands of years. Although many of us are perhaps apprehending what this means, and the trauma this violation imbues for the first time today, it is nothing new. If you find it morally, ethically abhorrent, I am glad you are learning of it today, because we need more people who are willing to make the ethical choice to step free of those dynamics, to choose that they no longer wish to benefit from them and to let them permeate unchecked.

"As my colleagues have alluded to, these are the same power imbalances, the same deals with the devil, that lead undocumented immigrants and migrant workers to risk their lives and face almost certain assault to find work here. The same patterns that have violated the treaties formed under duress and broken with impunity between our federal government and the indigenous sovereign nations of this land. The same patterns that have defined white American personhood and liberty at the expense of the black and brown bodies nonconsensually sacrificed; enslaved, raped, and imprisoned for its benefit to this day. The foreign policies that have allowed us to subvert the economic and cultural autonomy of sovereign nations abroad to serve our own.

"This is hegemony, the understanding that society is set up to benefit the few at the expense of the many, and that the perspectives of those not at the center are to be controlled and coerced into the technicality of consent, if only to take away their— our—ability to dissent, to offer another narrative, to say, as so many brave young people did in these films, that what happened was *not* ok, that it was *violent*, that it was *coercive*, that it was *rape*.

"The only choice we can make as actors striving for ethicality in a rape culture is to each strive for consent every day. Not merely to end rape, although this is a noble aim, since there will always be exploitation and we do not wish to silence those who have experienced rape from coming forward and seeking the help and support they deserve, but to each practice consent a little more each day. Thank you."

People throughout the auditorium were nodding, snapping in agreement with Miriam's final points, and as she finished, the crowd, and the rest of the panel, broke into applause.

"Thank you, Professor Lenard!" said Professor Thanh. "Unfortunately we're already over time, so we won't be able to have a Q&A today, but I encourage you to linger for a few minutes if you'd like to connect with any of the panelists. Thank you to all of you for spending your Saturday engaged in critical dialogue around the issue of sexual violence! On behalf of the Feminist Studies, the Black Studies, and the Philosophy Departments, I bid you to go forth, practice consent, and never stop asking questions!"

Another round of applause, and the audience began to dissipate. Michael sat for a moment, digesting what Miriam had said. She was so brilliant... she was probably the most brilliant person he had ever met... would ever meet. He felt so fortunate to be taken under her wing, to have the opportunity to work with her. He was glad he had come to the Symposium, too—Miriam's monologue had resolved so many of his lingering inner conflicts after the other speakers, and he was already thinking about how he would redraft his abstract to incorporate the new insights he had into desire, power, mutuality and reciprocity.

Part Five

Michael looked around, and saw the event staff cleaning up. He went to check in with one of them, and was asked to help pack up the wires and mics. He set himself to coiling up the wires, placing them in small plastic tubs. The audiovisual tech had needed to leave at five, so Michael would need to bring the equipment back to the Phil department for safekeeping over the rest of the weekend.

He looked up and saw that most of the audience had left, save a couple small clusters of students gathered around the two remaining counselors and Lolo. Professor Thanh, Professor Nkrumah, and Charlie were also deep in conversation with a few other student activists Michael recognized, and Miriam... Miriam was still seated at the table, chatting with Marsha Grossman, Michael noted with some surprise. Should he interrupt? Miriam had the key to the department; he still didn't have his own copy. He looked around, ensuring everything else in the auditorium was in place—the event staff had all left.

Michael approached the table, and both Miriam and Marsha looked up.

"Is everything alright, Michael?" asked Miriam.

"Yes, I'm just finishing up and I wondered if I could grab the department key from you to put the A/V equipment in the office. The tech asked me to hang onto it over the weekend." He added, quickly, "I loved what you said... I wondered how you were going to tie all that together."

Miriam gave him a little smile, then checked her watch. "Goodness! It's nearly seven! I left my bag and jacket in my office, I'll walk over with you and let you in."

She turned to Marsha, and said, "Please excuse me! It's been lovely to talk with you some more; you have my card."

Michael nodded at Marsha, then asked, "Everything is ok with your stay? Your hotel, and the flight tomorrow?"

Marsha smiled, "It's just fine. I'm taking the bus over to Peoria and flying out in the morning."

Michael replied, "Well, thank you for coming! It was interesting to have your perspective on the panel."

Marsha chuckled, a little wryly. "Not everyone seemed to think so," she said.

"This is Blakeley!" cut in Miriam, "People can be a bit blunt, but it means they respect your unique perspective, and want to let you know where they're coming from so you can take that into account moving forward. It can be a little hard to get used to, right, Michael?"

"Definitely," said Michael. He remembered when his literature professor had made a diagram of a comment he had made in class his first week at Blakeley. She had mapped out how his remark intersected with colonizing scripts and frames within the literary imaginary, and had told him that they were there to discuss the work, not propagandize.

Michael had been mortified, but when he

stayed after class to apologize, she had applauded him for having the courage to speak in class, and had thanked him for providing a learning moment for the whole group. It was similar to what had happened to Marsha, he thought, and since the learning moment impacted no one more than the person who raised the point, it hadn't been at her expense, even though she might feel somewhat aggrieved for a while, as he had after the lit theory experience.

Miriam and Michael said a brief goodbye to Marsha, Professor Thanh, Adelaide, and Charlie, ensuring that one of the professors would stay until the custodian locked the hall. They collected the equipment, and finally took their leave of the Humanitas building.

"So... what did you think? Things got pretty heated today!" Miriam asked, looking over at Michael as they walked side by side along the lamplit path back to Philosophy Hall, plastic tubs awkwardly in tow.

Michael responded, "I really appreciated how you tied that all together. I think you're right; it all comes down to consent and coercion, and who has the power to consent and coerce. It seems to me like everyone on the panel is advocating for the same thing, really; a system in which consent is possible, which isn't an exclusionary position, of course. I think if all these positions were able to coexist, to strengthen each other in a multipolar framework that didn't pit one issue or lens of analysis over another, that they *could* change the whole culture."

Miriam chuckled, and said, "Ahh, feminists have been paralyzed by that since the days of suffrage and abolition; sometimes it seems with little progress, for all our dialogue... It's frustrating to a degree that approaches absurdity, seeing the clash between gender- and race-based analyses play out over the years."

She paused for a moment, then continued speaking, "What I wish could be clarified is exactly what you pointed out—that these approaches are non-exclusionary, but that it is necessary to frame the dialogue in a way that doesn't preclude resolution, and regardless of whether your aims are cultural, institutional, or social change; if you make your lens about sexual violence, you *must* take into account the historical patterns of sexual violence, particularly with regards to race and colonization, and if lens is gender, it *cannot* prioritize the gender of 'women' over trans* and gender nonconforming people! Either you're talking about rape, or you're talking about gender; with this "Women's Movement Against Sexual Assault," it's like it's 1974, like we haven't had any breakthroughs whatsoever in the past forty years... All this framing of Title IX and institutional access. When you think about all the LGBT kids bullied and pushed out of the school system... Aren't they protected under Title IX? And if you're talking rape, how can you ignore or exclude the most vulnerable, the most susceptible, the most targeted?"

Miriam was impassioned, raising her voice as she spoke. Michael sensed that her personal politics had been a bit ruffled by the days' course. She changed tack, asking Michael, "What did you think of the rest of the Symposium?"

"I... I thought it was very interesting. I learned a lot. It helped me realize a lot of things about myself and the culture... I think I need to rework my abstract," Michael said.

"Do tell!" said Miriam, laughing slightly. She seemed more full of life than Michael had seen her in a while, and he thought about how different today, packed full of discourse and companionship with colleagues and community, must have been from most of her Saturdays.

"Well, at first I felt terrible," Michael said, "It got at the core of what I've been dancing around for years—that desire is not a source of pain and tension because all desires can never be fulfilled or satisfied, but that desire is a source of suffering because of what it leads people to do to each other, to prioritize their own enjoyment and satisfaction over that of another person, and even to turn that person into an objectified other for the purpose of one's own external validation. For privileged actors, for male and masculine actors in a patriarchy—and clearly for white actors within a racial hierarchy—what does that say about desire?"

"You're getting at a link between desire and exploitation... asking whether desire *is* the desire to exploit, to conquer, to oppress, to subjugate..." Miriam responded pensively.

"Especially sexually," continued Michael, "I had been including sexual desire in my analysis, but not... centering it in the way it should be, perhaps, with how... compartmentalized my own view of it has been." He didn't look at Miriam, but he was resolved to share with her the insights he had gleaned, no matter how self-incriminating they might prove to be.

"With my background—and my mother—and my own feminist lens, I suppose maybe it's been almost too centered in my analysis," Miriam laughed, "but I can see how that isn't the case for most people."

Michael continued, "Seeing all these films, and hearing what the panelists had to say about sexual dynamics and the culture, was really different for me... It really made me think about how I learned about sex, about how I've communicated with women, about what they've told me, and what they haven't, and about how I've communicated about sex with other men—communicated with other men about sex! not about sex with men! I'm not gay! I would tell you if I was.. If I were," he concluded hurriedly.

Miriam chuckled slightly, then caught herself and continued to nod in affirmation.

Michael said, "I.. You know, my parents never talked about sex. I can't remember them *ever* talking about sex in a way that acknowledged that people were having it and it was ok; only when it became a problem... If someone was having sex with someone they shouldn't, or had gotten pregnant, or was having sexual troubles, they might talk about it, or to say that my sister and I shouldn't have sex, or hang out with kids who had sex, or that there was too much sex in the culture—

especially American culture. I thought it was cultural, Taiwanese, and that maybe I was repressed—a lot of Americans seemed *too* obsessed with sex, though, and I think today is the first time I've really thought about the American sexual culture, and how it's unique, and how it's affected me."

"Our simultaneous puritanism and hyper-sexuality is a quandary to many cultures, I'm sure," said Miriam.

Michael went on, "But... it has affected me. I've watched that stuff—online porn—since I was twelve, if I'm honest with myself, and it really does shape you... Shapes what you think is normal, what you think sex is, how you think of your partner. I'll tell you—I've only been with one person, my girlfriend in college. She was Taiwanese too, and we both tried to just have a 'normal' sexual relationship. She wanted to make me happy, and I wanted to prove I could do it... could perform, I guess, could be a 'normal' guy. The chemistry was never there, though, and as long as I'm telling you all this, I might as well tell you that I was in love with someone else, in love with her friend—her roommate, actually—Emily. She was American, and I thought about it a lot—about whether it was real love I felt, or whether I just wanted her validation—or if I just wanted to rebel against my parents. They wanted me to settle down with a nice Taiwanese girl, like Astrid. Maybe it was about proving my Americanness, or proving my masculinity. Especially after coming to the US when I was a little kid, and then growing up here, I felt like I wasn't strong enough, big enough, loud enough... confident enough... to be an American man."

"That makes sense," said Miriam, nonjudgmentally, it seemed. She had surely theorized enough about masculinity to not be shocked by what he was saying, thought Michael, although it made him feel quite exposed to think of her understanding him and his personal life in this way.

They had reached the building, and Miriam unlocked the door, balancing her tubs awkwardly in one arm. Michael, arms laden with several tubs himself, tried to help open the door with his foot, but it only seemed to underscore his masculine insecurity, and he took a deep breath and ceased his efforts. Miriam was an adult woman; a professional and a feminist. She could handle opening a door, he thought. She held the door for him and he entered the dimly lit vestibule.

"Go on," Miriam prompted as they continued towards her office.

Michael said, "Well, it seems to me that a lot of the subtext today was about masculinity, as well as consent; rape culture, as we're describing it at least, seems to be a culture of toxic masculinities. And the way the finger was pointed at athletes, at jocks, at entitled, privileged guys—at Alpha males— makes sense, when you think about whose perspective is valued, and who is likely able to exert their will, their desires over another person. Guys who are used to getting what they want."

"Sure, the arbiters of the patriarchy," said

Miriam. She unlocked her own office door, and they entered, setting the tubs in the corner, and looking at each other with some uncertainty.

"Would you like a drink, Michael?" Miriam asked, "It doesn't seem like you've finished your thought, and I could really use a drink—it's been quite the day and I'm not sure I could just go home right now."

Michael had never really been so casually offered 'a drink' in his life. It sounded adult, sophisticated, eternally chic—like something a character on Mad Men would say.

"Ok," he responded, his voice pinched; kicking himself for not being more relaxed, more comfortable. He didn't want her to think he was *un*comfortable socializing with her alone, at night... He hoped they would have many such intimate collegial evenings discussing theories, manuscripts throughout their research together.

Miriam sat down in her desk chair and opened the bottom left drawer, pulling out a bottle of Tanqueray. "James got this for me last spring, so the department could toast my new manuscript, and it hasn't been touched since," she said, a bit wistfully.

James Horton was the chair of the philosophy department, and was an intellectual giant in his own right as the father of Hortonian Systemic Objectivism. Michael had only taken his lecture classes, and seen him at departmental functions, but he knew Miriam had a personal relationship with the man, and it still made Michael feel a little star-struck to hear her reference him so casually.

"Let me go grab some glasses and ice from the department kitchen," Miriam said. She left the office, leaving the door ajar.

* * * * *

Michael paced around the room several times, putting his hands in his pockets, then crossing his arms. Stay calm, he told himself. He could tell her what he'd realized without making it about his crush on her. And she wanted to hear what he thought! He was honored, especially after her incisive commentary on consent.

Miriam returned, holding two glasses, with a plastic bottle pinched under her arm. "We're in luck! There was tonic water in the fridge," she said, flashing him a warm smile and closing the door behind her. She sat in her desk chair, placed the ice-filled tumblers on the corner of her desk. Michael leaned against the desk, several feet from her, striving for casualness. Miriam opened the green bottle, and poured some into each glass.

"So I was thinking about masculinity," he began.

"Of course! Go on," replied Miriam. She added a splash of tonic to both glasses, swirled them around, and handed one to Michael.

He took a drink, bolstering his courage, and continued, "Well, as I said, it seemed like the perception today was that it's Alpha guys committing serial offenses—and that seems to be true. But have you heard of beta-ness, or beta guys?

I don't know if it's just a reddit thing..."

"I'm not sure, what is it?" Miriam asked.

Michael explained, "Well, broadly speaking, it's the guys who aren't king of the hill in a patriarchy, and therefore feel the pressure even more, like I was saying. Guys who are raised in a culture that tells them to be loud, confident, tough, strong; to not show their feelings, and to validate their superiority over women. Guys who identify as 'nice guys,' but resent it; who see that as something to overcompensate for, as a weakness. Guys who complain about being put in the 'friend zone.' There's this whole thing, called pick up artists, or PUA, online, where guys strategize about how to overcome their betaness, how to be more Alpha, and that means..."

"Conquest mentality," finished Miriam, "of course... We have a construct of hegemonic masculinity, but the ones who struggle to claim it are the ones whose claim to it is undermined, or threatened, and these are the ones most likely to adopt aggressive or apathetic means of self-expression and dissent. I think Connolly would concur with you; although, of course, he does have his discontents... You know, feminists are always saying that boys are the ones most affected by patriarchy; in how they're socialized to conceal their feelings and strive for control over their environments."

Michael said, "Well, so if I'm claiming my subjectivity within that—within hegemonic masculinity, and within American masculinity—here I am, I came here from Taiwan, a shy little kid who liked to play video games, whose best friend was a socially awkward tomboy who never left the house, and I felt I could never achieve what people expect of boys here, could never be loud, never be confident enough, never grow into a man like that. So I settled on at least being a good immigrant, striving for the American Dream; working hard, doing well in school, trying to make the most of the opportunities I had here, and I didn't think much of my sexuality."

He continued, "I thought it was *normal*, and I guess that's what I was going for. Like I said, I watched porn, but it seemed like pretty normal stuff—and I thought I had a crush on Lin, back in Taiwan, since we were still so close. She—he—was the only person I was really opening up to. I didn't have anything romantic with the girls at my high school, and I started to feel self-conscious about it, like women, especially American women, wouldn't like me because I wasn't the right kind of guy, wasn't Alpha enough—maybe because I was Asian. After Emily didn't want to be with me in college... that really got in my head, and I started reading a lot of that stuff online, talking with other guys about how to be respected as a man, how to seem 'less Asian,'—I know that's messed up!—how to seem confident around women, and most of all, how to score, how to attain that sexually... And a lot of that stuff, about how to get laid, seems like the same tactics people were talking about in that rape movie, and with what Charlie was talking about; about isolating someone, developing a personal connection with them, minimizing their opportunities to say no, pushing the boundaries, so that even if they think it goes too far or don't want to go that far, they can't technically call it rape—guys are coaching each other in how to do that online, all so they can all feel better about their masculine insecurity, their betaness…"

Miriam sipped her drink, and asked, "How did that make you feel about your relationship with your… friend?"

Michael felt a bitter smile curl the corner of his mouth. "Emily?" he asked, "You know? It made me realize I didn't even want to have sex with her so much as I wanted to be close to her. I was looking for something like I had with Lin, where you tell someone what's going on with you, confide in them, and they do the same to you, and it seemed to me that when you're adults, that means sex, too, being open to someone in that way. Women open up to someone they're sleeping with, and that's what I wanted with Emily. I didn't just want to be her friend, to hang out with her and share stories, to go to things together; I… I think I really loved her. I wanted to know her, and I wanted her to know me, and it felt like she never really saw that as a possibility, and that's what got me, and I thought it must be because I was Asian, because I wasn't the kind of guy she was looking for…"

He took another drink. "But then I started dating Astrid, and we did have sex, but we never had intimacy. I mean, we did, sort of, and I cared about her, and she's a very nice person, but… she never showed herself to me, never opened up, never told me what was really going on with her. She was trying so hard to be a good girlfriend, and so happy to have a boyfriend, that it felt like it was all head games, all about our relationship being what each of us was looking for, that it was never about us being together, and it started to remind me of my parents' relationship, and then I..." he trailed off, unsure about whether to finish his sentence, then deciding he might as well, "I couldn't get it up, and we broke up."

Michael's eyes had been on his brown loafers, and as he finished, he shot a nervous glance over at Miriam. He was sure she had heard worse, although he had never told anyone this story, and had no idea how she would react.

Miriam was shaking her head slightly.

"I apologize if I over-shared," said Michael quickly.

"No, It's not that..." she said, "You're right, what gets lost in all this conversation about the rape culture is what sex is *supposed* to be—what it *can* be. Not just the presence of consent, or even the mutuality of desire. Those are the preconditions, the ingredients—but what are you trying to create? That's what gets lost in an anti-sex culture, in an anti-woman culture, and even in an anti-rape culture! Feminists used to advocate for pleasure, as well as the dismantling of patriarchy, sexual harassment, and rape culture."

Miriam continued, "You know, *I* almost forgot that was what sex was about. It's sad, because when I was young, that's what everyone was talking about, at least in the circles I was in—

about sexual liberation, and the possibilities of human connection, and of pleasure, and intimacy—and somehow, over the last twenty years, in my own life, my own marriage, I've forgotten all of that. You're lucky you recognized that wasn't the type of relationship you were looking for... I thought Linda and I were looking for the same things, and that justified the compromises we both made to be together, and I think prevented me from realizing that the intimacy wasn't there for a long time, even when we were still having sex. Once the sex was gone, I thought that was the problem, and that *that* was what I missed—but if sex is about achieving anything, its about achieving intimacy—creating a shared window of perception, opening to another. Without that, it's just fucking, and if that's what we're talking about, the conversation shifts to whether she wanted to 'let him' do one sex act or another, and that's why the dialogue about the sexual culture has become so much about rape and technicalities of consent, rather than shared pleasure and intimacy... My mother and her friends would be disappointed."

Michael was surprised to hear Miriam curse, and he reflected on how different their frames of reference were, trying to get over his shock over her sex-positive mother.

Miriam continued, "It seems my generation is so intent to pin 'what's wrong with sex' these days on the hook up culture, as though people haven't always been 'hooking up.' It's not that pleasure and intimacy have to take place in some sacrosanct union—some of the most transformative experiences can happen in a fling, or a hook-up, and it's not as though marriage is necessarily intimate..."

"Linda could never understand..." Miriam continued with a bitter little laugh, "will never understand why what we have, what we've had isn't enough for me. And it's not that she's a woman! It really isn't! That's what people will think, but it's not her—it's the life we've built. It's not enough. Oh, that's terrible to say—My daughter is wonderful, she is! And Linda is a good parent, and we have a nice house, and we're both doing so well in our work... but I feel so alone."

It looked as though she were about to cry for an instant. "I've felt so alone for so long, and that isn't what I signed on for. We said we would support each other; that we would create a sanctuary outside of our work together, but for Linda, our home isn't a sanctuary; it's a place to hide! To hide from herself, and especially from me."

She took a drink. "I feel as though we haven't been intimate—and not just sexually—in years. That we haven't had a real conversation, a real connection in years. With her research, and the move, and the breakthrough, and the award; and now, the transition... during all that, I've been on my own. Sure, I stand by her side through it all, but she's doing it on her own; that's how she sees it. She doesn't confide in me, and she doesn't listen to me—for all her brilliance, she doesn't understand what I do enough to know how to support me in it, besides to give me space. If it weren't for Lisa, I wonder if we'd still be together... It's funny how a child can make it all seem worth it for so long."

Michael nodded. "I can't believe my parents are still together. My sister and I are long out of the house, and they've been making each other miserable for thirty years now. I don't think either one of them knows what's really going on with the other, or even what they *do* want; they both just gossip to their friends about how terrible the other one is. I wonder if it will be like that forever."

Miriam sighed. "It's not that there's any inherent value in staying together forever; the experiences one has in a marriage, no matter how short-lived, can make it worth it—and especially a child. But I wonder—as a mother, should I weigh the potential negative impact of a separation on my child more than the freedom it would give me to take back my life? I've always worried I was too selfish to be a good mother, that it would have a negative effect on her... I suppose I always suspected my own mother was too selfish though, always out saving the world, protesting, boycotting..."

"You can still take care of yourself and be there for another person," said Michael. "It was almost better for me as a child when my mother started working full time, and we weren't together all the time... She did that for herself; she couldn't stand to not work, and my dad appreciated her coming back to help at the business... But I always thought, what if they were free of each other? What if they divorced? Because they both made each other so miserable so much of the time, and it seemed to me that the only time I saw either of them happy, was on their own, away from the other."

"You're right, what kind of feminist have I become?" Miriam responded, "I want Lisa to aspire to more than I have right now—I want her to see that I can be happy and fulfilled and comfortable with myself, just like Linda."

Miriam trailed off, and met Michael's eyes again. "Thank you for telling me all that," she said, "It can't have been easy, and I appreciate that we have the kind of relationship where we can be open and honest with each other. There are some papers I'm going to send you, some literature about non-hegemonic masculinities. I think you'll find it quite interesting, considering the questions you've been asking. You're a brilliant young man, Michael."

Michael's head was spinning now. It sounded like Miriam was planning to leave Linda, and that she might even like... him? He said, "I thought I could tell you, with how open you've been with me. It was nice to get it off my chest. It's nice not to just have to... keep that inside of you. I never thought I'd tell anyone, but it's nice not to feel so alone."

Miriam said, "It reminds me of what you said about intimacy; that beneath all our insecurities, we all desire intimacy, especially in such an isolating culture."

"Certainly," responded Michael, "Even in most relationships, you might spend a lot of time together, but it can just scratch the surface, with no real intimacy, and you wonder if you even know the person, if there's any realness to the relationship."

They continued talking, Michael on his feet, leaning against her desk, half-seated; Miriam in her desk chair, sipping from their tumblers of gin and tonic. Finally at ease with her, Michael's eyes found themselves lingering on Miriam's lips as she spoke, over her fingers as she held the glass, raising it to her lips. With a burst of panic, he felt his penis begin to stiffen. There was no hiding it from this angle; he was standing right in front of her, his growing bulge nearly at her eye height. She must have noticed his face fall flat, his eyes dart from side to side, looking for some escape, some way out... somewhere he could run and hide to avoid ruining this situation. He had told her how much he admired her, what an honor it was to work with her, even hinted at how he had started to develop feelings for her—but getting a boner in her office was a different matter altogether. Should he run to the bathroom? Would she say anything? He tried to discreetly adjust himself from his pocket, but it was painfully obvious with her sitting right in front of him.

Miriam's eyes flicked over his bulge. He watched her carefully, as first her eyebrows raised slightly, then as what appeared to be the hint of a smile curled her lips. She took a drink, averting her eyes. Michael also took a drink. He felt vulnerable, exposed. Miriam sat only feet in front of him, so close... He had hoped his erection would subside, but sitting there in such close proximity to her, it only seemed to be growing harder. Certainly she had noticed… He moved his glass to cover himself, striving for nonchalance, discretion. They hadn't said anything for several moments, and the silence felt like it was buzzing in Michael's head like a swarm of bees. What should he do? What should he say?

Miriam looked up at him. "Do you desire me, Michael?" she asked directly.

"Yes," he stammered quickly, caught off guard by her question.

She looked away, taking another drink. "I'm leaving Linda," she said, "I don't know if that was clear from what I said earlier. It's over. It was over between us a long time ago."

Michael was nonplussed, standing there, awaiting her every word. Did she mean…?

"Would you laugh if I told you I desired you too?" she asked.

Michael felt dizzy. "Laugh? No…"

She continued, looking into her drink, occasionally glancing up at him, "I've been thinking about it, trying to pick out what part of me just wants validation; to be close with a man again, to feel desired, wanted, not just put up with… You remember, Linda and I haven't been together like that in a long time, and it was an even longer time since she wanted to do anything a man might want to do with a woman with me… I'm sorry to beat around the bush. I probably shouldn't be saying anything…"

"Please go on," said Michael earnestly.

She met his eyes, and continued, "It's not just that, though. It's not just that I want to be with a man after so long, because I've thought about that, and a big part of me isn't ready... It's you, Michael. I think you're charming, and you remind me of how much I cared about philosophy, about figuring it all out at your age. I really don't want to make you uncomfortable; given my position, I'm not sure we should even be having this conversation..."

He felt as though he was about to pass out. "We're subjective actors first and researchers second..." Michael began, "I haven't felt close to a woman.. to someone I desired... ever, really... and I don't want to ruin our relationship if that's what I'm looking for; intimacy, a way to be close to you, and not just intellectually... but you're the woman of my dreams, Miriam. This isn't just some crush. I've tried to tell myself it is, but you're what I've been looking for my whole life. I hope this isn't presumptuous, but I don't just see you as my professor, I see you as my colleague, on this quest for knowledge together with me, and I'd like to see you as a friend, to have a personal relationship with you," He fell silent, looking down. It had come out alright, but he was shaken by his nerve.

Miriam scooted forward in her chair until she was right in front of him. She set her tumbler on the desk, and cautiously placed her hand on his forearm reassuringly, looking up into his eyes. "I want to be close to you, Michael."

It was as though there was an unspoken question in her voice, her eyes, and Michael nodded, looking down at her, setting the glass he'd been holding over himself on the desk next to him.

He reached out and stroked her cheek. "I want to be close to you, too," he said, his voice cracking slightly.

Miriam placed her hands against his hips, at the level of his waistband, and Michael sighed. She was touching him! Was she going to... touch him? Should he do anything? Did she want him to make a move? She moved her hands to the front of his pants, fingers trailing over him, and he gasped.

"Do you want me to?" she asked, out loud this time.

Michael nodded again. "Yes, please," he choked out. So maybe she didn't mind being in charge, didn't mind him just standing there.

She unbuttoned his pants, and he could feel the fabric tugging against his erection. He couldn't believe she was about to... He could feel excitement swelling in him already, and he began to breathe in slow measured paces. He didn't want to come prematurely, or worse, while still in his pants... She was so confident, so sexy, and he couldn't believe she was going to touch him... Or maybe she would put him in her mouth... another wave of excitement swept through him. He decided to focus on what was happening and not to let his fantasies take him further than he wanted to go when what was happening was already the stuff of his deepest desires.

Miriam unzipped his khakis, looking up at him again to make sure it was alright as she reached in, through the slit in his boxers, and closed her hand around his hardness.

"Ah!" he gasped.

"Are you sure this is alright with you?" Miriam asked again, her hand resting against him.

"Yes, it's more than alright, please don't worry about it," Michael choked out.

She pulled out his penis to stand erect in front of her face. She held it in her hand, gripping it firmly, and Michael breathed deeply, acclimating himself to the sensations.

"May I?" she asked again, leaning forward, bringing her lips closer to him…

"Yes! Yes, yes, yes," said Michael. He was unsure of what to do with his hands. They rested on either side of him on the desk he was half-seated on.

Miriam closed her eyes, and leaned forward, placing her lips around the head of his penis. His breathing quickened, and he again, tried to calm himself. He, too, closed his eyes for a moment, just feeling her close to him, and it was as though they were within a force field of energy, of desire, of magnetism. It was as though she was bewitching him, pulling him into her, sliding her mouth over him, squeezing him rhythmically.

"Oh, Miriam," he gasped. He looked down. More than half of him was in her mouth now, and she didn't seem nervous anymore, didn't seem self-conscious. She seemed confident, in control.

Her hands held his hips, stimulating him with only her mouth now, and he moved his hands to rest over hers, holding them, intertwining their fingers together. She held his in return, looking up at him for a moment. Their eyes met, and it was as though they were really seeing each other for the first time, looking deeply into the other's eyes, searching, sharing. She took more of him in her mouth, and he threw back his head, letting out a groan.

When he looked back down, her eyes were closed again, and he watched for a moment as she sucked on him, thinking about how much better this was than any video he had watched, any time he had jerked off... This was what he had been looking for, for a moment of unexpected, exposed intimacy, for a woman who knew what she wanted.

Michael closed his eyes again, feeling Miriam's hands in his, her mouth warm and wet around him. He began to slip away in waves of pleasure, groaning slightly as his balls began to tighten. He could tell he was about to orgasm. Should he say something? Was it too much to come in her mouth? Astrid had preferred him to tap her shoulder, then come into a tissue, or his hand... He started to say, "I'm-" but it was too late.

Michael let out a cry and clenched her hands in his as he came, feeling her lips around him; her warmth, her closeness... He hoped she didn't mind. His body pulsed with electricity, trembling as he finished, thankful he was sitting on the edge of the desk for support. He didn't think he had ever had such an intense orgasm, despite years of solo practice.

He was gasping for air, and opened his eyes, looking down to see, to feel Miriam letting go of his hands, withdrawing her mouth from him. She placed her hand over her mouth, laughing slightly, and leaned over to spit into the trashcan, then wiped her mouth with a tissue. She didn't seem upset.

Michael tucked his softening penis back into his boxers and zipped, then buttoned his pants. He broke the silence, saying, "Wow!" They were both laughing slightly at the impropriety, the taboo of what had happened between them.

"Well, that's something I never thought I'd do. Would you like another drink?" Miriam asked.

"Yeah, sounds good," said Michael.

Miriam leaned over, opening the desk drawer and topping off their glasses with the bottle of Tanqueray. She added a splash of tonic, and handed him the glass. Michael was still stunned. He clinked his glass against hers, and took a sip. She did the same.

He felt like he should thank her, but wasn't sure if it would come out right. "Was that ok? For you?" he asked.

"I enjoyed it," she said with a little laugh, "I know it might seem a bit strange, but just to have an experience like that after not feeling wanted, desired for so long was just what I needed."

"Do you... want me to do anything to you?" he asked, wanting to be polite, mature, considerate.

"No! That's quite alright," she said quickly. Michael felt a little rebuffed, even though he hadn't quite known what he wanted to do to her. "It's... it's Linda," she continued, "I know it sounds odd, considering what I just did, but it feels like it would be too much of a betrayal for me to do anything more before I tell her, before I end things."

Michael nodded. God, they were having an affair, he thought. She was married. And she was his boss. How could this sound so wrong, but feel so natural, so comfortable? It was as though they were hanging out now, enjoying each other's company as they sipped their drinks, having found solidarity, understanding in the indiscretion they had just shared. "No, I understand," he said, adding, "Maybe this is crazy, but would you want to get some dinner?"

"Oh…" Miriam paused for a moment, "Dinner might be… too much."

Feeling more confident, Michael replied, "Well, there's a diner around the corner that serves breakfast all day. Do you know wafflebär? It's casual… and it's not technically dinner!"

Miriam laughed, "You know, that sounds all right. I'd like that."

Michael felt a rush of excitement. They were going on a date, it seemed, if even a casual one!

"It's vegan, is that alright with you?" he asked.

"You know, I used to be a vegetarian back in my hippie days," said Miriam.

There was a giddy energy—the electric potential of being seen, understood by another—between them as they gathered their things, locked the office and the building, and walked off campus together.

****

PREVIEW
MILLENNIAL SEX VOLUME 2:
WE'VE NEVER DONE THIS BEFORE

*****

6: QUINN

Respect

Trigger Warning: Power Play, Rape
Fantasy

Part One

Erin looked over at Quinn, smiling coyly. It was a Wednesday in October, and the two were having a mid-morning brunch at wafflebär to celebrate Quinn's 19th birthday. It was also the approximate six-month anniversary of their first meeting last spring, which they used as the informal beginning of their relationship. They had stayed in touch online over the summer, then Quinn had asked her to be his girlfriend, to be only with him, their first week at Blakeley.

"So..." Erin began, "The tickets were the first part of your present, but I told you there was another part... I've been thinking about what you said about your fantasy, about having..." She leaned forward and lowered her voice to a whisper, "anal sex."

Quinn's heart skipped a beat. Just hearing the words come from her mouth, he felt an instant rush of blood begin to stiffen his penis. Why was she bringing this up now? In public? at a diner? "Wha—What were you thinking about it, babe?"

Erin blushed and picked at her waffles. "Well," she continued, "I was thinking about how it's your birthday... and how we've been together for six months... and how I want to do everything with you... and that I want to do it with you. I want to try it."

Quinn's mind flashed to that manhandle.com video that he'd been watching on loop for the last couple weeks, the one where the male actor bent the woman over the couch, and pinned her arm behind her back and held her head down while he pushed himself first into her vagina, then, as she protested and tried to fight him off with her free hand, into her ass. He blinked several times, and thought that he should probably stop watching so much porn... After all, he had a girlfriend now, and the sex was better than he could have imagined, better than it had ever been with Risha, his high school ex back in Portland.

The porn felt addictive; scene after scene, endless variety, endless stimulation, always something new to get him off. It was how he relaxed, how he took study breaks, how he put himself to sleep when Erin wasn't staying over. He acted out some of the scenes with Erin, ones he thought she'd be into, or wouldn't find too extreme.

There were other scenes, though, scenes that pushed him over the edge, that weren't things he could bring up to Erin and wouldn't want to act out with her at all... ways he would never want to hurt her. He imagined Erin, bent over his bed as he took her anal virginity, thinking about how she had looked last night as he fucked her doggy style, hands tied behind her back, how much he had wanted to put it in her ass... and now she wanted to let him fuck her that way. He definitely had an erection, and his hands were beginning to sweat.

"Um... Wow! That's great... I'd love that. Thanks for... thinking about it and telling me. What... When would you want to do it? Today? ....Now?" An image of her, bent over the table flashed through his head.

"Well, not right now! I have my Ecosystems

class in an hour. Maybe tonight? I was thinking... Maybe I could come over after my bio group meeting and stay over tonight, if that's ok with you."

"Ok, babe. I'll finish my paper before so we can... hang out." He swallowed, thinking about the clip again... eyes flicking across the curve of her breasts, the hollow of her neck.

They had finished eating, chatting about their Environmental Justice seminar, Erin's sister's new dog, the Mumford and Sons concert on Friday that she had gotten them tickets for. Over and over in his head, the refrain looped, "Erin wants me to fuck her ass." Fortunately his erection had subsided as they chatted, but it threatened to return as Erin stood up, as he checked out her ass as they walked out the door, as he grazed her with his hand as they kissed goodbye on the sidewalk.

That evening, he waited nervously, wondering if he should jerk off before she came so he could last longer, or whether that might make him unable to perform. He decided not to, but he still opened a browser to analvirgins.tumblr.com and flicked back to it in between paragraphs of his paper, taking in image after image of women, on their knees, bent over, taking cocks in their asses in looped 3-second gifs.

They probably weren't actually anal virgins, he thought, if someone had filmed and uploaded it, but you never knew. Did it matter? It was all in his imagination anyway, what excited him, what got him hard, and had little to do with the actual people in the porn. His mind wandered, thinking about things he might want to do to Erin later that night... until he heard a knock on the door, and hurriedly pressed the close browser tab.

Part Two

"Come in!" Quinn said, willing his erection down, pretending to finish a sentence of his paper. The biodegenerative properties of ethylated mercury... He read over and over, then looked up to see Erin standing in the door.

"Hey!" She came over and gave him a kiss, then sat on the end of his bed.

He smiled at her nervously, and she broke the ice by saying, "So, I... uh, cleaned down there... I Googled it and it turns out that's what a douche is for. It's, like, a real thing. I went to the CVS. It was a really... uh… interesting... experience."

"I'll bet," Quinn laughed. He was relieved that it had been on her mind too, that she had brought it up, that she had prepared, that she still wanted to try it.

They chatted briefly about their day, then a lull fell in the conversation and Quinn said, "I want you to strip for me. Take off everything."

"Ok," Erin said, standing and slowly beginning to remove her clothing as he watched from the chair.

She slipped off her flats, then pulled off the transBlakeley t-shirt she was wearing and unbuttoned and slipped off her jeans. She unclasped her bra, letting it fall to the floor, then dropped her underwear too until she stood there completely naked.

"Lie over the bed. Bend over and spread your legs," Quinn commanded, and Erin followed his instruction, turning around and leaning forward, resting her upper body on the bed.

Quinn looked at her, naked, exposed from across the dorm room and he began to grow hard, feeling his cock, his balls begin to pulse as he saw her lying there, ready to submit to him.

"Spread your ass with your hands," he said and she shivered slightly and complied, exposing herself to him even more. He could see her asshole, tight, clenched, pink, waiting for him.

He strode forward and dropped to his knees behind her. He liked to lick her, to make her come for him, to feel her let go under his tongue, swelling and releasing until she was ready to take him deep and hard. This time, he wanted to eat her ass too, to feel how tight it was, to feel her open up to him. He had been a little squeamish about it, but felt better knowing that she had washed, that he wasn't going to wind up with a mouthful of... better not to think about it...

He reached out with his tongue and stroked her perineum, flicking down over her vagina, hearing her moan softly, then seeing her hands clench as he licked upwards over her ass.

"Ah!" she cried out, and he smiled, and licked again.

He felt her ass twitch as he lowered his lips to meet it, running his tongue around the opening. Erin was gasping, moaning, squirming under his tongue, and he imagined how she would react as he pushed his cock into her. The girls in the videos sometimes screamed, sometimes cried. How much would it hurt Erin? Would she enjoy it?

He wanted her to enjoy it, not to feel like it

was just something she had done because he wanted it... and she often enjoyed when he was rough with her, when he made her scream, even cry... but would there be any pleasure in it for her this way? What if she hated it?

He thought of the clip again, and imagined Erin's face over the girl's; Erin, fighting him off, crying, and felt a pang of sadness. He wouldn't want anyone to make her feel that way, to do that to her... but didn't he want to do that to her? She seemed so vulnerable, so trusting. She believed he wouldn't push her farther than she could take, that this was how he showed how much he cared for her.

Did she ever wish he was more of a normal guy? Quinn wondered. Did she wish that he could not just fuck her, but... make love to her? It sounded stupid, romantic. They were together because they respected each other, because they were attracted to each other, because of the explosive energy between them, not because they wanted some conventional romantic relationship.

Quinn pressed his tongue against her perineum, licking over her vagina, her clitoris as she relaxed slightly, rocking against his tongue. His cock felt stiff, pounding, constricted, against his boxers, and he slipped them down from his hips, letting his erection spring up.

"Mmm," he moaned, sliding his tongue back up over her ass, licking it again and again before pushing the tip of his tongue into her, feeling her constrict against him, then relax a little. He bobbed his chin, sliding incrementally further inside as

Erin's gasps and moans intensified.

"Oh my god," she cried, spreading her legs further, and he decided to try penetration. He slowly withdrew his tongue, feeling her pressing around him, a metallic, earthy taste in his mouth.

He stood up, tracing his fingers over her thighs and between her legs. He picked up the little bottle of lube from the end of his bed and squeezed some out onto his fingertips. Erin trembled in front of him, still holding her ass with both hands, spreading it for him as he worked the lube between his forefinger and thumb to warm it, then spread it slowly, deliberately over her asshole, pushing his finger in slightly as she let out a moan. It seemed like she had enjoyed this so far, but how would she feel about having his cock back there? This was where an actor in the porn he liked would grab her hips, or better, her wrists, or her hair, and would shove his cock inside her, rough fucking her over her cries of pain, but he wasn't sure that's what he wanted anymore. Maybe his fantasy had shifted from the one he had shared with her a couple weeks ago, now that she wanted to do it with him...

Erin lay before him, her legs spread, her eyes closed. He placed one hand on her mid-back, partially to comfort her, partially to hold her down, and rubbed the rest of the lube over his cock. Since they had become monogamous, they had decided to be fluid sharing, that is, to not use condoms, since Erin took the pill anyway, and he was excited by the thought of pushing his naked cock into her, feeling her hot against him. He was swollen and ready to fuck her.

Quinn inhaled sharply and moved his hips so that the head of his cock was held against her ass. Erin let out a soft whimpering sound, and as he shifted his weight and began to lean forward, pressing into her, she said in a panicked tone, "Orange!"

Quinn exhaled and pulled back, removing the pressure against her.

"What's up, babe? How are you doing?" he asked.

Erin stayed bent over the bed, not looking at him, and said in a small voice, "Quinn, what if it hurts too much? What if I can't do it like you want?"

Quinn looked at her, lying there, face down. He took another deep breath and said, "Sit up. Talk to me."

Erin gingerly pushed herself up and turned around, sitting on the edge of the bed. Quinn sat next to her and stroked her hair, saying, "You don't have to do anything you don't want to, babe, and we don't have to... do it like that, like I described it... I'll... be gentle... If you still want to try. Maybe if you like it this way, we can try it that way next time."

Erin sighed, "I don't want to ruin it for you. I just... You don't want to rape me, do you?"

Quinn froze, a chill running through him. This was his worst fear, that Erin thought the sexual things they had done had been fucked up, coercive and violent. He didn't say anything, and she continued.

"I went to that symposium my professor

had, the one I got the extra credit for, about the rape culture... And they talked about porn, about how it sexualizes more and more extreme violence against women. And then guys watch it from a young age and become desensitized, and sexualize violence and a lot of them end up... raping girls they know, or girls they're dating, and thinking it's normal because of the extreme media they've been exposed to and the lack of sex ed. And it happens a lot in college. And watching that, all those movies, just made me feel kind of scared. Because some of that stuff is stuff we do, stuff you like to watch. And I trust you, and you make me feel safe, and you respect my boundaries, and I don't think it's like that between us. I just wonder if there's something wrong with me, that I'm a bad feminist or a bad woman or something because I like it and because I think it's sexy. I'm sorry to bring this up now... I've just been freaked out since I went to that thing over the weekend, and I haven't been sure how to tell you. I didn't want you to think I was saying... I don't know. I really do want to try it, I just feel kind of weird."

Quinn's stomach sank a little. Was he disappointed? No, he hadn't really even wanted to do it hard this time, and more than that, maybe there was something unhealthy between them if she'd been afraid to bring that up and had then let him do what he had done the night before, to suggest they do what they were about to do. But she was telling him now, and she had thought about it, and she wasn't upset about what he had done, necessarily, just weirded out by what it said about her as a feminist. That was why they had had the safe words from the start, why he had always stopped the moment she used one, or seemed to be signaling one to him. They always talked about what they had done, and she was always smiling, no matter how far it had gone, always laughing about what an intense an orgasm she had had, how excited she had felt, how much the pain, the fear had heightened her senses. Was that weird? Probably. He wanted to be inside her; his cock was aching, softening slightly.

"No... no, babe. I'm glad you said something. I don't want you to do something you don't want to just because you think it would make me happy. We have to be honest to be able to trust each other. I wish you'd told me about all that earlier, before we tried that bondage yesterday. I hope you don't feel afraid of me. I can always stop, you know? I'm always more than willing to stop if you want to. I don't even mind. I'd rather you say something, if you don't like it or want something different. Movies like that are talking about people getting exploited, or doing things they don't want to do but are forced to. And that although some of the stuff we like seems like that, seems like... rape, or like role-play or whatever, the fact that we both want it means that it's not, and it's ok for you to want what you want. It doesn't make you a bad woman, or a bad feminist.

"Maybe I'm fucked up for being a guy and sexualizing that. I've been feeling bad about the stuff I watch lately, not knowing if those women are actually being hurt or acting, you know. Who they are. Part of me worries that it's my fault for sexualizing that, for internalizing it, and for making you do that with me, making you do something you didn't want to do because you liked me."

"Quinn, I chose to hook up with you. I wanted to hook up with somebody, and I liked you the moment we met. And I thought you were really sexy, especially after you fucked me. And I thought about you all summer, and touched myself thinking about you holding me down and... doing what you did. And when I got to campus, I knew I wanted to be with you. So please don't apologize. You taught me how to do things I didn't think I could be comfortable with, and that's why I'm with you now. And why I really do want to try this with you. If you're not too uncomfortable now."

Quinn replied, "I'd... I'd still like to try it if you'd like to, but we don't have to act out anything, or do it hard or anything. I just want to be close with you, to do this with you."

Seeing her sitting there at his side, anxious, self-conscious, a sudden burst of emotion ran through him and he felt protective, affectionate, towards her.

Impulsively he blurted, "I love you, Erin."

She did a double take and stammered, "What?"

"I... I love you. I really care about you, and I'm so glad we met, and have been together these last few months, and I wanted you to know.. And I don't want to hurt you... unless you want me to."

Erin was taken aback, then responded

quietly, "I love you too, Quinn."

"Well, that's... good. Glad we both feel that way," Quinn said, leaning forward to kiss her, pulling her against him.

The two kissed, slowly, intimately, falling back onto the bed, and Quinn rolled on top of Erin. She spread her legs as they kissed, chests pressed together, held in each other's arms. They began to grind together with a slow burning heat, and Quinn reached down to press his finger against her lubricated ass.

She moaned as he traced it again, then slipped his finger inside, fingering her slowly as she wrapped her legs around him. She was pulling him in this time, not fighting him off, and he felt magnetically drawn to her, pushing his finger deeper into her. She relaxed, and he slowly began to push in a second finger as her moans rose in pitch.

"I want... to try it..." she gasped.

Quinn sat up briefly and squeezed out some more lube into his hand, rubbing it over his cock, then over her entrance again before settling against her, kissing again, and blindly using his one hand to guide his erection to push against her. This time she was pushing against him too, legs wrapped around him, hands in his hair as the pressure built between them until the head of his cock slipped inside her and she let out a sharp cry, wrapping her arms around him.

"You ok?" Quinn whispered in her ear.

She replied, "Yeah, it feels big though. Please go slow."

Quinn slowly pushed another inch or so into her, and removed his hand, placing it over her clit where it rested against her while her hips twisted under him. Her cries built, a mix of pleasure and pain as he penetrated her. She held him close, arms wrapped around him, eyes closed and face contorted.

"Ah! Ah!" she cried out as he sunk deeper into her.

Quinn felt her ass, impossibly tight but relaxing around him, and held her close as he slid inside, aided by the lube. He watched her to see if he was going too fast, if her cries turned to distress. She was held against his chest, her arms wrapped around him, her face buried in his neck, and he felt protective, like he was claiming her for his own.

He had told her he loved her! Quinn remembered suddenly, and he felt the feeling growing inside him again as he looked at her, face buried in his neck, gasping and moaning as she accommodated him inside her, arms and legs clasped tight around him. She was his girl, and he would rather be with her than with anyone else. It had become more than just sex between them, much more, although maybe it had been about more than sex from the first time they hooked up.

Erin was brilliant, she was funny, she shared enough of his interests to be companionate, and had enough of her own to maintain her own life, and she not only put up with him sexually, but seemed to appreciate him as he was. More than that, though, she was what had made his first few months away at school feel like a fantasy, like he had entered into a world with no supervision, boundless support for his queries into how the world worked and why, and the girl of his dreams by his side, as into him as he was into her. He felt her, soft in his arms, soft around his cock, and he groaned as he felt the last bit of his shaft slide into her and she let out a little yelp.

"That's all, that's all the way in," he gasped.

"Wait a moment, let me get used to it, ok?" she replied.

He rested there, buried inside her ass, feeling her contracting around him, pulling him deeper and deeper... He could feel an orgasm beginning to build, and he hoped he would last long enough to stroke into her a few times. He breathed deeply, but everything around him, whether it was her breasts pressed against him, his face in her neck, the smell of her hair, her legs wrapped around him, the soft cries she was emitting and the way she was gently rolling her hips... pushed him closer to the edge. He had never felt turned on by intimacy like this, but the newness and excitement of this experience heightened all his senses, made him feel her in a whole new way.

"Ok," she murmured.

Just before he came, Quinn managed to pull out an inch and thrust back in.

Erin let out another yelp, and he felt her, pressing around him, squeezing him as he came deep inside her, spasming and releasing, held close in her arms. He felt ashamed about coming so quickly, and thought maybe he should have jerked off before after all…

"Sorry—" he began.

Erin cut him off, "Don't apologize. It's ok for me. It was already intense enough for this time. Just having you inside me like this is enough. I feel so close to you, and guess what?"

"What?" Quinn asked,

"I liked it," Erin said, "and we can try it again."

ABOUT THE AUTHORS

A. Lea Roth and Nastassja Schmiedt are the creative duo Phoenix Moment. The two come from very different backgrounds—Lea grew up in Minnesota, and Nastassja was raised in Miami—but they hit it off immediately when they met at a national LGBT organizing conference in 2012. Both students at Dartmouth College, the two began dating, and started to interweave their organizing, academic interests, and personal lives. After leaving school, Lea and Nastassja were inspired to create their own social enterprise to imagine alternatives to the current state of higher education and co-founded Spring Up, a multimedia activist collective creating a space of learning and healing. Together, Nastassja and Lea are the co-authors of the MILLENNIAL SEX trilogy. They are also the curators of Global Portals and the Imagine a World Campaign, and co-host the Phoenix Moment Podcast.

Learn more about all of Lea and Nastassja's creative projects—and get weekly sneak previews of upcoming MILLENNIAL SEX stories—on their Patreon community page: www.patreon/phoenixmoment

30559376R00224

Made in the USA
Middletown, DE
29 March 2016